刘惟 ● 著

英汉语主句现象对比研究

A Contrastive Study of
Main Clause Phenomena
in English and Chinese

厦门大学出版社 国家一级出版社
XIAMEN UNIVERSITY PRESS 全国百佳图书出版单位

图书在版编目（CIP）数据

英汉语主句现象对比研究 / 刘惟著. -- 厦门 ：厦
门大学出版社，2024.2
　　ISBN 978-7-5615-9277-9

　　Ⅰ．①英… Ⅱ．①刘… Ⅲ．①英语-语法-对比研究
-汉语 Ⅳ．①H314②H146

中国国家版本馆CIP数据核字(2024)第017894号

责任编辑　高奕欢
美术编辑　李嘉彬
技术编辑　许克华

出版发行　**厦门大著出版社**

社　　址　厦门市软件园二期望海路39号
邮政编码　361008
总　　机　0592-2181111　0592-2181406(传真)
营销中心　0592-2184458　0592-2181365
网　　址　http://www.xmupress.com
邮　　箱　xmup@xmupress.com
印　　刷　厦门市金凯龙包装科技有限公司

开本　720 mm×1 020 mm　1/16
印张　14.25
插页　2
字数　295 千字
版次　2024 年 2 月第 1 版
印次　2024 年 2 月第 1 次印刷
定价　56.00 元

本书如有印装质量问题请直接寄承印厂调换

厦门大学出版社
微信二维码

厦门大学出版社
微博二维码

序　言

　　主句现象限制研究作为语言学研究的一个热点问题已经持续了很多年。许多语言学家在主句现象限制领域展开研究并给出了不同的解释。英语和其他欧洲语言中的主句现象限制已经有了广泛而深入的研究，然而汉语中的主句现象限制还没有为人所注意。中国的语言学家并没有系统研究过汉语中的主句现象限制，也未给出过令人信服的原因来解释这种限制。此外，主句现象限制在英语和汉语中表现出一些相似性和差异，但以往的文献几乎没有涉及过这些具有对比性的句法现象。

　　本书在制图理论框架下探讨了英语和汉语状语结构和补足语从句中主句现象的相似和差异，试图对话题化和高位情态词这两种典型的主句现象在两种语言中不同的句法表现进行解释。

　　观察发现话题化与英语时间和条件状语从句以及叙实和名词补足语从句均不能兼容，但是话题化与汉语的这四种从句均能兼容。高位情态词的情况更为复杂。虽然英语和汉语的条件和时间状语结构不能嵌入高位情态词，但是在叙实和名词补足语从句中，按照叙实谓词和名词的不同特征，高位情态词展现出不同的兼容状态。

　　Haegeman 在她的一系列研究中（2007, 2009, 2010a, 2010b, 2012a, 2012b, 2014a）指出，状语从句和补足语从句中的这些主句现象来自算子移位以及由此带来的阻碍效应。虽然她的分析在主句现象研究领域很有代表性，但研究发现这一分析并不适用于汉语，因为主句现象在汉语状语从句和补足语从句中的分布与英语不完全相同。

研究从英语和汉语条件状语从句和时间状语从句中的主句现象入手，指出高位情态词与这两类状语从句不能兼容是由于阻碍效应（Haegeman 2009，2010b）。与之相对应地，英汉两种语言的状语结构中，话题化分布的不同则是由于英汉语在标句层短语（CP）分裂方面存在参数差异。当其分裂时，许多不同的功能性短语被进一步分裂出来。然而，这些功能性短语的具体构成在不同语言之中会存在不同之处，并导致参数差异。因此，话题化不能与英语的状语从句兼容，但是可以与汉语的状语结构相兼容。此外，汉语的时间状语是由两个不同的介词"在"和"当"引导并进一步构成"在……的时候"和"当……的时候"的结构，这两种结构都包含一个以"时候"为中心语的定语从句。研究指出，汉语的时间状语是介词短语，而这两种时间介词短语在主句现象和高低位解读方面也表现出差异。借鉴方位介词短语的制图理论，本书从句法角度对这两类时间介词短语进行了对比分析，认为这种差异源自介词"在"和"当"在介词短语中处于不同的制图层级。

本书接着讨论了叙实补足语从句和名词补足语从句中的主句现象。出于同样的原因，英语叙实和名词补足语从句不能兼容话题，而汉语相应的从句中话题的出现完全合法。高位情态词在这两类补足语从句中的分布较为复杂，呈现出不同的兼容状态。这种状态实际上与引导这些从句的叙实谓词和名词的特征直接相关。因为以往的文献中对于叙实和叙实性的界定并不清晰，本书对其进行了重新分类。通过引入可能世界语义学以及对于已然和未然的区分，将以往文献中的叙实谓词划分为真叙实谓词和指称（但不叙实）谓词。在此基础上，进一步将引导名词补足语从句的中心名词划分为真叙实类型和指称（但不叙实）类型。有了这样的重新分类，本书指出高位情态词能够与指称（但不叙实）谓词和指称（但不叙实）名词引导的补足语从句兼容。与之相对应，高位情态词不能与真叙实谓词和真叙实名词引导的补足语从句兼容是由于语义错配。具体来说，叙实谓词和名词要求发生在补足语从句中的事件是事实性的，而高位情态词则要求该事件是非事实性的。

本书主要涉及汉语和英语中条件状语从句、时间状语从句、时间介词短语、叙实补足语从句和名词补足语从句中的主句现象。由于语言学家尚未关注汉语中主句现象的分布和限制，因此这一研究是对现有语言学研究空缺的一次重要补充。通过分析汉语和英语中主句现象的相似和差异，发现在标句层短语分裂方面，英语和汉语存在重要的参数差异。这个发现深化了对于不同语言小句左缘结构的认识。另一项重要发现是汉语时间状语结构"在……的时候"和"当……的时候"产生区别的根源，这一问题长久以来为语言学家所关注，却一直未得到合理的解释。此外，本书将叙实性与指称性区分开来，并在此基础上解决了以往语言学家们所忽视的高位情态词与一些叙实补足语从句和名词补足语从句相兼容的问题。所有这些研究成果都对现有的制图方案做出了一定的贡献。

笔者

Contents

I/IP/InflP	inflection/inflection phrase/inflection phrase
MCP	main clause phenomena
ModeDirP	mode of directional preposition
ModP	modal phrase
N/NP	noun/noun phrase
OP	operator
P/PP	preposition/preposition phrase
PAC	peripheral adverbial clause
PERF	perfective
PF	phonetic form
PL	plural form
PPI	positive polarity item
PREP	preposition
Q	question
Q-feature	quantificational feature
R/RP	relator/relator phrase
RelViewP	relative viewpoint preposition
rev.	revised
RIDE	root-like indirect discourse embedding
SFP	sentence final particle
SpOA	speaker oriented adverb
Spec	specifier
Sta/StaP	stative/stative preposition
t	trace
T/TP	tense/tense phrase
TOP/TopP	topic/topic phrase
V2	verb second
VP	verb phrase

Chapter One
The Research History of MCP

Main clause phenomena (henceforth MCP) refer to the syntactic phenomena restricted to main clauses instead of subordinate or embedded clauses.[①] The most representative MCP in English are high modal (speaker-oriented modal) markers and topics. These two constituents are restricted to main clauses but not subordinate or embedded clauses as the following (1) and (2) show:

(1)
a. George *probably* comes.
b.*If George *probably* comes, the party will be a disaster.

(Haegeman 2012a: 224)

(2)
a. *This handout*, I have finished.
b. *I won't take time off until *this handout* I have finished.

(Haegeman 2012a: 155)

The high modal marker *probably* can exist in the matrix clause in (1a).[②]

---

① A subordinate clause is a clause that is linked by a subordinating conjunction (or conjunctor) such as when, although, since, because, while, after, etc. (Crystal: 462, rev.). A subordinate clause is a clause that depends on the main clause to complete its meaning, and that cannot form a sentence on its own (Sinclair: 649). An embedded clause is a clause that is included

② A matrix clause refers to the superordinate sentence within which another sentence is embedded (Crystal: 297). A main clause is an independent clause, i.e. it can stand on its own as a sentence (Crystal: 292). At the same time, a main clause can also refer to a part of a complex sentence. A complex sentence refers to a sentence consisting of a main clause and at least one subordinate clause (Crystal: 95). In this dissertation, the terms "matrix clause" and "main clause" refer to the same type of clauses if there is no specific illustration.

However, the sentence is ungrammatical when the same marker exists in the embedded conditional clause in (1b). The fronted topicalized constituent *this handout* is well accepted in the main clause in (2a), but the similar topicalization leads to ill-formedness in the subordinate temporal adverbial clause in (2b).

Why are such phenomena restricted to main clauses? Many linguists have provided a variety of accounts for these MCP restrictions from different perspectives. And there is a long-standing controversy over the source of MCP restrictions. Some linguists, starting from Emonds (1970), argue that MCP can be accounted for in terms of syntactic operations, while others, represented by Hooper and Thompson (1973), believe that semantic factors play the role. Unfortunately, up till now, neither side has prevailed and can provide a comprehensive and convincing argumentation.

According to Emonds (1970) and Hooper and Thompson (1973), MCP in English can be classified into several types, which are generally forbidden in certain (but not all) embedded clauses. Their classification of MCP can be generalized as preposing (like VP preposing, negative constituent preposing, directional adverb preposing, etc.), inversion (like subject-auxiliary inversion, etc.), dislocation (like adverb dislocation, left dislocation, right dislocation, etc.), topicalization, high modal markers, etc.[①] However, there is no clear-cut correspondence between the MCP in English and those in Chinese. On the one hand, some classical MCP in English, like topicalization, are in fact not MCP in Chinese. Topicalization is accepted in Chinese embedded clauses. See the following sentences:

(3)

a. *If *these exams* you don't pass, you won't get the degree.

(Haegeman 2010b: 599)

(embedded) in another, i.e. in syntactic subordination (Crystal: 166-167). It can be seen that "embedding transformations handle subordination" (Crystal: 208). In this book, the terms "subordinate clause" and "embedded clause" refer to the same type of clauses if there is no specific illustration.

① The specific classification and discussion will be in sections 3.2-3.3.

b. Ruguo zhexie kaoshi ni   meiyou tongguo,   ni   jiu   bu neng na-dao   xuewei.
   if   these exam you not   pass   you then not can   get-PERF degree
   'If *these exams* you don't pass, you won't get the degree.'

c. Zhexie kaoshi ni   meiyou tongguo.
   these exam you not   pass
   'These exams, you didn't pass.'

In the English conditional clause in (3a), the fronted topicalized constituent *these exams* makes the clause ungrammatical. In contrast, the existence of the topic *zhexie kaoshi* (these exams) in the Chinese conditional clause in (3b) is accepted. Similarly, the topicalized constituent *zhexie kaoshi* in the main clause in (3c) is also well accepted. Thus, this phenomenon cannot be regarded as a kind of MCP in Chinese because topicalization is grammatical in embedded clauses (3b) and also in main clauses (3c) in Chinese.

On the other hand, some English MCP are forbidden in main clauses in Chinese. That means they are fundamentally not accepted syntactic behaviors in Chinese. They are ungrammatical not only in embedded clauses but also in main clauses. Like subject auxiliary inversion, it is a kind of MCP in English, but it is forbidden in main clauses as well as embedded clauses in Chinese. See the following sentences:

(4)

a. When may her husband visit her?

b. *Mary forgets when may her husband visit her?   (Emonds 2004: 105)

c. *Mali wang le   hui ta-de zhangfu shenme-shihou lai   kan ta?
   Mary forget ASP may her   husband when   come visit her
   'Mary forgets when may her husband visit her?'

d. *Hui ta-de zhangfu   shenme-shihou lai   kan ta?
   may her   husband   when   come visit her
   'When may her husband visit her?'

e. Mali wang le   ta-de zhangfu shenme-shihou hui lai   kan ta?
   Mary forget ASP her   husband when   may come visit her
   'Mary forgets when her husband may visit her?'

    f. Ta-de zhangfu shenme-shihou hui lai kan ta?
       her   husband when   may come visit her
      'When her husband may visit her?'

In the interrogative clause in (4a), the auxiliary verb *may* moves to the pre-subject position, while in the embedded clause in (4b), moving the auxiliary verb *may* to the pre-subject position is forbidden. However, the similar movement of the auxiliary *hui* (may) is forbidden in both the embedded clause (4c) and the main clause (4d) in Chinese. Thus, this phenomenon cannot be regarded as a kind of MCP in Chinese because subject auxiliary inversion is absolutely ungrammatical in Chinese. The auxiliaries can never be preposed before the subject in Chinese. They can only follow the subject no matter in the embedded clause (4e) or the main clause (4f).

These observations show that the distributions of MCP in English and Chinese are not strictly corresponding, and there is a series of differences between English and Chinese in MCP restrictions. So the book will focus on these issues and make a contrastive study of MCP distributions in English and Chinese and attempt to provide a promising account for the MCP restrictions in these two languages.

1.1 The origin of the MCP research

Emonds (1970), in his pioneering work, first notices MCP (root transformations in his term). He distinguishes two types of transformations: structure-preserving transformation and root transformation. The former preserves structure in the sense that a constituent of a specific category is moved to a position that hosts constituents of the same category. That is, the operation is constrained to be structure-preserving. The latter, however, can create new positions, but only in root clauses, so it is called root transformation (the current MCP), and this initial work more or less influences the subsequent syntactic analysis of such phenomena.

Further crucial development is found by Hooper and Thompson (1973), who observe these phenomena from the semantic perspective. Contrary to Emonds (1970), they claim that these MCP can also occur in a subset of embedded clauses, not just in matrix clauses. They further argue that MCP's being confined to matrix clauses and certain types of embedded clauses is a natural consequence of their emphatic function because many embedded clauses cannot be emphatic. By virtue of their emphasizing function, MCP are constrained to assertive contexts and prohibited in presupposed clauses. According to them, the semantic property assertion is the decisive factor that influences the distribution of MCP. Hooper and Thompson's (1973) analysis provides us with a new horizon for the issue. It arouses many other linguists to follow this semantic tradition and utilize semantic or pragmatic approaches to analyze MCP. The subsequent researchers in this field always take assertion into consideration as long as they take the semantic approaches.

1.2 Present concerns about the MCP restriction

The next advances in MCP research are Haegeman's two different attempts under the framework of the cartographic program (Rizzi 1997, 2004; Cinque 1999, 2004; among others), and these attempts can still be seen as the syntactic solution. As her first attempt, Haegeman (2003a, 2003b, 2006a, 2006b) proposes a truncation account for MCP restriction in adverbial clauses. According to her, the lack of certain syntactic behaviors like topicalization in the clauses can be attributed to the truncated (reduced) left periphery of the clauses. She modifies this account in her later works (2007, 2009, 2010a, 2010b, 2012a, 2012b, 2014a) and puts forward an intervention account as her second attempt. In this proposal, the embedded clauses are free relatives that are derived by different operators, and the MCP restriction is thus a result of the intervention effect. That is, the moved constituents intervene in the movement of the operators that derive the embedded clauses. Following this line, the reduced left periphery is the by-product of the derivation of the embedded clause. In this way, Haegeman's works offer a syntactic account for the phenomena that have been previously considered to belong to the domain of semantics or pragmatics.

Being a focus of recent syntactic research, MCP attract many other researchers. They have proposed various accounts for MCP restriction in

English and other European languages (Krifka 2001; Emonds 2004, 2012; Heycock 2006; Ernst 2007; Basse 2008; de Cuba 2010, 2017; Bianchi and Frascarelli 2010; Cinque and Rizzi 2010; Haegeman and Ürögdi 2010a, 2010b; Frey 2012; Authier and Haegeman 2013; Lahousse, Laenzlinger and Soare 2014; Endo and Haegeman 2019; among others). Besides, some Chinese linguists (Pan and Paul 2018; Wei and Li, 2018a, 2018b, 2018c) discuss the distribution of MCP in Chinese and provide some tentative accounts for the restriction. All these accounts can be further divided into three different lines. They are the syntactic account, semantic account and cartographic account. Among these accounts, different linguists focus on MCP in different languages. Some of the researchers focus on the related phenomena in English. Some other researchers try to find cross-linguistic evidence for the phenomena, striving to investigate the problem from other perspectives.

With more linguists from different countries concentrating on MCP and examining MCP in various languages, now the understanding of MCP is more intensive and comprehensive. In today's MCP research, utilizing cross-linguistic materials to study is undoubtedly a new tendency and a more efficient approach. However, present concerns about this issue have not yet been extended to Mandarin Chinese to the best of my knowledge. In the previous literature, linguists have not yet analyzed MCP constraints in Chinese embedded clauses and the different syntactic behaviors between English and Chinese embedded clauses. Accordingly, this book will make a contrastive study of MCP in adverbial clauses and complement clauses and provide an account for the similarities and differences of MCP distributions and restrictions in English and Chinese.

1.3 The questions to be answered

This book will make a contrastive study of MCP in English and Chinese adverbial clauses and structures and complement clauses. To be specific, the book will discuss the MCP restrictions in conditional adverbial clauses, temporal adverbial clauses, temporal preposition phrases, factive complement clauses and noun complement clauses in English and Chinese. The reason why I choose these types of clauses and structures is that MCP are deeply involved with these ones. Moreover, there are similarities and differences in terms of MCP distribution in these clauses and structures in English and Chinese. See the following examples, (1b) is repeated here as (5a), and (3a) is repeated here as (6a) for convenience:

(5)

a. *If George *probably* comes, the party will be a disaster.

b. *Ruguo Qiaozhi *dagai*   lai,   wanhui jiang-hui shi yi-chang zainan.
   if   George probably come party will-may be one-CL disaster

(6)

a. *If *these exams* you don't pass, you won't get the degree.

b. Ruguo   zhexie   kaoshi   ni   meiyou   tongguo,   ni   jiu   bu   neng
   if   these   exam   you   not   pass   you   then   not   can

na-dao   xuewei.
get-PERF   degree[①]

In (5), the high modal marker *probably* and its Chinese counterpart *dagai* (probably) are not compatible with the embedded conditional clauses. This is because both English and Chinese conditional clauses exclude high modals. However, the situation is different in the aspect of topicalization. As (6a) shows, the topicalized constituent *these exams* cannot exist in the conditional clause in English, while the corresponding Chinese topic *zhexie kaoshi* (these exams) can be embedded in the conditional clause in (6b).

It can be seen that the distributions of MCP in English and Chinese embedded clauses demonstrate some similarities as well as differences. For example, some MCP in English (like high modal markers) show similar distributions with their Chinese counterparts. In contrast, the distributions of other MCP in English (like topics) do not pattern with the corresponding

---

① Due to space limitations, here I just choose the conditional clause as the example. Other types of clauses also show these MCP restrictions, and there are minor differences in the distribution of these MCP in other types of clauses. The elaborate discussion will be in the following chapters.

Chinese clauses. These similarities and differences lead us to the first question in this book:

I. What are the syntactic similarities and differences of MCP distributions in English and Chinese embedded clauses and structures?

Aiming at these MCP, many linguists have researched how MCP are excluded from the embedded clauses. Various accounts have been provided to explain the absence of MCP in these clauses (see Chapter 3). These accounts can be summarized as two main lines. One is the syntactic analysis in which MCP restriction is seen as a consequence of certain operations in deriving the embedded clauses. The other is the semantic analysis in which the lack of MCP in non-matrix clauses results from a semantic mismatch between MCP and the property of the embedded clauses. Both of these lines give their argumentation, and neither side can gain ascendancy until now.

Reviewing the literature, I find that it is rare to see the related research in Chinese. As a hot topic in today's linguistic research, the restriction of MCP in English and other European languages has been studied comprehensively and profoundly. However, Chinese linguists have not yet systematically studied the issue of MCP restriction in Chinese and have not given convincing argumentation about the reasons for the restriction.

Because there are still controversies, MCP restriction and the true essence of the restriction are not that clear. So consistent research on this issue is still necessary for English and other European languages. At the same time, because there are similarities and differences in terms of MCP restrictions in English and Chinese, and also because the research of MCP in Chinese is not concerned by Chinese linguists, it is necessary to step into the field of MCP in Chinese embedded clauses and make a contrastive study of MCP restrictions in English and Chinese.

Therefore, on the one hand, the research outcomes on MCP in English cannot be entirely applied to the corresponding Chinese clauses and structures. On the other hand, the Chinese linguists have not studied MCP systematically.

The current research status brings about the second question of this book:

II. Why are there MCP restrictions in English and Chinese?

English and Chinese demonstrate sharp differences in resisting MCP in embedded clauses and structures. However, the previous literature seldom concentrates on these differences and does not provide convincing argumentation to account for the differences.

Noticeably, MCP are not isolated syntactic behaviors in the study of the left periphery of the clauses. And just because there is a cluster of grammatical phenomena in the left periphery of clauses, it is reasonable to see whether the analysis in this proposal can be extended to other associated language phenomena in the left periphery, whether there is any regularity behind the intricacies of these different phenomena, and whether there is a unified account. All these problems will surely deepen the understanding of the left periphery of the clauses in English and Chinese. This expectation will direct at the third and also the final question of the book:

III. What are the similarities and differences between English and Chinese in the structure of the left periphery of clauses?

For the sake of convenience, the three research questions that this study endeavors to answer are collected in (7):

(7)
a. What are the syntactic similarities and differences of MCP distributions in English and Chinese embedded clauses and structures?
b. Why are there such MCP restrictions in English and Chinese?
c. What are the similarities and differences between English and Chinese in the structure of the left periphery of clauses?

1.4 Two guiding theories

The theoretical framework of this book is the cartographic program proposed by Rizzi (1997) and the subsequent cartographic research (Cinque 1999, 2004; Rizzi 2004; Cinque and Rizzi 2010; Rizzi and Cinque 2016; among others). The cartography of syntactic structures is the line of research which addresses this topic: it is the attempt to draw maps of syntactic configurations as precise and detailed as possible (Cinque and Rizzi 2010: 51). Currently, the cartographic research is more concerned with the functional elements of the clause such as the distinctive projections in the left periphery, the features of different syntactic constituents, etc. Through adopting certain methodologies and hypotheses on the nature of syntactic structures, it forms a well-defined research direction. The heuristic guideline of this direction is in accord with the issues in this book and is naturally the theoretical framework for the study.

1.4.1 Introduction to the cartographic theory

The cartographic theory develops from the syntactic analyses of functional heads under the principle and parameter framework. The first critical step is the full-fledged extension of X-bar theory to the functional elements as a complementizer phrase (CP)-inflection phrase (InflP or IP)-verb phrase (VP) structure (Chomsky 1986); and the observation that nominal expressions are amenable to a hierarchical structure with a lexical projection embedded within a functional structure (the DP hypothesis, Abney 1987) (Cinque and Rizzi 2010: 51). According to Abney (1987), the traditional noun phrase (NP) should be substituted with the determiner phrase (DP) because the domain of a DP covers not only the noun phrase, but also other phrases like the determiner phrase, possessive phrase, numeral phrase, etc. So the syntactic structure of a DP is in fact a hierarchical structure with several layers of different functional projections. Besides, the determiner, rather than the noun, should be the head in the structure of a DP.

If the first step is the idea that clauses and phrases are formed by a lexical structure and a higher functional structure, both corresponding to elementary building blocks hierarchically organize. The second crucial step is the observation that the functional structure typically consists of more than one head (Cinque and Rizzi 2010: 52). An inflectional phrase zone can be further decomposed, leading to the splitting of InflP (IP) into more elementary components (the Split-Infl hypothesis, Pollock 1989). By contrasting the structures of verb phrases in English and French, Pollock (1989) shows that assuming a single Infl (I) position does not provide enough space to account for the different positions which can be occupied by different morphological forms of the verb in French. Thus, he argues that an inflection phrase can be further split into a tense phrase (TP) and an agreement phrase (AgrP). The verb can be attracted to different functional positions to pick up affixes and get properly inflected, thus changing its position with respect to adverbs and other elements. Although Chomsky (1995) argues that AgrP does not carry the interpretable features and thus excludes AgrP from the functional categories, splitting the existing phrases becomes a new tendency in formal linguistic studies. The same logic soon leads to a later splitting of the complementizer phrase into more articulated hierarchical sequences of functional projections (the split-CP hypothesis, Rizzi 1997). The proposal of the split-CP hypothesis is the first and the most influential work under the genuine cartographic framework. Rizzi (1997) in this work, first involves the research with the information structure and accommodates the functional elements like illocutionary force, mood, modality, focus and topic. By this means, he offers a comprehensive cartographic spectrum of the different projections in the left periphery of the clause. It is generally acknowledged that Rizzi (1997) first puts forward the cartographic approach (Tsai 2019: 28).

Since the split-CP hypothesis, the cartographic program has been applied to other grammatical categories such as the preposition phrases (Koopman 2000; Svenonius 2006, 2007, 2008a, 2010; den Dikken 2010; Cinque 2010a), adjective phrases (Svenonius 2008b; Cinque 2010b), adverbial phrases (Cinque 1999, 2004), noun phrases (Cinque 2002; Kayne 2007b) and even the pragmatic elements (Speas and Tenny 2003; Hill 2007a, 2007b, 2014; Haegeman 2014b; Heine 2016). Many linguists follow the line and more or less contribute to the cartographic research of syntactic structures. With ascending research outcomes from different linguistic categories under the framework, the cartographic program attempts to make a unified analysis of the individual linguistic systems like mood, modality, tense, aspect, lexical items and the information structure and further demonstrates the mapping relationships among the syntax, semantics and pragmatics. In this period, the most comprehensive and in-depth research domains are the left periphery of the clause and the features of the functional elements. And these two domains are closely related to the studies of this book. Therefore, the following sections will discuss these two domains, respectively.

1.4.2 Split-CP hypothesis

The starting point of the cartographic approach is the analysis of the left periphery of the clause (the split-CP hypothesis, Rizzi 1997). Rizzi (1997) gives original thinking for the syntactic status of various kinds of fronted constituents in the left periphery of the clause. He proposes that CP is split into different phrases and can host these fronted constituents. This hypothesis and the analysis of the left periphery are closely related to the discussion of MCP restriction in this book.

According to the hypothesis, the CP layer can be split into several independent phrases, ForceP, TopP, FocP and FinP, which should follow the sequence of "ForceP>TopP*>FocP>TopP*>FinP".[①] In the subsequent work, Rizzi (2004) adds ModP between FocP and FinP.

Among these phrases, ForceP hosts constituents that express illocutionary force, marking the sentence as declarative, interrogative or imperative. TopP is the landing site for fronted topicalized constituents. FocP is the landing site for fronted focalized constituents. FinP hosts the elements that indicate finiteness, defining the sentence as finite or non-finite. Lastly, ModP hosts modal markers that are related to the speaker's attitude. The constituents that express illocutionary force and finiteness occupy the head position of ForceP and FinP, respectively. In contrast, topicalized constituents, focalized constituents and modal markers occupy the specifier positions of

---

① A unique focal head can project its X-bar schema (FocP) in between C (ForceP) and FinP and topics can freely be adjoined to FinP and FocP (Rizzi 1997: 296).

TopP, FocP and ModP, respectively.

The following syntactic tree (8b) clearly shows the distribution of the different phrases when they appear all together in an English sentence.

As (8b) shows, the verb *prayed* in the main clause takes a complement clause introduced by the complementizer *that*. The complementizer *that* occupies the head position of ForceP, indicating that the clause is declarative. The topicalized constituent *atrocities like those* moves from the base position within TP to the specifier position of TopP and the focalized constituent *never again* moves in a similar way to the specifier position of FocP. Simultaneously, the auxiliary verb *would* moves from the base position within TP to the head position of FocP. Thus, the surface structure of the complement clause derives from the linear order of ForceP>TopP>FocP>TP.

(8) a. He prayed *that atrocities like those, never again would* he witness.[1]

(Radford 2009: 330)

b.

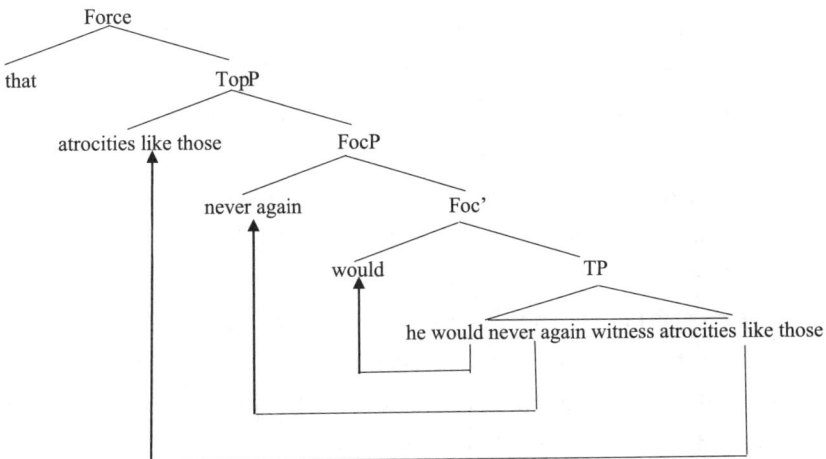

---

[1] The declarative complement clause introduced by declarative predicate is usually considered as a root-like indirect discourse embedding (RIDE) (Emonds: 2004, 2012), i.e. the main clause. Therefore, subject auxiliary inversion is compatible with this complement clause.

The split-CP hypothesis is very influential throughout the history of cartography of syntactic structures. With the introduction of the split-CP hypothesis, formal linguistic studies are not constrained in the field of syntax. It begins to accommodate the linguistic elements that traditionally belong to the fields of semantic and pragmatic research. Therefore, the formal syntax extends the domain of research and surely is more closely integrated with the current tendency of linguistic study.

The split-CP hypothesis is closely related to the research of this book. The classical MCP like topics and high modal markers are generally believed to be on the CP layer. When CP is split, TopP hosts the topicalized constituents and the ModP hosts the high modals. So the research of the book will surely implement under the framework of the split-CP hypothesis.

1.4.3 Locality principle

Another significant breakthrough of the cartographic theory is the modification and extension of the locality principle (Tsai 2019: 33). It is admitted that the modification and extension of the locality principle are based on the analysis of the features of different syntactic configurations. The development of locality theory is virtually the modification of the features carried by the syntactic configurations occupying argument positions and specifier positions, A-positions and A'-positions in the standard terminology. More importantly, the later feature-based locality principle based on the modification is particularly associated with the issues in this book.

The locality principle is first mentioned by Chomsky (1964). He proposes the A-Over-A Principle and an early version of the wh-island constraint, which are seen as subtypes of the locality principle. Then, Chomsky (1973) introduces the subjacency condition, which can be seen as the prototype of the locality principle, as the following (9) shows:

(9)
No rule can relate X and Y in the following structure:
... X ... [B ... [B ... Y ...]
where X is separated from Y by more than one bounding node B.

Chomsky proposes that bounding nodes S and NP (correspond to TP and DP under current assumptions) are cyclic nodes. To define the bounding nodes, Chomsky (1986) defines barriers in terms of Blocking Categories (BC):

(10)
X is a barrier for Y iff (a) or (b):
a. X immediately dominates Z, Z is a BC for Y (X is a BC for Y iff X is not L-marked and X dominates Y);
b. X is a BC for Y, X ≠ IP (IP corresponds to the earlier S and the later TP).

In order to understand how these definitions work, a definition of L-marking is needed:

(11)
X L-marks Y iff X is a lexical category that θ-governs Y.

θ-government is the relation between a lexical head and its sister. The basic form of subjacency remains the same, in that movement across two barriers is not permitted.

The next advance in locality research comes from Rizzi (1990). He proposes the innovative relativized minimality, the central idea of which is that Z intervenes between X and Y when X C-commands Z and Z C-commands Y, and Z is of the same structural type as X. The subsequent researchers combine this analysis with syntactic features and gradually form the feature-based locality principle (Strake 2001; Rizzi 2004, 2013; Friedmann, Belletti and Rizzi 2009). Here, Strake's (2001) contribution to the locality research should be noticed because he first discovers that a more richly specified element can be extracted from the domain of a less richly specified element, but not vice versa.

Based on Strake's (2001) distinguished work, Rizzi (2004) argues that the typology of syntactic configurations is the typology of the licensing substantive features and thus distinguishes four different features as the following (12) shows:

(12)

a. Argumental: person, number, gender, case

b. Quantificational: Wh, Neg, measure, focus…

c. Modifier: evaluative, epistemic, Neg, frequentative, celerative, measure, manner…

d. Topic

(Rizzi 2004: 243)

The argumental features of (12a) are the traditional Phi-features: they define the positions relevant for the argumental system. And just as (12b-d) show, the typology amounts to splitting the class of A'-positions into three classes: quantificational, modifier, and topic. By this means, Rizzi (2004) abandons the classical typology in terms of the A/A'-distinction for it is too strict and then provides a precise typology of structural positions for the theory of locality. And this modification can be seen as the most critical step towards the feature-based locality principle.

Absorbing all these assumptions about the feature typology, Rizzi (2013: 179) illustrates the locality principle as follows:

(13)

A local relation (e.g., movement) cannot hold between X and Y if Z intervenes and Z fully matches the specification of X in the relevant morphosyntactic features.

Rizzi (2013) regards morphosyntactic features as the critical factor to illustrate the locality principle. According to him, the availability of the movement operation depends on the syntactic features that these moved constituents carry. A syntactic constituent will block the movement or extraction of another constituent if this constituent has the same features as the moved one.

The locality principle is always the focus of formal linguistic studies. And the feature-based locality principle is, to some extent, an essential modification to the traditional locality theory. Now, it is widely adopted by other linguists in related syntactic analysis. The core concepts of this principle deeply influence the analysis of syntactic operations like argument movement, topicalization, focalization and other movement behaviors. Generally speaking, the licensing of the movement operation depends mainly upon whether the movement obeys this locality principle.

The feature-based locality principle is also interconnected with the study in this book. The movement operations like topics and high modal markers that are regarded as typical MCP are deeply involved with the locality principle. The intervention effect arises when the fronted constituents and the operators that derive the adverbial clauses carry the same syntactic features according to the locality principle and the MCP in these adverbial clauses are thus absent.

1.4.4 Assumptions adapted in the present study

The last sections discuss the cartographic theory and introduce the split-CP hypothesis and the locality principle, which are the most influential outcomes in the cartography of the syntactic structures. So far, the cartographic theory gradually forms a coherent body of a series of assumptions and hypotheses and becomes a vital schema for linguistic studies. In Cinque and Rizzi (2010), they describe clearly the cartographic studies as follows:

> The cartographic studies can be seen as an attempt to "syntacticize" as much as possible the interpretive domains, tracing back interpretive algorithms for such properties as argument structure..., scope, and informational structure (the "criterial" approach defended in Rizzi 1997 and much related work) to the familiar ingredients uncovered and refined in half a century of formal syntax. To the extent to which these efforts are empirically supported, they may shed light not only on syntax proper, but also on the structure and functioning of the cognitive systems at the interface with the syntactic module.
>
> (Cinque and Rizzi 2010: 63)

The analysis in this book will be under the framework of cartography (especially under the guideline of Split-CP hypothesis and the feature-based locality principle), concentrating on MCP such as fronted topicalized constituents and high modal markers in the embedded clauses in both English and Chinese. Attempting to account for the distinctive syntactic behaviors between English and Chinese embedded clauses is the first obligation in this book. Further analyzing the similarities and differences of the fine-grained structures of the left periphery in English and Chinese should be the second. The last and also the most significant task is to contribute something meaningful to the cartographic program.

1.5 The outline of the book

In Chapter One of the book, a brief introduction to MCP is presented. It reviews the origin and present concerns of MCP and then puts forward the research questions and the theoretical framework. It is noticeable that the book is under the cartographic program, especially the split-CP hypothesis. The remaining part of the book will be organized as follows: Chapter Two summarizes the previous studies and evaluates their outcomes. Generally speaking, the research of MCP can be divided into three different lines: the syntactic account, the semantic account and the cartographic account. Based on the previous study, Chapter Three accounts for MCP restriction in adverbial clauses and structure, and Chapter Four accounts for MCP restriction in complement clauses. The book shows the similarities and differences of MCP distributions and attempts to give a reasonable explanation for MCP restriction in English and Chinese. Finally, Chapter Five is the concluding remarks.

Chapter Two
The Previous Studies of MCP

The previous research on MCP falls mainly into two lines. One is to seek the syntactic account (strictly speaking, the cartographic analysis is also one kind of syntactic account), and the other is to seek the semantic account. In this chapter, the cartographic account of MCP will be presented independently because MCP research, particularly in recent years, is mainly under the cartographic framework.

2.1 The syntactic account of MCP

Ever since Emonds (1970) distinguishes two types of transformations: structure-preserving transformation and root transformation (the current MCP), it has been acknowledged that a range of syntactic phenomena are by and large restricted to occurring in root clauses. Emonds's early works focus on identifying these phenomena and the syntactic factors that underlie their distribution. To explain the asymmetry of the distribution of MCP in root and embedded clauses, Emonds (1976) proposes the Structure Preserving Constraint: major grammatical transformational operations are either root or structure-preserving operations (Emonds 1976: 5), which means that root transformations operate on the root S (current TP) node; hence they can only be applied in a root clause. The phenomena discussed in Emonds (1976) are primarily instances of the movement to the left periphery of the clauses and include the following constructions:

(14)

a. Leftward movement to pre-subject position with no verb inversion (English but not German): topicalization, VP-preposing, exclamative wh-fronting, directional PP preposing (*Away John ran*).

b. Leftward movement to pre-subject position with obligatory finite verb fronting: English direct question formation and preposed negative constituents; German topicalization.

c. Finite verb inversion: German "Verb Second"; English auxiliary inversion and V inversion for quotes and directional PPs as in *Away John ran*.

d. Leftward movement (or expletives) with clause-final subjects: preposing of AP over *be* and of locative PPs; there-insertion with clause-final subjects.

e. Left dislocated phrases with commas: left dislocation; sentential complement preposing, yielding clause-final parentheticals as in *Bill was late, it seems to me*.

f. Phrases in final position with comma intonation: right dislocation; parenthetical PPs; English tag questions.

g. Phrases moved to clause-final position with comma intonation: rightward movements over internal parenthetical and appositive relative clauses.

(Emonds 2004: 78-79)

Emonds (2004) signals that though root transformations are restricted to unembedded clauses, they are possible in certain embedded clauses, which are essentially characterized as the indirect discourse, hence his label "root-like indirect discourse embedding (RIDE)". He also proposes that the unspecified categorical discourse shell (which he calls A-categorical shell) can explain why some maximal projections can move to the specifier positions and why such category-free movements occur in root contexts only. In the following work (2012), he further postulates a set of A-categorical root projections (discourse shells) and argues that root movements target the specifier or head positions of these A-categorical projections.

Emonds's work is the starting point of root transformations/MCP research, so it is natural to launch the discussion with his study. His original work discovers a new kind of grammatical phenomenon with great acuteness and creates a prospective field of study that lasts for a long period of time and attracts so many linguists to engage in it. His work definitely lays the foundation of MCP research and influences the followers when they dedicate themselves to this domain of linguistics. Emonds's contributions in this field are mainly identification and classification. He identifies MCP, defines them for the first time, and classifies them into several types. As for the reasons behind the MCP restriction, however, he hardly touches on the topic. His Structure Preserving Constraint stipulates that MCP should only apply in root clauses without providing a reasonable explanation. Thus, his analysis cannot form convincing argumentation and reach explanatory adequacy.

Whether they approve Emonds's idea or not, the subsequent linguists in this field are influenced by Emonds's work more or less. One group of linguists continue to divide MCP into more specific subtypes, like Heycock (2006) and Miyagawa (2012). The former distinguishes between structural phenomena—which include topicalization and negative preposing, as well as verb second in German, and certain Japanese and Korean topic markers—and non-structural phenomena like particular adverbial adjuncts and interjections as these are often associated with the speaker's attitude. The latter believes that MCP and root phenomena are syntactically distinct, stemming from different structures and giving rise to different effects. Therefore, some MCP (mainly involving moving a constituent to an articulated CP position) that occur in a subset of embedded domains and root environments are totally different from root phenomena (mainly involving encoding the relationship between the speaker and the hearer), which are strictly unembeddable.

Other groups of researchers, however, pay more attention to the stipulated rules that constrain MCP distribution. They find cross-linguistic data to investigate the related language phenomena, particularly in the Germanic languages. In their works, Higgins (1973), Williams (1974), Koster (1975), and den Besten (1983), among others, point out that there is no need for a stipulative distinction between root and non-root transformations. According to them, an important subset of Emonds's root transformations is analyzed as involving the movement of some element to the complementizer position; the presence of a lexical complementizer blocks such movement. From this perspective, the root/non-root distinction is only an artifact of the typical, but not entirely general, correlation of lexical complementizers and embedded clauses (Heycock 2006: 175). These findings mainly come from the observation of the Germanic verb second (V2) phenomenon. With these findings, the question of defining MCP distribution becomes more complicated.

The status of MCP research from the syntactic perspective makes the linguists realize that a purely syntactic analysis without considering the semantic and pragmatic factors cannot perceive the regularities and constraints behind MCP distribution. Against this background, the semantic and pragmatic account of MCP steps onto the center of the stage. So the next section of the book will concentrate on the semantic account of MCP.

2.2 The semantic account of MCP

Emonds's (1970) work incurs dissenting opinions quickly. Hooper and Thompson (1973) point out that the MCP identified by Emonds are sometimes embeddable and argue that the crucial licensing factor for MCP is a semantic/ pragmatic one: MCP depend on assertion, which is a property of declarative root clauses. To be compatible with MCP, embedded clauses must be asserted (that means they will have the property of root clauses). A corollary is that the clauses that are presupposed (i.e., not asserted) are incompatible with MCP. Hooper and Thompson (1973) also make a similar classification of MCP as (15) shows, though there are some adjustments to the corresponding Emonds's one:

(15)
    a. VP preposing
    b. Negative constituent preposing
    c. Directional adverb preposing
    d. Preposing around *be*
    e. Participle preposing
    f. Prepositional phrase substitution
    g. Subject replacement
    h. Direct quote preposing

i. Complement preposing

j. Adverb dislocation

k. Topicalization

l. Left dislocation

m. Right dislocation

n. Tag question formation

o. Subject auxiliary inversion   (Hooper and Thompson 1973: 466-468)

They state that these MCP must be in the asserted sentences, and sentences may contain more than one assertion (in the case of coordination); also importantly, some subordinate clauses can be asserted, too. Based on this notion, they provide a five-way division of predicates taking sentential complements or sentential subjects, as (16) shows:

(16)

a. Class A predicates (e.g., "say", "report", "be true", "be obvious"). The verbs in this group are all verbs of saying. Both the verbs and the adjectives in this group can function "parenthetically", in which case the subordinate clause constitutes the sentence's main assertion. However, it is claimed that if the subordinate clause occurs in the subject position (as in, e.g., That German beer is better than American beer is true), it is not asserted.

b. Class B predicates (e.g., "suppose", "expect", "it seems", "it appears"). In this group, the predicates can function parenthetically, and in this case, the subordinate clause is asserted. The distinction between this class and Class A is not made entirely clear, although it is noted that Class B predicates allow "Neg raising" and tag questions based on the subordinate clause.

c. Class C predicates [e.g., "be (un)likely", "be (im)possible", "doubt", "deny"] have complements which are not asserted.

d. Class D predicates (e.g., "resent", "regret", "be odd", "be strange"). These factive predicates have complements which are argued to be presupposed, and hence not asserted.

e. Class E predicates (e.g., "realize", "know"). These semi-factives (factives that lose their factivity in questions and conditionals) have a reading on which the subordinate clause is asserted.   (Heycock 2006: 189)

The assertion hypothesis means that temporal clauses, conditional

25

clauses, complement clauses of factive predicates, subject clauses, and complement clauses of noun phrases are incompatible with MCP. Hooper and Thompson further claim that reduced clauses (infinitives, gerunds, and subjunctive clauses) are not asserted. Restrictive relative clauses on definite heads are argued to be presupposed (and therefore never asserted); non-restrictive relatives, and restrictive relatives on indefinite heads, are not presupposed (and maybe asserted). An adverbial clause itself may be ambiguous between presupposed (hence not asserted) and non-presupposed interpretations. MCP can apply when the clause is non-presupposed.

Initiating a new approach to investigate MCP, Hooper and Thompson (1973) significantly impact the subsequent linguists who adopt the semantic or pragmatic approach to study MCP. Their influence even finds followings in the attempts to syntacticize the analysis (Cinque and Rizzi 2010). Although they solve some problems brought about by Emonds's work to some degree, they still have to face some challenges. Firstly, by their own admission, Hooper and Thompson (1973) have not given an accurate definition of assertion (which is the key point of their account). And a vague definition is always a fatal problem. Secondly, their analysis (that the failure of root transformation to occur in non-asserted clauses is due to the incompatibility of emphasis with non-assertion) has always been doubted by the counter-evidence (like clefting construction, which is in presupposed environments but can be embedded in factive complement clauses, e.g., We regretted that *it was precisely this book* that had been destroyed).

Though Hooper and Thompson (1973) cannot yet uncover the veil of MCP ultimately, their work is a milestone of MCP research. Their assertion hypothesis is so influential that the subsequent linguists, whether they adopt the semantic or syntactic approaches to study MCP, will consider the property of assertion. Their influence finds a following in the literature in Green (1976, 1980), Ernst (2007), Larson and Sawada (2012), de Cat (2012), etc. Among them, Green is the first one who puts forward a pragmatic hypothesis: embedded root phenomena are licensed just in case that the proposition they affect and therefore emphasize, is one which the speaker supports. At the same time, she also admits that this is only one constraint out of many affecting the acceptability of these phenomena.

Following Giannakidou (1999) and Nilsen (2004), Ernst (2007) puts forward a new program towards the MCP research. He points out that the speaker-oriented adverbs (henceforth SpOAs) fit the pattern for positive polarity items (henceforth PPIs) and respond primarily to whether they are in the scope of veridical, nonveridical, or antiveridical operators. And the licensing conditions for PPIs require that PPIs cannot be in the scope of a nonveridical operator, and this condition accounts for the unacceptability of SpOAs in negative, interrogative, and conditional contexts because negation, question, and conditional operators are nonveridical operators. Thus SpOAs cannot be within their scope.

Larson and Sawada (2012), following Krifka (2001), adopt the quantificational approach to MCP restriction. They argue that root transformations are available in adverbial clauses that correspond to the scope of quantification, but not in those corresponding to the restriction. Based on Johnston's (1994) analysis on temporal adverbial clauses and Larson's (2004) analysis on causal adverbial clauses, they suggest a semantic closure account in which root transformations trigger an existential closure in an adverbial, binding all available variables in a restriction and all but the main variable in the scope. As a result, root transformations induce a vacuous quantification violation in the first case, but not in the second.

The last work in this line that should be mentioned is de Cat's (2012) in which she explores MCP with an interpretive import, and identifies three kinds of data that go unaccounted for under purely syntactic approaches: the gradience in acceptability of MCP in different clause types, the variable behavior of peripheral adverbial clauses, and the existence of root phenomena in "fragments (utterances that are not propositional syntactically)". She argues for an interface account, where most of the burden of licensing falls on the interpretive components.

Many linguists engage in the analyses of MCP in European languages, especially in English. In contrast, the analyses of MCP in Chinese are still sporadic. Shi (2000) perhaps is the first to notice such differences between English and Chinese, but his focus is on other related phenomena rather than MCP.

Following Shi (2000), Tang (2008) systematically studies MCP in Chinese relative clauses. In his work, he presents some comparisons between English and Chinese and makes a detailed description of the licensing conditions of these MCP in relative clauses in Chinese. Most of these conditions are semantic and pragmatic ones instead of syntactic ones.

The semantic proposal solves some problems that are not amendable to solve by the syntactic account. However, the semantic approach does have a critical theoretical defect, namely, what is the property of assertion and how to define the property of assertion? Accordingly, the analysis based on this vague definition is fragile to the criticism from other perspectives, and the conclusion cannot hold water. Therefore, though it seems reasonable, such an analysis cannot provide a satisfactory solution to the problem of MCP restriction. Observing this, many linguists turn to the cartographic approach to study MCP. Therefore, the next section will present the MCP research from the cartographic perspective.

2.3 The cartographic account of MCP

This section will present the cartographic account of MCP. Strictly speaking, the cartographic account can also be considered as one kind of syntactic approach. However, there are still some specific differences between the cartographic account and the traditional syntactic account. Firstly, in accounting for the MCP constraints, the traditional syntactic approach does not concentrate on the internal structure of the left periphery of the clauses. Thus, it cannot give a detailed description of the CP structure. On the contrary, with the split-CP hypothesis, the cartographic account provides a well-defined structure of CP and the syntactic status of various kinds of fronted constituents on the CP layer. Secondly, the traditional syntactic approach ignores the features of the moved constituents and the issues of locality are thus neglected. However, just as the feature-based locality principle indicates, the movement operations that are involved with MCP must obey this principle. Thus, the locality principle and the associated intervention effect play a critical role in deciding the distribution of MCP in different types of embedded clauses. It can be said that the cartographic account is more appealing and efficient in solving the problem of MCP restriction in comparison with the traditional syntactic approach.

Besides, the cartographic account contributes more than the traditional syntactic and semantic proposals to MCP research, particularly in recent years. Therefore, it is necessary to present this account independently. The following sections will present the cartographic account with elaborate illustrations and empirical evidence.

2.3.1 The truncation account

There are two eras in the period of the cartographic analysis of MCP. The first era starts from Haegeman (2003a, 2003b). She argues that the lack of MCP in the embedded clauses can be attributed to the truncated structures of the clauses. Because these embedded clauses do not have full-fledged left peripheries, they cannot hold the fronted constituents like topics or high modal markers. Hence, the analysis in this era is usually called the truncation account.

The second era begins with Haegeman (2007). She modifies her truncation analysis and then provides a movement account for MCP restriction. She first hypothesizes that the embedded clauses are derived from the movement of the related operators. Then she proposes that MCP is forbidden in these embedded clauses because the fronted constituents intervene in the movement of the related operators according to the feature-based locality principle. Thus, the intervention effect arises, and the embedded clauses cannot accommodate these fronted constituents. Therefore, the analysis in the second era is generally called the movement account.

The truncation account is first put forward by Haegeman (2003a, 2003b), who proposes that a truncated left periphery of the embedded clauses lacks the related projections that can host the moved constituents. She argues that this is the reason for the absence of MCP in these embedded clauses. In Haegeman (2003a), she first distinguishes event-conditionals and premise conditionals. Then she claims that the left periphery of the event conditional clause lacks the functional head Force, which encodes illocutionary force with which MCP is compatible. And in the other work (2003b), she discovers that while English fronted arguments are typically restricted to root clauses or clauses with root properties, different fronted adjuncts do not have the unified restriction. This is because the short fronted adjuncts function as scene setters of the higher clauses. However, the long fronted adjuncts pattern like fronted arguments rather than short fronted adjuncts.

Haegeman (2006a, 2006b) provides similar accounts of MCP restriction. She argues that the left peripheries of these clauses are reduced or truncated; as a result, there are no associated landing sites for the moved syntactic constituents. She (2006a) contrasts English argument fronting (topicalization) and Romance Clitic Left Dislocation (henceforth CLLD). Then she argues that the former is MCP while the latter is not. English argument fronting is excluded from central adverbial clauses (henceforth CACs), which are closely integrated with the main clauses that they are associated with and resist MCP; in contrast, there are peripheral adverbial clauses (henceforth PACs), which are less integrated and allow MCP. She further proposes that the English argument fronting is related to the functional head Force in the left periphery. Whenever the left periphery is structurally reduced, Force is not projected, and topicalization becomes illicit. On the contrary, CLLD does not depend on Force but is licensed through the lower head Fin. In contexts in which Force is not projected but in which Fin is projected, CLLD remains licit. In her later works, she labels the asymmetries of argument fronting versus adjunct fronting and English argument fronting versus Romance CLLD as a double asymmetry and often utilizes this as a diagnostic tool to test MCP.

Later Haegeman (2006b) shows that the conjunctions introducing adverbial clauses may select a reduced complementizer phrase (CP), in which case such clauses lack MCP; or the conjunctions may select a full-fledged CP, in which case the adverbial clauses are compatible with MCP. And this analysis can be extended to the clausal complements of factive predicates, which can be shown to instantiate the reduced structures. According to Haegeman (2006b: 1666), the left periphery of the factive complement clause is a truncated CP structure.

(17)

Complements of factive predicates: that ModP FinP[1]

As (17) shows, the complement clause of factive predicates is a reduced CP structure in which TopP and FocP are not projected. Therefore, the topics and foci cannot exist in these clauses and such clauses lack these MCP.

Haegeman's truncation account provides a train of thought as follows. Because the left periphery in the embedded clauses is truncated or reduced, it has no space for some specific constituents which can be hosted in the root clauses, the left periphery of which is complete. Thus the absence of MCP in these embedded clauses can be accounted for reasonably. This analysis opens a new horizon for MCP research under the cartographic framework and can be seen as a new solution to the MCP constraint. Moreover, the analysis is based on comprehensive and systematic observations of MCP in different subordinate clauses in English and many other languages. Therefore, the explanation for MCP distribution is more convincing and compelling.

Though it seems reasonable, the truncation account is not without controversies. The first defect is that this account is stipulative instead of explanatory. In this sense, the truncation account is still far from explanatory adequacy. The truncation account indeed has empirical adequacy; however, this adequacy is largely achieved by defining the left periphery of adverbial clauses in such a way as to ensure the availability of CLLD in Romance and left periphery adjuncts in English while excluding English argument fronting. It is proposed that English argument fronting depends on the presence of Force, but this dependency is stipulated, just as Haegeman herself admits.

---

[1]   Haegeman (2006b) utilizes Mod and Fin here. However, I believe ModP and FinP are more appropriate.

In more general terms, the status of the syntactic representation of Force is not uncontroversial. Zanuttini and Portner (2003) and Gartner and Steinbach (2006), among others, doubt the validity of postulating a syntactic projection for Force. Their argumentation further shakes the foundation of the truncation hypothesis.

The other weak point of the truncation account is that the presence of Force is not sufficient to allow MCP such as topicalization. The clauses that can be used to illustrate this point are root yes-no questions, root wh-questions and imperatives, etc. These clauses are associated with illocutionary force and should be compatible with MCP, but the fact is just the opposite. (e.g., *This book, leave on the table.) It can be seen that the clause is associated with imperative force, and the illocutionary force is projected, thus topicalization should be licit according to the truncation account. However, the topicalized constituent *this book* makes the clause ungrammatical. The apparent counter-example shows that the truncation account is not without problems.

Another challenge comes from the criticism of Haegeman's (2002) division between CAC and PAC. The precise implementation of the division brings about another thorny issue for the truncation analysis, i.e., the asymmetrical classification of adverbial clauses cannot lead to a unified solution to MCP distribution.

Although it still has many problems and is not anywhere close to perfection, Haegeman's truncation account does provide new ideas towards MCP research and is subsequently explored by quite a number of other scholars (Carrilho 2005, 2008; Munaro 2005; Bentzen, Hrafnbjargarson, Hroarsdottir and Wiklund 2007; de Cat 2007; Hernanz 2007a, 2007b; Abels and Muriungi 2008; Basse 2008; Cardinaletti 2009; Wiklund, Bentzen, Hrafnbjargarson and Hroarsdottir 2009; Bianchi and Frascarelli 2010; Cinque and Rizzi 2010; de Cuba 2010, 2017; Nasu 2012; Hill 2012; Coniglio and Zegrean 2012; Endo 2012; Laskova 2012; Frey 2012; among others). Some of them find cross-linguistic evidence to support this account.

Based on careful observation of related language phenomena in French, de Cat (2007) proposes that there is a distinctive property or projection (discourse projection) of the root clause which licenses the MCP (similar to Haegeman's analysis of defining Force as the property in root clauses). So the absence of this property or projection is why MCP are excluded in non-root clauses. She argues that the dislocated element is merged by adjunction to a discourse projection (defined as a maximal projection with root properties). Their own discourse properties, therefore, determine the distribution of dislocated elements.

Basse (2008) argues for a minimalist analysis of factive complement clauses. He argues that the presupposition associated with factives is not a discrete feature itself but is a reflex of the absence of matrix subject assertion feature in ForceP of the embedded clauses. The missing feature causes the subordinate clause to become a defective phrase, which is shown to resist movement to its left edge.

Bianchi and Frascarelli (2010) discuss the question of whether topics are necessarily restricted to root clauses. Following Reinhart's (1981), Büring's (2003) and Krifka's (2008) discussion on conversational common ground and adopting the typology of topics by Frascarelli and Hinterhölzl (2007), they derive the root restriction from the necessity of illocutionary force (i.e., the impact on common ground management). Generally speaking, topics affect the management of the conversational common ground and should appear in the clauses with illocutionary force (root clauses). However, because the familiar/given topics (G-topics) do not affect the conversational dynamics, they are not restricted to root clauses. In this way, there are root restrictions in English because there are no familiar/given topics, which have no impact on common ground management. So the absence of topics in English non-root clauses is reduced to the lack of familiar/given topics.

Inspired by Hooper and Thompson's (1973) work, Cinque and Rizzi (2010) put forward a similar truncation account. They attempt to redefine assertion as a functional projection in the left periphery. Therefore, that MCP cannot exist in the non-root environments is a natural result of their being lack of this functional projection.

Nasu's (2012) work is based on the syntactic and pragmatic

characteristics of topic particle stranding in Japanese, whereby a topic particle appears in the sentence-initial position without an overt topic phrase. He argues for the existence of a projection above ForceP in the CP domain and believes that topicalization occurs in TopP while topic particle stranding occurs in the projection above ForceP. This higher projection constitutes the outermost periphery of a clause and appears only in root clauses. Thus, the absence of MCP in the embedded clauses is attributed to the lack of this higher projection.

Hill (2012) (in the same volume) adopts a similar approach to MCP distribution. Her analysis capitalizes on the proposal that a field for encoding conversational pragmatics is projected at the left periphery of the clause above ForceP.

Coniglio and Zegrean's (2012) attempt to account for MCP constraints by splitting CP into more articulated layers. They present data on discourse particles in Romance and Germanic languages, which support the splitting of Rizzi's (1997) ForceP into two distinct projections: Illocutionary Force Phrase (ILLP) and Clause Type Phrase (CTP). They think that each particle can occur in certain clause types but not in others, and they are only licensed in clauses with root properties. Further, they show that the discourse particles interact with the illocutionary force of the clause. Hence, they are typical MCP and can only appear in root contexts.

De Cuba (2017) focuses on noun complement clauses and claims that such clauses are referential clauses that have a syntactically truncated left periphery, which can account for the lack of MCP in these noun complement clauses. In his term, MCP can be captured by the cP structure (the extra structural position to provide a landing site for MCP). Therefore, the referential clauses are incompatible with MCP because they do not have this specific cP structure. Thus the left periphery of the referential clauses is also a truncated structure.

Another group of linguists attempts to re-classify the two types of adverbial clauses (CAC and PAC) distinguished by Haegeman (2002) and illustrates the MCP distribution from a new perspective. Inspired by the insights from the traditional descriptive Japanese grammarian (Minami 1974) who identifies three basic types of adverbial clauses, Endo (2012) shows that there is gradience in the functional structure of adverbial clauses ranging from these three types which correlate with the availability of MCP: the more functional elements a given adverbial clause contains, the more it allows MCP.

Then, Laskova (2012) discusses the two types of adverbial clauses in relation to the properties of the Bulgarian non-past verbal form. She focuses on the high modal markers and argues that the Bulgarian non-past verbal form is an instantiation of the subjunctive mood and its distribution correlates with the distribution between CAC and PAC. Additionally, she further distinguishes two subtypes of peripheral clauses (adversative and premise clauses) and argues that the former contains epistemic modals, which are typical MCP. On the contrary, the latter prohibits such subjective modals.

The last work following this line that cannot be ignored is Frey's (2012). He shows that, apart from PAC (which allows certain MCP) and CAC (which does not), another class of adverbial clauses (which he calls the non-integrated adverbial clauses) should be distinguished. In Germany, the clauses allow more MCP than the peripheral adverbials and show indications of greater independence. He argues that while CAC and PAC are differently licensed syntactically (the former by the host's verbal projection, the latter by Force in the host's periphery), non-integrated adverbials are not syntactically licensed at all. Instead, they are "orphans", being only semantically linked to their associated clauses by a specific discourse relation.

Similar to Haegeman's truncation account, a strand of works attempts to explore the syntactic encoding of the semantic concepts as the illocutionary force. Among them, Han (2000) extends this truncation analysis to imperative clauses. Citing Sadock and Zwicky (1985) and Palmer (1986), he points out that imperatives are root phenomena that never occur in embedded contexts. She attributes this to the existence of an imperative operator located on the complementizer layer. This layer includes a directive feature that expresses the illocutionary force. Thus, she assumes that the illocutionary force can only be expressed in unembedded clauses.

It is gratifying to see that some Chinese linguists follow the truncation line to research MCP distribution. Lu (2003, 2008) is the first one (to the best of my knowledge) who notices the different distribution of MCP between English and Chinese in adverbial clauses. She attempts to replicate Haegeman's (2002) test of argument fronting for Chinese for the sake of distinguishing between CACs from PACs. She postulates that adverbial clauses preceding the main clause involve PACs, whereas adverbial clauses merged below the subject of the matrix clause instantiate CACs. Accordingly, object topicalization, a typical MCP, will be expected to be possible in the former, but not in the latter.

Pan (2015) makes a general study of the syntax-discourse interface in Mandarin Chinese. Although he does not concentrate on MCP directly, he indeed explains MCP restriction. According to him, Chinese has the following hierarchy for functional projections in the left periphery: AttitudeP1>AttitudeP2>Special QuestionP>Illocutionary ForceP>Only FocusP>Sentential.AspectP>TP. These projections host sentence final particles (SFP) or null operators. When the compared projections are both head-final, the syntactic word order reflects the relevant hierarchy; when the compared projections are not uniformly head-final, their scope interaction reflects the order. And the study finally shows that the higher a projection, the more subjective its interpretation and the harder it can be embedded.

The linguists following the truncation line contribute to the truncation hypothesis and even to the split-CP hypothesis, deepening the understanding of MCP restriction and the structures of the left periphery of the clauses. They revise some layers in the left periphery and define the accurate structures of the CP domain, on the basis of which they propose more precise restrictions on MCP distribution.

However, Haegeman's truncation account and the subsequent research along this line have to face an unavoidable issue all the time, namely, the simplicity of the theory. As Haegeman herself admits, such an analysis is stipulative rather than explanatory. As it stipulates the articulated structures of the left periphery, the truncation approach has to carry the burden of specifying which clause type has an impoverished left periphery, and which projections are missing, and further illustrating in which language, and why. Indeed, all these questions should be considered, and hence such an analysis will add the theoretical burden. Besides, the answers to such questions are usually assumed to be related to illocutionary force or discourse-related features. However, these concepts are still not syntactically encoded and thus have not yet been fully formalized. Therefore, the analysis will naturally raise a lot of problems of implementation. Maybe just because of these intractable problems, Haegeman keeps modifying her own accounts. The following part will present her new solution to the issue and other linguists' works along the line.

2.3.2 The movement account

Haegeman modifies her truncation account and then provides a better one (at least for her) for MCP restriction (2007, 2009, 2010a, 2010b, 2012a, 2012b, 2014a), that is, the movement account. In her work (2007), Haegeman analyzes MCP constraint by contrasting argument fronting in English and Romance CLLD. Following Geis (1970, 1975), Larson (1987, 1990), Dubinsky and Williams (1995), Penner and Bader (1995), Citko (2000), Zribi-Hertz and Diagne (2003) and Demirdache and Uribe-Etxebarria (2004), she proposes that an adverbial clause is derived by the movement of an operator to its left periphery and the intervention effect is thus predicted in English because the movement of the operator interacts with the movement of the fronted arguments. Contrary to this, no such intervention effect will arise with Romance CLLD as it does not give rise to the same intervention effect.

Then, Haegeman (2009, 2010b) extends this analysis to temporal adverbial clauses and conditional adverbial clauses, respectively. She argues that the temporal operator (which derives the temporal adverbial clause) and the world operator (which derives the conditional adverbial clause) move from a TP internal position to the left periphery. This movement interacts with the movement of the fronted arguments. Therefore, the intervention effect accounts for the absence of a number of fronting phenomena in temporal and conditional adverbial clauses in English. As she (2010b: 606) indicates, high modal markers share the same Q-feature with the moved world operator, which leads to incompatibility of high modals with conditional clauses:

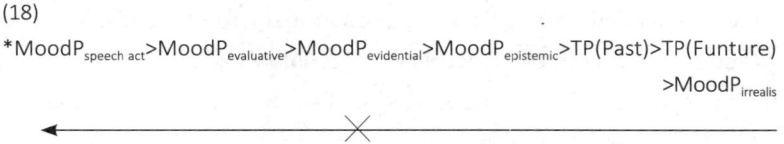

(18)

$*MoodP_{speech\ act} > MoodP_{evaluative} > MoodP_{evidential} > MoodP_{epistemic} > TP(Past) > TP(Funture) > MoodP_{irrealis}$

As (18) shows, the moved world operator that has the Q-feature moves from the position MoodPirrealis to the leftmost position of the clause. However, this movement operation is blocked by high modal markers that have the same Q-feature according to the feature-based locality principle. The intervention effect arises and the conditional clauses cannot host high modal markers. Topicalization, as another kind of MCP, is also absent in these clauses for the same reason. Then, she further predicts that this movement analysis can be extended to other domains that resist fronting operations in English, like factive complement clauses.

Haegeman (2010a) continues to concentrate on the internal syntax of adverbial clauses and generalizes the movement analysis for temporal adverbial clauses and conditional adverbial clauses. According to her, the unavailability of MCP in these adverbial clauses in English can be accounted for in purely syntactic terms if one adopts the hypothesis that the movement of the related operators derives the relevant adverbial clauses. The fronted arguments intervene in the movement of the related operators and the intervention effect arises, and thus the adverbial clauses become ungrammatical.

Haegeman (2012b) develops the intervention account for MCP and contrasts it with the original truncation account. In the intervention account, the effect of truncation is no longer stated as a primitive but is syntactically derived. That is to say, the truncated left periphery is a natural result of the intervention effect brought about by the movement operation.

Based on these observations and analysis, Haegeman compiles a book (2012a) concerned with the composition of the left periphery of adverbial clauses and the MCP constraints. Concentrating on the internal and external syntax of adverbial clauses, she mainly discusses why a subset of adverbial clauses is incompatible with MCP.

The next extension of MCP research appears in Haegeman and Ürögdi (2010a, 2010b). They extend the movement analysis to finite complement clauses (some of which, factive complement clauses in particular, also resist MCP). Following de Cuba and Ürögdi (2009, 2010), they propose that factivity has referential properties and thus should be substituted by referentiality. In their work, they use the term referentiality in substitution of factivity in the previous literature.[1] Then, they develop a movement derivation pattern for such referential embedded clauses, showing that their referential property can be made to follow from event relativization, which in turn accounts for the constraints on the syntax of their left periphery. Adopting this movement analysis that pays much attention to the feature make-up of the operator, they make fine-grained predictions with respect to the availability of various MCP in these clauses and finally prove that referential clauses are derived by the movement of the operator and MCP are forbidden in these referential clauses by the intervention effects.

Finally, Haegeman (2014a) gives a unified account of the incompatibility of MCP with some embedded clauses. She proposes that MCP are excluded from clausal domains derived by the movement of a TP-internal operator to the left periphery. In this view, the ban on MCP in such domains—and the apparent unavailability of the projections that host them—follows from the locality principle on movement. Thus, the MCP restriction is completely due to the locality principle. The truncated left periphery of the specific embedded clauses is the natural consequence of the operator movement and the resulting intervention effect in these clauses.

Haegeman's movement account has tremendous significance in MCP

---

[1]   I will discuss the property referentiality and the relationship between factivity and referentiality in section 4.2.3.3.3.

research and deepens the understanding of the articulated structure of the left periphery, contributing a lot to the cartographic theory. Based on the distinction between CAC and PAC, she gives convincing argumentation on the restriction of MCP in some adverbial clauses. She then extends this analysis to complement clauses, especially factive complement clauses and complement clauses of NP, finally giving a unified account of the absence of MCP in these embedded clauses. Haegeman investigates many cross-linguistic data for the sake of observing MCP more clearly and comprehensively. And these data indeed prove her account from other perspectives and make her argumentation firmly supported.

Haegeman's movement proposal solves some problems of the truncation account and, in a sense, reaches explanatory adequacy. Nevertheless, this proposal still can not yet tackle the problem of MCP restriction thoroughly. Firstly, Haegeman's movement proposal does not have a solid theoretical foundation. Her analysis is based on the make-up of the features carried by the different specifiers. However, the features of the specifiers (especially the features carried by topics) are not always clear enough. Haegeman's movement proposal for adverbial clauses is based on the spirit of Kayne (2008) and Arsenijević (2009), who claim that the adverbial clauses are derived by operator movement, and therefore such clauses are hidden relatives. Following Melvold (1991), Watanabe (1993, 1996) and Hiraiwa (2010), among others, Haegeman further argues that the movement of the operator derives factive complement clauses and noun complement clauses. Haegeman then proposes that the fronted argument and the high modal marker, which are regarded as typical MCP, share the same quantificational feature (henceforth Q-feature) with the moving operator, so the intervention effect arises and leads to incompatibility. The idea of the fronted argument (equivalent to the topicalized constituent) sharing the same Q-feature with the operator is against the analysis of the typology of specifiers proposed by Rizzi (2004), who claims that topics are not quantificational, which are different from the wh-operator, negative operator and focus that are classified as quantificational specifiers (Rizzi 2004: 243). In this case, whether a topic has the Q-feature is still uncertain. Nevertheless, the movement analysis is just based on the make-up of the features carried by the moved constituents. Thus, the uncertainty will impair the convincing power of the analysis.

Secondly, there are many counter-examples from other languages that Haegaman's analysis cannot account for though she covers many cross-linguistic data. For example, de Cuba (2017) points out that in some languages like Swedish and Basque (where the morphological form of the relative complementizer is tied to the presence of a relative operator in the left periphery of the clause), a declarative complementizer shows up in factive complement clauses and noun complement clauses. The operator movement account, which explicitly proposes a relative operator movement in such clauses, obviously makes the incorrect prediction that the relative complementizer should appear. This phenomenon shows that at least complement clauses are not relatives and thus undermines the basis of Haegeman's analysis. Besides, Liu and Zhang (2019) find that topics are compatible with conditional adverbial clauses in Chinese. Thus, if the movement account is correct, the availability of topics in Chinese conditionals will become unexplainable.

Lastly, Haegeman has not yet located the original position of the operator in the embedded clauses, which makes the whole analysis seem somewhat illusory. As a result, the conclusion drawn on this analysis does not appear that concrete.

Subsequent researchers who favor the movement analysis adopt similar approaches in the investigation into MCP from other perspectives (Aboh 2010, Authier and Haegeman 2013, Fernández and Miyagawa 2014, Lahousse et al. 2014, Endo and Haegeman 2019). Through investigating the language data in Gungbe whereby factive complements are completely transparent to movement, Aboh (2010) argues that the contrast between factive clauses (which disallow MCP) and non-factive clauses (which allow MCP) in English is not derived from the lexico-semantics of the selecting verbs in the matrix, but from the syntax of the embedded clauses. In other words, the fronted argument in the embedded clause may bear an event feature, which is a strong form in Gungbe and thus can be attracted by a relevant head within the C-domain. However, the event feature carried by the argument in English is weak and hence cannot be extracted.

Auhier and Haegeman (2013) turn their attention to the related language phenomena in French and argues that while a spelled out fronted TP is an intervener for wh-movement in adverbial clauses, leading to a phonetic form (PF) crash, the ellipsis of this fronted TP leads to a convergent derivation via Bošković's (2011) mechanism of rescue by PF deletion. This account entails that adverbial clauses involve wh-movement and that the landing site for TP topicalization is available in a non-root environment in French.

Fernández and Miyagawa (2014) argue that in Spanish and Japanese, the discourse feature of the topic is inherited from C to T (as opposed to English where the discourse feature stays in C). Therefore the topic preposing to TP (which forms topicalization) and the operator movement to CP (which derives embedded clauses) in the former two languages does not lead to competition for the same syntactic position. In contrast, in English the topic feature stays in C. As a result, the topic fronting and the operator movement vie for the same position, which leads to the absence of topics in embedded clauses where the operator movement has occurred.

Lahousse et al. (2014) develop the feature-based locality principle to illustrate the gradient availabilities of topics in different clauses. In their opinion, the make-up of the features carried by the related elements may be diversified. They believe that adding a C-feature (contrastive feature) to the features of Q (quantificational) and δ (discourse-linking) which are already used in the literature can account for the distribution of contrastive topics and foci in English. Accordingly, a preposed C-bearing element is not an intervener for a Q-bearing element. Thus, a contrastive topic is acceptable in non-assertive clauses, while a non-contrastive topic is excluded.

The latest publication about the MCP constraint along this line is Endo and Haegeman (2019). Starting from the distinction between CAC and PAC and drawing from the traditional literature on Japanese data (Minami 1974; Noda 1989, 2002; Endo 2012), they adopt the movement derivation of adverbial clauses and propose that the merger of an adverbial clause with the associated main clause is determined by the derivational history, i.e., the external syntax of an adverbial clause is determined by its internal syntax.

It is encouraging to see that some Chinese linguists have done some related research into MCP constraints. Following the movement line, Wei and Li (2018a, 2018b, 2018c) systematically study complex sentences in Chinese and pay much attention to the relative order of the adverbial clauses with the related main clauses. Based on the observation that intervention effects are operative in relative clauses but not in appositive clauses, they indicate that the Chinese temporal clause contains a relative clause while the purposive clause introduces an appositive clause. As a consequence, topicalization is possible in the latter but not in the former. Another interesting finding in their research is that they divide the standard adverbial clauses into two types, the real adverbial clauses (including S-final conditional clauses) and the in-fact root clauses, which are traditionally labeled as adverbials but actually are not adverbials at all (including S-final reason and concessive clauses). Further, the tests of TP-internal discourse particles and the scope-related tests enable them to argue that the distinction between CAC and PAC, which has been proposed for European languages like English and German, also holds in Chinese.

These researchers along Haegeman's movement line have more or less contributed to the movement hypothesis. They modify the make-up of features of some constituents and thus more reasonably and flexibly utilize the locality principle to study the MCP constraint. Moreover, they have provided some better solutions to MCP restrictions in different contexts and different languages and have shown us a bigger picture of MCP distribution.

Nevertheless, all these analyses still cannot tackle the specific problem of MCP research, namely, the gradient availabilities of MCP in different types of embedded clauses. Theoretically speaking, understanding the cause of this gradience is the key to understanding the nature of MCP. In this sense, the previous researchers have not offered a panorama of the relationships between the MCP occurrence and the different types of embedded clauses. Therefore, drawing a clear-cut demarcation line between the embedded clauses that are compatible with MCP and those incompatible are necessary in this field.

At the same time, it is not very hard to notice that the MCP research in Chinese starts more recently and is not as systematic and comprehensive as the corresponding researches in other languages that have lasted for a long period of time. Many problems related to MCP distribution in Chinese have not been touched (like the incompatibility of high modal markers with conditional clauses and the asymmetry of topicalized constituents between English and Chinese factive complement clauses). Therefore, this book will concentrate on the syntactic discrepancies between English and Chinese in terms of MCP and discuss the MCP in Chinese and the reasons behind these phenomena.

2.4 Summary

In this chapter, I have reviewed the research outcomes of MCP restriction in the literature. All these analyses can be divided into three different lines. They are the syntactic account with Emonds (1970) as the representative; the semantic account with the representation of Hooper and Thompson (1973), and the cartographic account represented by Haegeman (2003a, 2003b, 2006a, 2006b, 2007, 2009, 2010a, 2010b, 2012a, 2012b, 2014a).

The chapter firstly reviews Emonds's (1970) syntactic account. He is the first linguist who notices MCP and his work can be considered as the starting point of MCP research. Undoubtedly, he lays the foundation for MCP research which lasts for a very long time. But, what he does mainly is identification and classification of these MCP. Basically, he does not explore the reasons for MCP restriction.

Then, the chapter discusses the semantic account. Hooper and Thompson (1973) argue that the semantic property "assertion" is the key element for MCP distribution. That means, to be compatible with MCP, embedded clauses must be asserted. Thus, the clauses that presupposed are incompatible with MCP because they are not asserted. Hooper and Thompson's proposal brings a new perspective to MCP restriction. But they cannot give an accurate definition of assertion, which undermines the convincing power of their argumentation.

Lastly, the chapter focuses on the cartographic account. The cartographic account can be further divided into two types. The first one is the truncation account (Haegeman 2003a, 2003b, 2006a, 2006b). Haegeman argues that the CP of the embedded clauses is truncated, so it cannot hold the fronted constituents like topics or high modal markers. However, just as she herself admits, this account is stipulative, not explanatory.

The second one is the movement account. Haegeman modifies her last account and soon puts forward this new account (Haegeman 2007, 2009, 2010a, 2010b, 2012a, 2012b, 2014a). According to this movement account, the moved constituents intervene in the movement of the operators that derive the embedded clauses because both the moved constituents and the operators have the same Q-feature. So these fronted constituents cannot be compatible with the embedded clauses. The most serious problem of this account is the weak theoretical foundation since topics are not always quantificational.

It can be seen that all these accounts cannot give satisfactory explanations to MCP constraints though most of them do provide some insightful ideas. Meanwhile, the current analysis of MCP do not extend to Mandarin Chinese. Many problems related to MCP distribution in Chinese have not been noticed. Therefore, the analysis of MCP in English and Chinese adverbial clauses will be presented in the next chapter.

Chapter Three
MCP in Adverbial Clauses and Structures

This chapter will discuss MCP in two types of adverbial clauses in English and Chinese and two types of temporal preposition phrases in Chinese, i.e., the conditional adverbial clause and the temporal adverbial clause in English and Chinese, and the temporal preposition phrases "*zai...de shihou*" and "*dang...de shihou*" constructions in Chinese. The first part of the chapter provides empirical arguments to classify the adverbial clauses into different types according to their specific properties and internal and external structures. With the division of CAC and PAC, the contrast between English and Chinese adverbial clause can be made for further MCP analyses. Then the chapter focuses on the conjunctions that introduce the adverbial clauses and analyzes the syntactic status of these conjunctions. It shows that the conjunctions in adverbial clauses in Chinese are complementizers instead of adverbs in traditional literature. Based on these findings, the following section discusses MCP in the conditional and temporal adverbials in Chinese and then contrasts them with the homologous phenomena in English. Finally, the chapter demonstrates that Chinese conditional and temporal adverbials are different kinds of syntactic structures and different from the structures of conditional and temporal adverbial clauses in English. All these differences result in different distributions of MCP in adverbial clauses and preposition phrases in Chinese and English.

3.1 Re-cognition of Chinese adverbial clauses and structures

Before stepping into the field of MCP research, I will first present a systematic description of different types of adverbial clauses and the conjunctions introducing these adverbial clauses in Chinese. With a re-classification of the Chinese adverbial clauses, the adverbials that resist MCP and those that do not can be distinguished from each other. The section then further investigates the MCP distribution in these adverbial clauses. Meanwhile, the re-definition of the conjunctions in Chinese is another challenge because the syntactic status of these conjunctions is controversial in traditional linguistic research. After careful observations and rigorous argumentation, it can be convinced that these conjunctions are complementizers instead of adverbs.

3.1.1 Re-classifying Chinese adverbial clauses and structures

Adverbial clauses refer to the ones that are used mainly to modify the main clauses. Sometimes they are also labeled as adjunct clauses, irrespective of whether they are actually syntactically adjoined to the main clauses or not. Among these clauses, conditional and temporal adverbial clauses in English are regarded as typical adverbials, while rationale and concessive adverbial clauses are not typical types. This is because, on the one hand, these different adverbial clauses are merged at different positions in the structures of the main clauses, and they also show different availabilities to MCP on the other hand.

The situation about Chinese adverbial clauses is more complicated due to the flexible orders of adverbials (adverbial clauses can be put before or after the main clauses and both are unmarked sequences, making a comparison with the fixed order of adverbials in English where they follow the main clauses) and the ambiguous syntactic status of conjunctions (conjunctions in Chinese can be classified as conjunctors/complementizers or adverbs, making a comparison with the clear status of conjunctions in English where they are usually regarded as conjunctors/complementizers).

Against this backdrop, it is necessary to discuss the typology of adverbial clauses at first. Haegeman (2002) proposes that adverbial clauses can be divided into CAC and PAC in English. CACs are closely integrated with the clauses that they are associated with and resist MCP, while PACs are less integrated and allow MCP. In other words, CACs are associated with the event structure of the main clauses, while PACs are associated with the discourse structure of the main clauses. Haegeman (2012a: 164) presents a table to illustrate the typology of adverbial clauses comprehensively (see Table 1):

It can be seen that the classification of CAC and PAC in English is not from conjunctions in the adverbials but from the degree of syntactic integration between the adverbials and the main clauses they are associated with. In this case, the typology of adverbial clauses deviates from the traditional types. Or in other words, the traditional typology of adverbials is not suitable for the MCP research and cannot reflect the relationships between the adverbial clauses and the associated main clauses.

Table 1   Central adverbial clause/Peripheral adverbial clause

Conjunction	Central adverbial clause	Peripheral adverbial clause
	Event structure	Discourse structure
(Al)though		Concessive
As	Event time	Cause/premise
Before/after	Event time	
Because	Event clause/reason	Rationale
If	Event-condition	Conditional assertion
Since	Event time	Cause/premise
So that	Purpose	Result
Until	Event time	
When	Event time	Contrast
Whereas	Concessive	
While	Event time	Concessive

As Table 1 shows, a temporal *while* clause modifies the event expressed in the matrix clause, so it is a CAC in (19a). However, the concessive *while* clause is regarded as a peripheral one in (19b). The conjunction *while* on its own cannot be used as the diagnostic tool to distinguish CACs from PACs.

(19)

a. According to Smith, a group of Arkansas state troopers who worked for Clinton *while* he was governor wanted to go public with tales of Clinton's womanizing.

(*Guardian*, G2, March 12, 2002: 3, col. 2-3)

(c.f., Haegeman 2012a: 160)

b. *While* his support for women priests and gay partnerships might label him as liberal, this would be a misleading way of depicting his uncompromisingly orthodox espousal of Christian belief.

(*Guardian*, March 2, 2002: 9, col. 1-2)

(c.f., Haegeman 2012a: 160)

Except for this, the difference between CACs and PACs is also embodied in the degree of availability of MCP. Although both of them are introduced by the conjunction *while*, the adverbial in (20a) resists MCP such as topics, whereas the adverbial in (20b) does not.

(20)

a. *While *this paper* I was revising last night, I thought of another analysis.

(Haegeman 2009: 397)

b. His face not many admired, while *his character* still fewer felt they could praise.

(Quirk, Greenbaum, Leech and Svartvik. 1985: 1378)

This MCP constraint can be extended to conditional clauses. Noticeably, there are subtypes in the conditional adverbials. The conjunction *if* in (21a) and (21b) are different though both adverbials are conditional clauses. In (21a), *if* introduces a condition for the event expressed in the main clause: the event expressed in the conditional antecedent is the cause of that expressed in the consequence. In (21b), on the other hand, the *if* clause provides the privileged contextual background assumption against which the proposition expressed in the associated clause is processed. Therefore, the adverbial clause in (21a) is a CAC while that in (21b) is a PAC:

(21)

a. If your back-supporting muscles tire, you will be at increased risk of lower-back pain.　　　　(*Independent on Sunday Sports,* October 14, 2001: 29, col. 3)

(c.f., Haegeman 2012a: 84)

b. We are seeing a fall in the incidence of crime, particularly serious crime, and I think we're right to say "What's going on? If crime is falling, why are we seeing a continuing rise in the prison population?" (*Guardian*, November 1, 2001: 2, col. 6)

(c.f., Haegeman 2012a: 161)

Similarly, a central conditional clause is not compatible with MCP like topics as (22a) shows; while a peripheral conditional is compatible with MCP as (22b) shows:

(22)

a. *If *these final exams* you don't pass, you won't get the degree.

(Haegeman 2003: 332)

b. If *some precautions* they have indeed taken, many other possible measures they have continued to neglect.　　　　(Haegeman 2012a: 232)

All these examples show that some conditionals and the temporal adverbial clauses in English are CACs and these clauses are not compatible with MCP. If some minor exceptions are ignored, conditional and temporal adverbial clauses can be labeled as CACs, while concessive and rationale adverbials are labeled as PACs. With this clear-cut classification, this book will concentrate on these CACs that are incompatible with MCP in English while putting aside those PACs that are compatible with MCP.

Interestingly, whether such a distinction between CAC and PAC exists in Chinese adverbials is still controversial. The distinction of Chinese adverbials is more complicated compared with the English one. It is challenging to seek the one-to-one correspondence between English and Chinese types of adverbial clauses. So it is necessary to depict the panorama of complex sentences in Chinese before going into the field of adverbial clauses.

According to Xing (2001), Chinese complex clauses can be classified into three groups. The first group is the generalized causal and the associated main clauses (including the causal, inferential, hypothetical, conditional, purposive clauses and the associated main clauses, etc.),[①] demonstrated in the following sentences:

(23)

a. Yinwei you ren   zhao ta, ta hen gaoxing. (causal clause)
   because have people visit him he very happy
   'Because someone visits him, he is very happy.'

b. Jiran   you ren   zhao ta, ta yiding   hen gaoxing. (inferential clause)
   now.that have people visit him he certainly very happy
   'Now that someone visits him, he certainly is very happy.'

c. Ruguo you ren   zhao ta, ta zhun hui hen gaoxing. (hypothetical clause)
   if   have people visit him he surely will very happy
   'If someone visited him, he surely would be very happy.'

d. Zhiyao you ren   zhao ta, ta ding   hui hen gaoxing. (conditional clause)
   if.only   have people visit him he certainly will very happy
   'If only someone visits him, he certainly will be very happy.'

e. Yiding   yao you ren   zhao ta, yibian   rang   ta   gaoxing
   certainly need have people visit   him so.that make him happy
   gaoxing. (purposive clause)
   happy
   'We certainly need someone to visit him so that we can make him happy.'

(Xing 2001: 39)

The second group is the generalized coordinate and the associated main clauses (including the coordinate, coherent, progressive, selective clauses and the associated main clauses, etc.). It is observed that the subordinate clauses in these sentences are generally not labeled as adverbial clauses. See the following sentences:

---

① For convenience, the following dissertation will just utilize the the causal, inferential, hypothetical, conditional, purposive clauses instead, without mentioning the associated main clauses.

(24)

a. Ji   you ren   zhao ta,   you you ren   zhao wo. (coordinate clause)

    both have people visit   him and   have people visit   me

    'Someone visits him and someone visits me.'

b. Xian you ren   zhao ta,   jiezhe you ren   zhao wo. (coherent clause)

    first   have people visit   him then   have people visit   me

    'First someone visits him, then someone visits me.'

c. Bujin   you ren   zhao ta,   erqie   you ren   zhao wo. (progressive clause)

    not.only have people visit   him but.also have people visit   me

    'Not only someone visits him, but also someone visits me.'

d. Huozhe you ren   zhao ta,   huozhe you ren   zhao wo. (selective clause)

    either   have people visit   him or   have people visit   me

    'Either someone visits him, or someone visits me.'   (Xing 2001: 43)

The last one is the generalized adversative and the associated main clauses (including the adversative, concessive, pseudo adversative clauses and the associated main clauses, etc.), as the following sentences show:

(25)

a. You ren   zhao ta,   dan ta bing bu   gaoxing. (adversative clause)

    have people visit   him but he yet   not happy

    'Someone visits him, but he is not happy.'

b. Suiran   you ren   zhao ta,   dan ta gaoxing bu   qilai. (concessive clause)

    although have people visit   him but he happy   not up

    'Although someone visits him, he is not happy.'

c. Xiangbi   you   ren   zhao ta,   fouze   ta   bu   hui   zheme

    presumably   have people visit   him otherwise   he   not will   so

    gaoxing. (pseudo adversative clause)

    happy

    'Presumably someone visited him, otherwise he would not be so happy.'

                                       (Xing 2001: 45)

It is not difficult to conclude that the subordinate clauses in the first group (i.e., the generalized causal clauses) and the subordinate clauses in the third group (i.e., the generalized adversative clauses) are the adverbial clauses in Chinese. In contrast, those in the second group (i.e., the generalized coordinate clauses) are not adverbial clauses.

After separating adverbials from other coordinate clauses, I will distinguish CACs from PACs in Chinese. Lu (2003, 2008) uses the special order of adverbials in Chinese to distinguish CACs from PACs. There are three different orders for the adverbial clause: (i) adverbial clause>main clause; (ii) main clause>adverbial clause; and (iii) matrix subject>adverbial clause>main predicate, i.e., the case where the adverbial clause appears below the matrix subject and above the matrix predicate. Observing these different orders, she postulates that the adverbial clause preceding the main clause involves PAC, whereas the adverbial clause merged below the subject of the matrix clause instantiates CAC. Accordingly, object topicalization would be expected to be possible in the former but not in the latter. See the following (26a-d):

(26)

a. ?Xiaohong ruguo ta-de nanpengyou   baba bu xihuan, jiu   hui feichang
   Xiaohong if   her   boy.friend   dad not like   then will very

   nanguo.
   sad

   'If her boy friend, her dad doesn't like, Xiaohong will be very sad.'

b. ?Ruguo ta-de nanpengyou   baba bu xihuan, Xiaohong jiu   hui
   If   her   boy.friend   dad not like   Xiaohong then   will

   feichang nanguo.
   very   sad

   'If her boy friend, her dad doesn't like, Xiaohong will be very sad.'

c. ?Xiaohong jishi   ta-de nanpengyou baba bu xihuan, ye   yao ba ta
   Xiaohong even.if her   boy.friend   dad not like   also will BA him

   daihui jia   qu.
   bring home go

   'Xiaohong, even if her boyfriend, her dad doesn't like, (she) nevertheless brings him home.'

d. ?Jishi   ta-de nanpengyou   baba bu xihuan, Xiaohong ye yao ba ta
   even.if her   boy.friend   dad   not like   Xiaohong also will BA him

daihui jia   qu.
bring   home   go

'Xiaohong, even if her boyfriend, her dad doesn't like, (she) nevertheless brings
him home.'   (Pan and Paul 2018: 149-150)

As demonstrated in (26a-d), the comparison is not borne out by the examples. Just as Pan and Paul (2018) indicate, there seems no sharp difference between these TP-external and TP-internal adverbial clauses: both marginally allow the topicalization (argument fronting) of the object. This is the first problem for Lu's attempt to replicate Haegeman's test of argument fronting to distinguish CACs from PACs. Besides, Lu's analysis of the distinction between CAC and PAC is based on the relative order of adverbial clauses associated with the main clauses. This classification does not relate the types of adverbial clauses to the distinction between CAC and PAC. Consequently, such a classification cannot uncover the truth of the differences between CAC and PAC and thus there is not a satisfactory approach to distinguish CACs from PACs.

Wei and Li (2018a) use another test to distinguish CACs from PACs. They first argue that a PAC has illocutionary force, but a CAC does not have illocutionary force. Thus the discourse particles in Chinese can occur in PACs but not in CACs. Then they take the discourse particle *you* (conveys the speaker's strong intention in persuading the addressee) as evidence to show that the inferential clause in (27a) is a PAC because it is compatible with the discourse particle *you* which express "you might as well forgive him (Zhangsan) since obviously he did not do this intentionally". In contrast, the conditional clause in (27b) is a CAC because it is incompatible with the discourse particle *you*.

---

① In Pan and Paul (2018), they use *nanpengyou* instead of *nan-pengyou* and boy.friend instead of boy-friend. According to the standard of this dissertation, these terms should be *nan-pengyou* and boy-friend, I copy their forms for consistence.

(27)

a. Jiran Zhangsan you   bu shi guyi   de, ni jiu yuanliang ta ba.
   since Zhangsan ATTITUDE not be intentional DE you then forgive   him SFP
   'Since Zhangsan obviously is not intentional (in doing something), you might
   as well forgive him.'

b. Ruguo Zhangsan (*you)   bu shi guyi   de, ni jiu yuanliang ta   ba.
   if   Zhangsan ATTITUDE not be intentional DE you then forgive   him SFP
   'You might as well forgive Zhangsan if he (*obviously) is not intentional (in
   doing something.)'   (Wei and Li 2018a: 210)

As (27a) shows, adding a discourse particle *you* in the inferential
clause in (27a) is acceptable. As a PAC has illocutionary force, it is natural
to conclude that a PAC has the syntactic position for the discourse particle.
Thus the inferential clause is a PAC with illocutionary force. However,
adding the same particle in the conditional clause in (27b) makes the
clause unacceptable, proving that the conditional clause is a CAC without
illocutionary force.

In a similar way, they continue to use another attitude discourse particle
ye (softens the tone of the speaker) to show the difference between CAC and
PAC. In (28a), with the particle *ye*, the context can also be of persuasion and
conveys the speaker's intention of pleading on *Zhangsan*'s behalf so as to
persuade the addressee that "you might as well forgive him (*Zhangsan*) since
after all, he did not do this intentionally". The inferential clause in (28a) is
compatible with the discourse particle *ye*. However, the occurrence of *ye* in
the conditional clause in (28b) is not acceptable.

(28)

a. Jiran Zhangsan ye   bu shi guyi   de, ni jiu yuanliang ta ba.
   since Zhangsan ATTITUDE not be intentional DE you then forgive   him SFP
   'Since Zhangsan is not intentional (in doing something) after all, you might as
   well forgive him.'

b. Ruguo Zhangsan (*ye)   bu shi guyi   de, ni jiu yuanliang ta ba.
   if   Zhangsan ATTITUDE not be intentional DE you then forgive   him SFP
   'You might as well forgive Zhangsan if he is not intentional (in doing
   something) after all.'   (Wei and Li 2018a: 210)

As (28a) shows, the existence of the discourse particle *ye* in the inferential clause is allowed, while the same particle in the conditional clause is not permitted, as (28b) shows. The contrast proves that the inferential clause is a PAC while the conditional clause is a CAC.

Besides, they also use the discourse particle *you* to test other types of adverbials like S-final reason and concessive clauses and prove the distinction between CAC and PAC in Chinese.[①]

Then, Wei and Li continue to use three scope-related tests to distinguish CACs from PACs in Chinese: quantificational binding, the scope of the negation/modal, and the scope of interrogative force. Through a series of tests, Wei and Li finally propose that the dichotomy of CAC vs. PAC in Chinese does exist. They argue that the distinction between CAC and PAC in Chinese is not based on lexical items (i.e., conjunctions), but on the semantic meaning that the adverbials express and the relationships that they are associated with the main clauses. In particular, CACs are either vP or TP adjunctions below the ForceP of the main clauses, whereas PACs are merged as the specifiers of DiscourseP that is the highest projection in the left periphery of the main clauses. It can be seen that this classification basically follows Haegeman's (2002) proposal in its nature.

Though Wei and Li's (2018a) analysis indeed proves the existence of the distinction between CAC and PAC in Chinese, it does not offer a panorama of CACs and PACs in Chinese because they do not accommodate all the types of adverbial clauses. In their opinion, only some but not all conditionals are CACs; S-final reason and concessive clauses are root clauses. You may also notice that many other types of adverbials are still not included in their analysis (like S-initial reason and concessive clauses, temporal clauses, etc.). How to classify these adverbial clauses? Are they CACs or PACs? It seems that Wei and Li deliberately ignore these problems.

Though Wei and Li's (2018a) analysis is not comprehensive, I basically agree with their classification of CAC and PAC in Chinese. There is no constant matching relationship between the classification of CAC/PAC and

---

① For the process of the tests, interested readers can refer to Wei and Li (2018a: 211-213).

the classification of types of adverbial clauses (like conditional, temporal, causal or concessive adverbial clauses). In other words, the distinction between CAC and PAC in Chinese is not based on the types of adverbials but on the semantic meaning that the adverbials express and the relationships that they are associated with the main clauses. On the basis of their study, the discussion is further widened to include temporal adverbial structures in Chinese for a more comprehensive analysis.

For this sake, it is necessary to address the syntactic structures of temporal adverbials in Chinese. The discussion above shows that in both English and Chinese, it is admitted that the conditional adverbial clause belongs to CACs (though the so-called premise conditional does not). However, the other kind of CAC in English, i.e., the temporal adverbial clause, cannot find a similar-structured Chinese counterpart.

The syntactic structures of the temporal adverbial clauses in Chinese are very complicated. These temporal adverbials are introduced by the prepositions *zai* (at) and *dang* (just at). And these two prepositions further form the structure "*zai...de shihou* (at the time when...) (henceforth *zai-X* structure)" and the structure "*dang...de shihou* (just at the time when...) (henceforth *dang-X* structure)", respectively. According to Wei and Li (2018a), both of these two structures are preposition phrases containing relative clauses with *shihou* (time) as the head noun. Thus, the temporal adverbial clauses in Chinese are preposition phrases instead of clauses syntactically, and the relative clauses are included in the preposition phrases. Because temporal adverbial clauses in English are relative clauses (Haegeman 2009), there is a sharp syntactic difference between English and Chinese temporal adverbial clauses, and a comparison should be made between the English temporal adverbials and the Chinese ones.

Meanwhile, extending the discussion to temporal adverbial structures in Chinese brings about a novel problem since these temporal adverbials are preposition phrases, not clauses. One can see that there are differences between English and Chinese in denoting the temporal concepts. In English, the adverbial clauses introduced by the complementizer/conjunction *when* are adopted to refer to time and modify the main clauses that they are associated with. While in Chinese, the temporal preposition phrases introduced by the prepositions *zai* and *dang* are the standard forms to express time. And the syntactic function of these preposition phrases is still to modify main clauses. It is noticeable that English temporal adverbial clauses and Chinese temporal preposition phrases both refer to the time that is related to the events in the main clauses and are thus seen as the adverbials of the main clauses. Therefore, it is reasonable to make a comparison between these two adverbial structures in English and Chinese.

It is necessary to initiate the re-classification of the adverbial clauses in Chinese in this section. It makes preparations for the studies of the similarities and differences of MCP distribution in English and Chinese adverbials in that the re-classification enables the comparison between MCP in English adverbial clauses and those in corresponding adverbial structures in Chinese.

After distinguishing CACs from PACs and covering the Chinese temporal adverbials in the discussion, I will select the CACs in English (conditional and temporal adverbial clauses) and compare them with the corresponding adverbial clauses and structures in Chinese for further analyses. The next section will re-define the conjunctions that introduce the adverbial clauses in Chinese.

3.1.2 Re-defining conjunctions in Chinese adverbial clauses

The controversy of the syntactic status of conjunctions in Chinese adverbial clauses is a long story in linguistic research. Conjunctions may be regarded as conjunctors/complementizers or adverbs in Chinese adverbials. The idea of defining conjunctions as adverbs goes back to Chao (1968). The most crucial evidence to argue for the adverb status is the observation that these conjunctions pattern with sentential adverbs, occurring either above the subject or in the canonical adverb position, i.e., below the subject and above the verb, as (29a-b) show:

(29)

a. Ruguo wo tongguo le   zhe-ci kaoshi, jiu   keyi na-dao   xuewei.

   if   I   pass   ASP this-CL exam   then can get-PERF degree

   'If I pass this exam, I can get the degree.'

b. Wo ruguo tongguo le   zhe-ci kaoshi, jiu   keyi na-dao   xuewei.

   I   if   pass   ASP this-CL exam   then can get-PERF degree

   'If I pass this exam, I can get the degree.'

In (29a), the conjunction *ruguo* (if) is above the subject *wo* (I) of the clause, and it can also exist below the subject *wo* and above the verb *tongguo* (pass) as (29b) shows. However, this comparison is just a sufficient but not necessary condition. Though it reflects that these conjunctions do behave like adverbs, it cannot yet prove that they are real adverbs. In fact, if we analyze the sentence-initial *wo* in (29b) as an external topic rather than the subject of the clause, the conjunction *ruguo* can be taken as the conjunctor/ complementizer of the adverbial clause.

In addition, more shreds of evidence have been found to show that these conjunctions are more like conjunctors or complementizers instead of adverbs. As I have mentioned above, there are different relative orders of the adverbial clauses with the associated main clauses. These adverbials can precede the main clauses or precede the predicate but follow the subject of the main clauses like (30a-b) show. However, if the conjunctions were identified as adverbs, this analysis could not account for the island effects in the following (30c-d), because the sentences should be acceptable if the conjunction *yinwei* (because) were regarded as an adverb for its not being able to block the extraction of the objects in the adverbial clauses.

(30)

a. [Yinwei Zhangsan tongguo le   zhe-ci kaoshi], [$_{\text{Matrix TP}}$ laoshi   hen gaoxing].

   because Zhangsan pass   ASP this-CL exam   teacher very happy

   'Because Zhangsan passes the exam, the teacher is very happy.'

b. [$_{\text{Matrix TP}}$ Laoshi [yinwei Zhangsan tongguo le   zhe-ci kaoshi], hen gaoxing].

   teacher because Zhangsan pass   ASP this-CL exam   very happy

   'The teacher, because Zhangsan passes the exam, is very happy.'

c. ?Zhe-ci kaoshi$_i$ [$_{Matrix\ TP}$ laoshi   [yinwei Zhangsan tongguo le t$_i$], hen gaoxing].
   this-CL exam   teacher because Zhangsan pass   ASP   very happy
   'The exam, the teacher, because Zhangsan passes the exam, is very happy.'

d. *[$_{Matrix\ TP}$ Laoshi [zhe-ci kaoshi yinwei   Zhangsan tongguo le t$_i$], hen gaoxing].
   teacher this-CL xam   because Zhangsan pass   ASP   very happy
   'The teacher, the exam, because Zhangsan passes, is very happy.'

The adverbial clause introduced by *yinwei* (because) precedes the main clause in (30a), while the adverbial clause in (30b) precedes the predicate *tongguo* (pass) but follows the subject of the main clause *laoshi* (the teacher). Both of these two sentences are acceptable. However, the sentence becomes degraded when the topicalized constituent *zheci kaoshi* (this exam) moves to the initial position of the clause in (30c). Furthermore, the sentence becomes unacceptable when the topicalized constituent *zheci kaoshi* moves to the position between the subject of the main clause and the predicate of the adverbial clause in (30d). If the conjunction *yinwei* were an adverb, the extraction of the topic *zheci kaoshi* should be acceptable because the adverb should not be an island for the extraction. Thus classifying the conjunctions as adverbs will make a wrong prediction. The syntactic behaviors in (30c-d) prove that the conjunctions in the adverbials in Chinese are not adverbs.

Following Pan and Paul (2018), I propose that the conjunctions—including *ruguo* (if), *yinwei* (because), *jishi* (even if), *jiusuan* (enen though), *suiran* (although/though), *jiran* (now that)—that occur in different types of adverbial clauses are heads, i.e., they are conjunctors or complementizers, not adverbs.

After classifying adverbial clauses and defining the status of conjunctions in these two sections, I lay a solid foundation for further syntactic analysis into MCP in adverbial clauses. The following section will go into the field of MCP research in conditional clauses in English and Chinese. The next section will first show MCP in English conditionals and review the analysis of the MCP restriction. Then, a comparison between the MCP in English conditional adverbial clauses and those in Chinese conditional clauses will be presented. The section finally proposes that the similarities and differences in terms of MCP distribution result from the parametric variation between English and Chinese in CP-splitting.

3.2 A contrastive study of MCP in English and Chinese conditional adverbial clauses

This section will make a contrastive study of MCP in English and Chinese conditional adverbial clauses. English and Chinese conditionals have similarities and also differences in MCP distribution. English conditional clauses forbid high modal markers and topicalization, while Chinese conditionals show similar availability to high modal markers and different availability to topicalization with their English counterparts. The following parts of this section will analyze the similarities and differences between English and Chinese conditional clauses and attempt to find the reasons behind these phenomena.

3.2.1 MCP in English conditional clauses

Two kinds of MCP have been noticed in English conditional clauses. One is the argument fronting (topicalization) shown in (3a), repeated here as (31a) for convenience; the other is the high modal marker shown in (5a), repeated here as (31b):

(31)
a. *If *these exams* you don't pass, you won't get the degree.
b. *If George *probably* comes, the party will be a disaster.

As (31a-b) show, the topicalized constituent *these exams* and the high modal marker *probably* cannot be compatible with conditional adverbial clauses. The most representative and influential analysis of this constraint is Haegeman's (2010b) world operator movement account. Following Bhatt and Pancheva (2006), Haegeman proposes that the conditional adverbial clause is derived by the movement of the world operator, which means that the event of the conditional adverbial clause happens in a possible world. Syntactically, the conditional clause is derived by the movement of the world operator from the original position [Spec, MoodP$_{irrealis}$] to the position [Spec, CP] in the left periphery of the clause. Haegeman attributes the ungrammaticality of sentences like (31a-b) to the intervention effect, i.e., the fronted argument (*these exams*) and the high modal marker (*probably*) intervene in the movement of the world operator that derives the conditional clause. In particular, the movement of the world operator disobeys the feature-based locality principle (also known as the relativized minimality) (Strake 2001, Rizzi 2004, 2013, Friedmann. et al. 2009) that requires a local relation (e.g. movement) cannot hold between X and Y if Z intervenes and Z fully matches the specification of X in the relevant morphosyntactic features (Rizzi 2013: 179). Because the topicalized constituent shares the same Q-feature with the moved world operator, it blocks the movement of the world operator. As a result, the topicalized constituent is incompatible with conditional clauses.

Take (31a) as an example, the topicalized constituent *these exams* and the world operator carry the Q-feature. When the topicalized constituent moves from its original object position to the left periphery of the conditional clause, it brings about the intervention effect to the movement of the world operator from the original position [Spec, MoodP$_{irrealis}$] to the position [Spec, CP] because the topicalized constituent *these exams* has the same Q-feature with the world operator. Therefore, (31a) is not acceptable.

As for the high modal markers, Haegeman (2010b: 606) adopts a similar approach and argues that these high modals share the same Q-feature with the moved world operator, which leads to incompatibility shown in (18), repeated here as (32) for convenience:

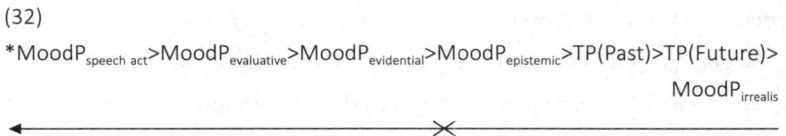

(32)
*MoodP$_{speech\ act}$>MoodP$_{evaluative}$>MoodP$_{evidential}$>MoodP$_{epistemic}$>TP(Past)>TP(Future)> MoodP$_{irrealis}$

◄―――――――――――――――――✕―――――――――――――――――

According to Cinque's (1999, 2004) cartographic hierarchy of modals, every modal has its own functional projection. The modals that express speech act, evaluative, evidential and epistemic modality are called high modals since they are on the relatively high layers of the hierarchy and express the speaker's attitude towards the proposition of the clause. As (32) shows, when deriving the conditional clause, the world operator will move from its original position [Spec, MoodP$_{irrealis}$] to the position [Spec, CP], and the high modal markers will block this movement because these markers have the same Q-feature carried by the world operator. So the high modal markers are not compatible with conditional clauses.

Take (31b) above as an example, the high modal marker *probably* is an epistemic one and thus is a high modal. Because this modal shares the same Q-feature with the world operator that derives the conditional clause, the intervention effect arises and the movement of the world operator is prohibited. Therefore, the high modal marker *probably* is incompatible with the conditional clause in (31b).

The analysis proposed by Haegeman (2010b) explains why these MCP are incompatible with conditional clauses in English. However, this analysis cannot apply to Chinese since topicalized constituents are acceptable in Chinese conditional clauses though high modal markers are not. The next section will concentrate on the MCP in Chinese conditional adverbial clauses and attempt to find the reasons for these similar and different syntactic phenomena in English and Chinese conditional clauses.

3.2.2 MCP in Chinese conditional clauses

Chinese conditional clauses show similarities and differences with their English counterparts in terms of MCP distribution. Specifically, high modal markers are incompatible with conditionals in both English and Chinese, while topicalization is compatible with Chinese conditionals but not with English ones. It can be seen that the topicalized constituent *zhexie kaoshi* (these exams) is acceptable in the conditional clause in (33a), but the high modal marker *dagai* (probably) is not in (33b):

(33)

a. Ruguo *zhexie kaoshi* ni   meiyou tongguo, ni jiu bu neng na-dao xuewei.

   if   these exam you not   pass   you then not can get-PERF degree

   'If these exams you don't pass, you cannot get the degree.'

b. *Ruguo Qiaozhi *dagai*   lai,   wanhui jiang-hui shi yi-chang zainan.

   if   George probably come party   will-may be one-CL   disaster

   'If George probably come, the party will be a disaster.'

I also find more examples in the corpus showing that the topicalized constituents do not obey the constraint of MCP in Chinese conditional clauses. See the following sentences from Center for Chinese Linguistics of Peking University:

(34)

a. Ruguo *zhe-jian shiqing* xiashu   bing meiyou chuli   tongyang

   if   this-CL thing   subordinates yet   not   deal.with well   again

   yizhao   ni-de xiguan hui piping   xiashu   gongzuo bu deli.

   according.to your habit will criticize subordinates work   not efficiently

   'If your subordinates do not yet deal with this thing well, again according to your habit, you will criticize your subordinates for not working efficiently.'

b. Ruguo zhexie hua   wo meiyou ting cuo,   na   women jiu tongtong

   if   these word I   not   hear mistakenly then we   just same

   shi zhe yi lei de ren   le.

   be this one type DE people SFP

   'If I have not misunderstood your words, then we are the same type of people.'

Different from English, the topicalized constituent *zhejian shiqing* (this thing) exists in the conditional clause, and the sentence is grammatical in (34a). And in (34b), the topicalized constituent *zhexie hua* (these words) can also appear in the conditional clause, and the sentence is still grammatical.

3.2.3 Accounting for MCP in English and Chinese conditionals

English conditionals and Chinese conditionals show similarities as well as differences in MCP distribution. Specifically, high modal markers are incompatible with conditional clauses both in English and Chinese, while topicalized constituents are compatible with Chinese conditionals but not with English ones. Following Liu and Zhang (2019), I propose that this is due to the parametric variation between English and Chinese in CP-splitting, and this argumentation will be built on the following three steps:

(35)

a. The intervention effect is the reason for the incompatibility of high modal markers with conditional clauses in English and Chinese, but not the reason for the incompatibility of topicalization with conditional clauses.

b. Topicalized constituents do not share the same Q-feature with the world operator (at least in Chinese); thus the topicalized constituents do not intervene in the movement of the world operator that derives the conditional clause.

c. There is the parametric variation between English and Chinese in CP-splitting, and this accounts for the different distributions of topicalized constituents in English and Chinese conditional clauses.

3.2.3.1 The intervention effect

I propose that the intervention effect is the reason for the incompatibility of high modal markers with conditional clauses, but not for the incompatibility of topicalization. The main evidence for my argumentation is that high modal markers do have the same Q-feature with the world operator while topicalized constituents do not. Some linguists have noted that high modals behave like focus-sensitive adverbs in that their syntactic distributions as well as semantic interpretations can be affected by the position of the focused elements in the sentences. Consider the following (36) and (37) from Krifka (2008: 254):

(36)

Fortunately, Bill spilled [white] F wine on the carpet.

According to Krifka (2008), a proper understanding of (36) should be:

(37)

Among the two alternatives, BILL SPILLED RED WINE and BILL SPILLED WHITE

WINE, the latter one was more fortunate.

As (37) shows, the interpretation of the high modal *fortunately* is affected by the position of the focused elements, thus showing that the high modal *fortunately* has a similar property with the focus adverb.

Similar observations can be found in Jackendoff (1972: 252) and König (1991: 12). This property of high modal markers is also manifested syntactically. Cinque (1999: 31) notes that most classes of higher AdvPs can be used as focusing adverbs. Firstly, like focusing adverbs, the high modals in Italian cannot occur after a finite verb (in a sentence-final position, unless they are "de-accented"):

(38)

a. *Gianni lo merita *francamente/fortunamente/evidentementa/probabilmente/ forse/* ...
   'Gianni deserves it frankly/luckily/evidently/probably/perhaps/ ...'

b. Gianni lo merita, *francamente/fortunamente/evidentementa/probabilmente/ forse/* ...   (Cinque 1999: 31)

Secondly, like focusing adverbs, these high modal markers can be fronted together under focus movement, or clefting in Italian and French, as (39a-c) show:

(39)

a. *Probabilmente* per questa ragione, lo hanno licenziato.
   'Probably for this reason (focus), they have fired him.'

b. E'*Probabilmente* per questa ragione che lo hanno licenziato.
   'It is probably for this reason that they fired him.'

c. C'est *heureusement* Paul qui a vendu sa voiture.
   'It's luckily Paul who sold his car.'

It can be seen that the high modals behave like focusing adverbs in European languages like Italian, French and English. In addition, Engels (2005) also shows that syntactic facts suggest high modals are focus-sensitive.

It is well known that focalized constituents carry the Q-feature (Rooth 1992, Cinque 2004), so the high modals are very likely to have the Q-feature.

Besides, other syntactic behaviors can also support that the high modal markers have the Q-feature. For example, Nakajima (1991) notices that the wh-constituents cannot be extracted from the domain of high modals, demonstrating that high modals share the same Q-feature with the wh-constituents. See the following (40a-b):

(40)
a. *How *probably* will he get here on time?
b. *How *unfortunately* he will not be there!   (Nakajima 1991: 358)

The ungrammaticality of (40a-b) suggests that the movement of the wh-constituents is intervened by the high modals. Since wh-constituents generally carry the Q-feature, the intervention effect shows that high modals also carry the Q-feature according to the feature-based locality principle.

The conditional clause is derived by the world operator and the world operator shares the same Q-feature with high modals, leading to the intervention effect. The intervention effect is the reason for the incompatibility of high modal markers with conditional clauses both in English and Chinese. However, topicalized constituents behave differently with the high modal markers in that they do not have the Q-feature. So it is hard to accept that the intervention effect is also the reason for the incompatibility of topicalization with conditional clauses in English. The next section will give more supporting evidence to illustrate this.

3.2.3.2 The Q-feature

Contrary to high modal markers' being regarded to be quantificational, topicalized constituents are not believed to have this property by some linguists. Rizzi (2004) claims that topic constructions belong to a distinct class in the typology of the specifiers and not of the same structural type as the quantificational specifiers. As he (2004: 243) indicates, topics are not quantificational. Topic and other quantificational specifiers differ with respect to the syntactic tests for quantificational elements.

Furthermore, the more direct evidence of topic's being not quantificational is the observation that topics do not bring about the intervention effect. For example, Cinque (2004: 245) shows that topics do not act as interveners on other kinds of A'-dependencies in Italian:

(41)

a. ?Non so a chi pensi che, tuo fratello, lo potremmo affidare
   'I don't know to whom you think that, your brother, we could entrust'
b. ?Non so come pensi che, tuo fratello, lo potremmo convincere
   'I don't know how you think that, your brother, we could convince him'

As he said, wh-extraction across a topic is slightly degraded. If topics share the Q-feature with other types of chain dependencies like wh-operator, we would expect intervening topics to give rise to the intervention effect, and (41) should be unacceptable. However, (41) shows that this prediction is not borne out.

Besides, Liu and Zhang (2019) also notice that topicalized constituents can occupy the specifier position of CPs that carry the Q-feature in the corresponding clauses in Chinese. Topicalized constituents can freely move to the specifier position of these CPs. See the following (42a-b):

(42)

a. Naxie qianiu-hua, yuehan shenme-shihou zhong de?
   those petunia   John   what-time   plant DE
   'Those petunias, when did John plant?'
b. zhe-ben shu, fang zai zhuo shang ba.
   this-CL book put PREP table on   SFP
   'This book, leave on the table.'   (Liu and Zhang 2019: 391)

It is well-acknowledged that there are interrogative and imperative operators on the CP layer of the interrogative and imperative clauses, which means that the CP layers of these clauses which have the Q-feature for the interrogative and imperative operators are quantificational by nature. However, topicalized constituents *naxie qianniuhua* (those petunias) and *zheben shu* (this book) can move from the base position to the specifier position of CP in these clauses. Apparently, the intervention effect does not arise, and these syntactic behaviors thus prove that the topicalized constituents do not have the Q-feature.

From (41) and (42), one can see that the topicalized constituents can be compatible with the interrogative and imperative CPs that have the Q-feature in Italian and Chinese. According to the feature-based locality principle, it can only be the case that the topicalized constituents do not have the same Q-feature with these interrogative and imperative operators. Then, suppose the world operator that derives the conditional clause is also one kind of operator with Q-feature, the topicalized constituents should be compatible with conditional clauses, and the intervention effect should not arise in the conditionals in English since the topicalized constituents do not have Q-feature. However, (31a) shows that this prediction is not correct. Topicalization is not permitted in English conditional clauses. Based on these findings, the book argues that the intervention effect is not the reason for the incompatibility of topicalized constituents with conditional clauses in English. Their incompatibility must stem from other factors.

3.2.3.3 The parametric variation of CP-splitting

The argumentation will be sequenced as follows. At first, the section shows that there is a competition of TopP and ForceP in English according to the split-CP hypothesis, and the elaborate syntactic analysis is followed. Then, the section proves that this is the reason why TopP is incompatible with the conditional clause in English. However, observation shows that TopP and ForceP can co-occur in Chinese. Thus, TopP is compatible with the conditional clause in Chinese. Finally, the section argues that there is a parametric variation in CP-splitting between English and Chinese, and this is the primary cause for the different distributions of topicalized constituents in English and Chinese conditional clauses.

3.2.3.3.1 Splitting up ForceP

Following Roussou (2000), Coniglio and Zegrean (2012), I will first split Rizzi's (1997) ForceP into two distinct functional phrases: Illocutionary Force Phrase (ForceP) and Clause Type Phrase (CTP).[①] Specifically, the former is where the speaker's intentions are encoded, and the latter is where features are presented, which ensures the realization of syntactic operations specific to each clause type.

The main evidence that CTP must be distinguished from ForceP comes from the mismatch between the illocutionary force of indirect speech act and its concrete syntactic realization. Although surfacing as an interrogative clause, (43) for instance is not a request of information, but a directive requesting an action on behalf of the addressee:

(43)
Could you close the window, please?
illocutionary force = directive (requesting an action); clause type = interrogative
(Coniglio and Zegrean 2012: 246)

Following Coniglio and Zegrean (2012), I further I suggest that CTP must be lower than ForceP because CTP conveys the information about the syntactic structure of the clause while ForceP encodes the speaker's attitude and intention and thus lies at the interface between syntax and pragmatics and is relevant at the discourse level.

It should be noticed that a certain type of illocutionary force is typically mapped into syntax by means of a specific clause type. Therefore, one can usually observe a one-to-one relationship between clause type and illocutionary force. In English, a particular illocutionary force typically corresponds to a certain type of clause. However, just as (43) shows, a speech act can be realized by means of a clause type that does not typically correspond to its illocutionary force. There can be a kind of mismatch between the illocutionary force and clause type.

---

① Coniglio and Zegrean (2012) adopt the term ILLP for illocutionary force phrase while I will still adopt ForceP for consistence. And in the rest of the dissertation, ForceP refers to illocutionary force phrase and CTP refers to clause type phrase if there is no specific illustration.

3.2.3.3.2 The competition of TopP and ForceP in English

I propose a parametric variation in CP-splitting in English and Chinese leads to the different distributions of topicalization in conditional clauses. The splitting-CP as the diagnostic tool can be utilized to test the compatibility of the topicalized constituents (TopP) with the illocutionary force (ForceP) in different types of clauses in English. In fact, observation shows that topicalization is not only incompatible with conditional clauses but also incompatible with some main clauses in English, as (44) shows:

(44)
a. *Those petunias, did John plant?
b. *Those petunias, when did John plant?
c. *This book, leave on the table.　　　　　　(Bianchi and Frascarelli 2010: 77)

As (44a-c) show, topicalization is not compatible with the main clauses that express the interrogative or imperative force. The extraction of the topicalized constituent *those petunias* from the object position of the main clause that expresses the interrogative force to the initial position in (44a-b) makes the clauses ungrammatical. Similarly, the extraction of the topicalized constituent *this book* from the object position of the main clause that expresses the imperative force to the initial position in (44c) also makes the clause ungrammatical.[1]

Except for this, topicalization cannot exist in many other complement clauses, as (45) shows:

---

[1]　The anonymous expert points out that the topicalized structure (especially the structure with resumptive pronouns) is compatible with interrogative clauses and exclamative clauses. He thus doubts whether TopP competes for the same syntactic position with ForceP in English.
(1)a. This kind of behavior, do you think I can tolerate it/who do you think can tolerate it?
　　b. This kind of behavior, how annoying it is!
However, the formation of the so-called topicalized structure with resumptive pronouns is not regarded as the operation of topicalization in the literature but is a kind of Clitic Left Dislocation (CLLD) (Haegeman 2006a). Therefore, it is beyond the range of discussion in this book.

(45)

a. *Do you think that *socialist theory* many Czechs would deny? (Emonds 1976: 31)

b. *How do you think that *this problem* we will solve? (Haegeman 2012a: 129)

c. *Tell them that *this book*, he has read.[①]

d. *Bill asked if *such books* John only reads at home. (Schachter 1992: 108)

e. *Robin knows where *the birdseed* you are going to put. (Culicover 1991: 5)

As (45a-c) show, topicalization is not compatible with the complement clauses embedded in the main clauses that express illocutionary force. The topics *socialist theory* in (45a) and *this problem* in (45b) move to the initial position of the complement clauses embedded in the main clauses that express the interrogative force, and the sentences are ungrammatical. It is also ungrammatical when the fronted topic *this book* exists in the complement clause embedded in the main clause that expresses the imperative force in (45c).

It can be seen that topicalization is not compatible with the complement clauses that express illocutionary force, either. In (45d), the topic *such books* appears in an interrogative clause introduced by *if*. This sentence is unacceptable. In (45e), the topic *the birdseed* exists in an interrogative clause introduced by *where*. This sentence is unacceptable, either.

The topicalized constituents cannot be compatible with interrogative or imperative sentences, whether they exist in the complement or the main clauses. Topicalization can only be accepted in the declarative main clauses or the complement clauses of the declarative predicates, as (46a-b) show in the following:

(46)

a. *This kind of behavior*, we cannot tolerate.

b. You must know that *this kind of behavior*, we cannot tolerate.

(Radford 2009: 335)

---

① I made this sentence to prove my hypothesis. During the period of the 26th Annual Conference of International Association of Chinese Linguistics in the University of Wisconsin-Madison in the United States of America, I tested 10 native speakers. They all considered this sentence as ungrammatical.

In (46a), the topicalized constituent *this kind of behavior* is in the declarative clause, and it is grammatical. In (46b), the same topicalized constituent is in the complement clause of the declarative verb *know,* and it is grammatical.

In the last section, I have mentioned that a certain type of illocutionary force is typically mapped into syntax by means of a specific clause type though there can be a kind of mismatch between the two. However, a declarative main clause sometimes can have different illocutionary force in different utterances. The clause (*The window is open*) for instance, can be declarative by nature, but it can also be assertive (to assert the fact that the window is open), directive (to ask other people to close the window because of coldness or other reason), expressive (to remind someone that something great or dangerous will come from the window), commissive (to promise that the speaker has opened the window), or even interrogative (to require the information why the window is not closed). It can be seen that a declarative main clause can perform all the categories of speech acts proposed by Searle (1975) and thus expresses a variety of illocutionary force.

Following Pesetsky & Torrego (2007), I will make use of the feature valuation mechanism and hypothesize that the ForceP of a declarative main clause has the unvalued feature before entering the derivation. A feature which refers to the speaker's intentions encoded in ForceP takes on the illocutionary force of a given declarative main clause and turns it into a different, more precisely specified illocutionary force in the utterance. That is to say, the feature of the ForceP of a declarative main clause is not valued and the ForceP is thus null in its essence. Therefore, the ForceP will not be projected when it does not yet enter the derivation in the utterance.

In (46a), the feature of the ForceP of the declarative main clause is unvalued and the ForceP is thus not projected. Because of this, the declarative main clause can be compatible with the fronted topicalized constituent *this kind of behavior.* The topicalization operation values the unvalued feature on the ForceP and the derivation then converges. Accordingly, TopP in the declarative main clause is accepted.

According to Radford (2009), the head of ForceP in the complement clause is spelled out as *that*, which means that the head of ForceP (that) is compatible with the topicalized constituent *this kind of behavior* in (46b). In other words, TopP and ForceP can be compatible in the complement clause of a declarative predicate. However, I argue that the word *that* in (46b) is not the head of ForceP but functions as other constituents.

The main evidence of this argumentation is that the word *that* can co-occur with other constituents that occupy the position of ForceP. See the following (47a-b):

(47)
a. I do wonder *that* if God ain't want us to make a little love.

(Corpus of Contemporary American English)

b. It has always been important to me *that* how people feel that I was doing.

(ibid.)

These sentences are from the corpus. In (47a), the word *if* which occupies the head position of ForceP should compete with *that* for the same syntactic position if the word *that* occupied the head position of ForceP. And this competition will lead to ungrammaticality. In (47b), the word *how* which occupies the specifier position of ForceP should precede the word *that* which occupies the head position of ForceP. However, (47a) is grammatical all the way and the word order of (47b) is on the contrary. All these indicate that the word *that* does not occupy the head position of ForceP in the complement clause.[1]

Following den Dikken (2006), Arsenijević (2009) and Kayne (2010b), I propose that the word *that* in the complement clause of the declarative verb

---

[1] From (47a-b), it can be seen that the word *that* is just a linking element that links the main clause and the complement clause. After the word that, there is a constituent that expresses the illocutionary force like *how*, *if*, etc. If this were the case, there should be a null ForceP in the complement clause of a declarative verb. This null ForceP is different from those constituents that express the specified interrogative force. It is a null constituent that is not valued.

is not the head of ForceP but a relator which functions as a linking word. Therefore, the grammaticality of (46b) cannot prove that the word *that* is the head of ForceP in the complement clause.

Because the interrogative and the imperative sentences have the illocutionary force and the related wh-operator and imp-operator will move from the original position to the position [Spec, ForceP] to mark the clause type and express the illocutionary force, the incompatibility of topicalization with the clauses in (44) and (45) illustrates that topicalized constituents cannot be hosted in a clause that already hosts the constituent that expresses the illocutionary force.

Simultaneously, because the word *that* is not the head of ForceP in the complement clause, the grammaticality of (46b) cannot prove that TopP and ForceP can be compatible with each other in the complement clause of declarative verbs. Thus, I can safely draw the conclusion that TopP is not compatible with ForceP in all types of clauses in English though sometimes it can be compatible with clause type phrase (CTP). Then, the only reasonable explanation is that TopP and ForceP both occupy the leftmost syntactic position of the left periphery, and they will compete for the same syntactic position. In other words, the left periphery can only have one position to host TopP or ForceP in English when CP is split. Therefore, the co-occurrence of TopP and ForceP will make the derivation crash, and the clause will be ungrammatical in English.

3.2.3.3.3 The syntactic analysis of the competition of TopP and ForceP in English

If this analysis is on the right track, I can make a syntactic analysis for the ungrammaticality of (43), repeated here as (48) for convenience:

(48)
a. *Those petunias*, did John plant?
b. *Those petunias*, when did John plant?
c. *This book*, leave on the table.

In (48a-c), the topicalized constituents exist in the main clauses that express the interrogative and imperative force, and the sentences are ungrammatical. Since the sentences express the speaker's illocutionary force, the sentences should be regarded as the maximal projection of ForceP. (48a) is a yes-or-no interrogative clause. The auxiliary verb *did* moves from T to C and occupies the head position of the leftmost phrase ForceP to express the interrogative force. Then, the edge feature of this CP is [+Q] (question). While the topicalized constituent *those petunias* which carries the [+TOP] feature will move to the specifier position of this leftmost phrase, then the feature mismatch will make the syntactic derivation crash because the edge feature of CP is [+Q] instead of [+TOP].

(48b) is a wh-interrogative clause. Similar to (48a), *did* in (48b) also moves from T to C and the wh-constituent *when* moves from its base position to the specifier position of ForceP. Then the moved topicalized constituent *those petunias* moves to the specifier position of the leftmost phrase and brings about the feature mismatch. Besides, the topicalized constituent vies for the same syntactic position with the wh-constituent *when*, so the derivation crashes, and the sentence is also unacceptable.

Lastly, (48c) is an imperative sentence. According to Rivero and Terzi (1995), Platzack and Rosengren (1998) and Han (2000), the verb in the imperative sentence should also move from T to C in English. Thus, the verb *leave* occupies the head position of the leftmost phrase ForceP to express imperative force. Then, the edge feature of this CP is [+Imp] (imperative). The moved topicalized constituent *those petunias* will bring about the feature mismatch and make the derivation crash. The sentence is then not grammatical. (49a-c) are the process of the derivation:

(49)
a. *[CP [$_{TopP}$ Those petunias$_i$ [+TOP] [$_C$ did [+Q] [$_{TP}$ John plant t$_i$]]]]?
b. *[CP [$_{TopP}$ Those petunias$_i$ [+TOP] [when$_j$ [+Q] [$_C$ did [+Q] [$_{TP}$ John plant t$_i$ t$_j$]]]]]?
c. *[CP [$_{TopP}$ This book$_i$ [+TOP] [$_C$ leave$_j$ [+Imp] [$_{TP}$ t$_j$ t$_i$ on the table]]]].

A similar analysis can apply to (44), repeated as (50) for convenience:

(50)

a. *Do you think that *socialist theory* many Czechs would deny?

b. *How do you think that *this problem* we will solve?

c. *Tell them that *this book*, he has read.

d. *Bill asked if *such books* John only reads at home.

e. *Robin knows where *the birdseed* you are going to put.

In (50a-c), the main clauses are interrogative or imperative, and the complement clauses are declarative. The main clause in (50a) is a yes-or-no interrogative one, while the complement clause is declarative. In (50a), the verb *do* in the main clause moves to the head position of ForceP and indicates that the edge feature of CP is [+Q]. According to den Dikken (2006), Arsenijević (2009), Kayne (2010b), the word *that* is the linking element that links the main clause and the complement clause. From (47a-b), it can be seen that there should be a zero constituent that expresses the null force (a null ForceP) after the word *that* (see section 3.2.3.3.2). Then the interrogative force of the main clause can percolate to the zero constituent and this zero constituent can inherit the interrogative force from the main clause. Therefore, the topicalized constituent *socialist theory* of the complement clause that carries the [+TOP] feature will mismatch the [+Q] feature inherited by the null ForceP. The sentence is then ungrammatical.

The analysis of (50b) is on a similar pattern. The main clause in (50b) is wh-interrogative, while the complement clause is declarative. In (50b), *how* and *do* occupy the specifier and head position of ForceP, respectively, percolating the feature [+Q] to the null ForceP in the complement clause. The null ForceP in the complement clause inherits the interrogative force from the main clause, and the feature mismatch leads to the incompatibility of the topicalized constituent *this problem* with the complement clause.

Lastly, (50c) is an imperative clause embedding a declarative complement clause. In (50c), the verb *tell* in the main clause occupies the head position of ForceP and percolates the feature [+Imp] to the null ForceP of the complement clause. Then the moved topic *this book* will bring about the feature mismatch. So a topicalized constituent is not compatible with a complement clause embedded in an imperative main clause.

The situation of (50d-e) is different. The main clauses are declarative while the complement clauses are interrogative. The topicalized constituent *such books* mismatches the feature carried by the interrogative word *if*, and the feature mismatch leads to the ungrammaticality of (50d). The same reason leads to the incompatibility of the topicalized constituent *the birdseed* with the interrogative clause introduced by *where* in (50e). The following (51a-e) show the derivation process:

(51)

a. *$[_{CP}$ $[_{C}$ Do [+Q] $[_{TP}$ you think $[_{RP}$ that $[_{CP}$ $[_{TopP}$ socialist theory$_i$ [+TOP] $[_{C}$ $\varPhi$ [+Q] $[_{TP}$ many Czechs would deny t$_i$]]]]]]?

b. *$[_{CP}$ How $[_{C}$ do [+Q] $[_{TP}$ you think $[_{RP}$ that $[_{CP}$ $[_{TopP}$ this problem$_i$ [+TOP] $[_{C}$ $\varPhi$ [+Q] $[_{TP}$ we will solve t$_i$]]]]]]]?

c. *$[_{CP}$ $[_{C}$ Tell [+Imp] $[_{TP}$ them $[_{RP}$ that $[_{CP}$ $[_{TopP}$ this book$_i$ [+TOP] $[_{C}$ $\varPhi$ [+Imp] $[_{TP}$ he has read t$_i$]]]]]]]?

d. *$[_{CP}$ $[_{C}$ $[_{TP}$ Bill asked $[_{RP}$ $[_{CP}$ $[_{C}$ if [+Q] $_{[TopP}$ such books$_i$ [+TOP] $[_{TP}$ John only reads t$_i$ at home]]]]]]?

e. *$[_{CP}[_{C}$ $[_{TP}$ Robin knows $[_{RP}$ $[_{CP}$ where $[_{C}$ [+Q] $[_{TopP}$ the birdseed$_i$ [+TOP] $[_{TP}$ you are going to put t$_i$]]]]]]?

Through these syntactic analyses, the distribution of topics in simple and complex sentences in English can be summarized as the following Table 2 and Table 3:

Table 2   Topics in simple sentences

Sentence type	Topic
Declarative	+
Interrogative	-
Imperative	-

Table 3   Topics in complex sentences

Main clause \ Subordinate clause	Declarative	Interrogative	Imperative
Declarative	+	-	N/P
Interrogative	-	N/P	N/P
Imperative	-	N/P	N/P

3.2.3.3.4 The incompatibility of TopP and the conditional clause in English

Now the discussion goes back to the conditional clause in English. As Haegeman (2010b) proposes, the world operator will move to the position [Spec, CP] to derive the conditional clause. According to the split-CP hypothesis, there are four different phrases on this CP layer. So locating the accurate position of the world operator is the issue at hand. Then I will utilize different types of sentences to test the landing site of the world operator. See the following (52):

(52)
a. *If did John buy this book, ...
b. *If when did you buy this book, ...
c. *If leave this book on the table, ...

(52a-c) show that the world operator *if* cannot be compatible with interrogative or imperative clauses. In other words, the world operator cannot be compatible with ForceP.[①] So the natural result of this syntactic behavior is that they also occupy the same position, i.e., the leftmost position of CP. This observation coincides with the idea that the movement of the world operator is similar to the wh-movement proposed by Haegeman (2010b). Therefore, I argue that the world operator is similar to wh-constituent, and the function of the operator carrier *if* is to introduce and type a clause. So it should be in the leftmost position of CP, that is, the [Spec, CP] or [Spec, ForceP]. The discussion above shows that both TopP and ForceP are in the leftmost position of CP. Then, the world operator, together with TopP and ForceP will compete for the same syntactic position in English. The consequence of this competition is that they cannot co-occur in any type of sentence no matter whether they are in main or subordinate clauses. Just because the world operator cannot co-occur with TopP in English, the topicalized constituents cannot be compatible with conditional clauses in English.

3.2.3.3.5 The co-occurrence of TopP and ForceP in Chinese

Compared with the ungrammatical sentences (42) and (43) in English,

---

① At present, I am not sure whether the world operator, Force and topic are in the same category. What I can say here is that the world operator should belong to the modal system because it expresses the irrealis modality. According to Cinque (1999, 2004), modals should also be put in the different positions in the cartographic hierarchy. Some of them are on CP layer, while others may be on TP or other layers. And the landing site of the world operator is just overlapped with Force. Although they may belong to different categories, they occupy the same syntactic position. Just like in Chinese context, the word yao that expresses dynamic modality occupies the same position as aspectual markers and they never co-occur. The following (1a-b) are both grammatical:

(1) a. Wo yao du yi-ben shu.
    I   want read one-CL book
    'I want to read a book.'

  b. Wo du le yi-ben shu.
    I   read ASP one-CL book
    'I have read a book.'

When they exist in the same clause, the clause will be ungrammatical, as (2) shows:

(2)* wo yao du le yi-ben shu.
    I   want read ASP one-CL book
    'I want to have read a book.'

As this book mainly concentrates on the syntactic positions of the world operator and ForceP, their categories and their interaction is out of the range of discussion.

the corresponding Chinese sentences are grammatical. The opposite syntactic behaviors indicate that the distribution of topicalized constituents in Chinese is different from that in English. As (53) and (54) show, the topicalized constituents can be embedded in these clauses:

(53)

a. *Naxie qianniu-hua* Yuehan zhong le   ma?
   those petunia   John   plant ASP SFP
   '*Those petunias*, did John plant?'

b. *Naxie qianniu-hua* Yuehan shenme-shihou zhong le?
   those petunia   John   what-time   plant ASP/SFP
   '*Those petunias*, when did John plant?'

c. *Zhe-ben shu*,   fang zai zhuo   shang (ba).
   this-CL   book   put PREP table on   (SFP)
   '*This book*, leave on the table.'

In (53a), the sentence final particle *ma* expresses the interrogative force, the wh-constituent *shenme shihou* (when) in (53b) expresses the interrogative force and the sentence final particle *ba* expresses the imperative force in (53c). It can be seen that these particles and wh-constituent already occupy ForceP in these three clauses. The topicalized constituents *naxie qianniu hua* (those petunias) in (53a-b) and *zheben shu* (this book) in (53c) can be allowed in these clauses, proving that TopP and ForceP can be compatible with each other in Chinese.

(54)

a. Ni   renwei *shehui-zhuyi lilun*   henduo jieke-ren hui   fouren ma?
   you   think   socialist   theory   many   Czech   will deny   SFP
   'Do you think that *socialist theory* many Czechs would deny?'

b. Ni   juede *zhe-ge wenti*   women yingdang zenme jiejue?
   you   think this-CL problem   we   should   how   solve
   'How do you think that *this problem* we will solve?'

c. Gaosu tamen (ba)   *zhe-ben shu*   ta   du   guo le.
   tell   them (SFP) this-CL   book   he   read ASP SFP
   'Tell them that *this book*, he has read.'

d. Bier wen shifou *zhexie shuji* Yuehan zhi zai jia du.
Bill ask if these book John only at home read
'Bill asked if *such books* John only reads at home.'

e. Luobin zhidao *zhexie niao-shi* ni yao fang zai nali.
Robin know these birdseed you are.going.to put PREP where
'Robin knows where *the birdseed* you are going to put.'

In (54a), the sentence final particle *ma* expresses the interrogative force, the wh-constituent *zenme* (how) in (54b) expresses the interrogative force and the sentence final particle *ba* expresses the imperative force in (54c). All the constituents that express the illocutionary force exist in the main clauses. The topics *shehuizhuyi lilun* (socialist theory), *zhege wenti* (this problem) and *zheben shu* (this book) are allowed to exist in the complement clauses.

On the contrary, some constituents that express the illocutionary force are in the complement clauses. In (54d), the interrogative conjunction *shifou* (if) expresses the interrogative force and the wh-constituent *nali* (where) expresses the interrogative force in (54e). The topicalized constituents *zhexie shuji* (these books) and *zhexie niaoshi* (these birdseed) exist in these complement clauses, and the sentences are grammatical.

The grammaticality of (53) and (54) show that the topicalized constituents are compatible with interrogative and imperative sentences, whether they exist in the main or the complement clauses. In the clauses that express interrogative or imperative force, the position of ForceP has been occupied. However, the topicalized constituents can still exist in these clauses, which proves that TopP and ForceP are independent projections and can co-occur in the same clause in Chinese. Contrary to English, they do not compete for the same syntactic position.[①]

In fact, TopP and ForceP, even FocP can co-occur in one clause in Chinese:

---

① For the syntactic analysis, readers can go back to section 3.2.3.3.3 for reference.

(55)

Zhe-jian	*shi,*	lian	*Zhangsan*	dou	meiyou	banfa	*ma?*
this-CL	thing	even	Zhangsan	DOU	not	solution	SFP

'Even Zhangsan cannot solve this problem, can he?'

In (55), *zhejian shi* (this thing) is the topic, the *lian...dou* (even) structure indicates that *Zhangsan* (the person's name) is the focus and sentence final particle *ma* expresses the interrogative force. The grammaticality of (55) shows that TopP, FocP and ForceP can co-occur in the same clause, and they are independent phrases in Chinese. Different from English, TopP is not in the leftmost position of the CP layer.

It is noticeable that sometimes they do not follow the linear order: ForceP>TopP>FocP>FinP in Chinese though CP is decomposed into independent ForceP, TopP and FocP. The order of these phrases in the surface structure is very flexible. In the interrogative clauses in Chinese, there is no T-to-C movement for the auxiliary verb or wh-movement for the wh-constituent. Besides, the sentence final particle *ma* typing the clause as interrogative also stays at the original position (Huang 1982; Tang 2015; Deng 2016). The various orders like ForceP>TopP>FocP, TopP>ForceP>FocP or TopP>FocP>ForceP can easily be found in Chinese sentences, as the following (56a-c) show:

(56)

a.
Wei-shenme	zhe-jian	shi,	lian	Zhangsan	dou	meiyou	banfa?
for-what	this-CL	thing	even	Zhangsan	DOU	not	solution

'Why cannot even Zhangsan solve this problem?'

b.
Zhe-jian	shi,	wei-shenme	lian	Zhangsan	dou	meiyou	banfa?
this-CL	thing	for-what	even	Zhangsan	DOU	not	solution

'Why cannot even Zhangsan solve this problem?'

c.
Zhe-jian	*shi,*	lian	Zhangsan	dou	meiyou	banfa	ma?
this-CL	thing	even	Zhangsan	DOU	not	solution	SFP

'Even Zhangsan cannot solve this problem, can he?'

Although the orders of these decomposed phrases in the surface structures are flexible, ForceP in these clauses still occupies the leftmost position in the logic form in Chinese. Just like the wh-movement in the logic form, the constituent that expresses illocutionary force stays at the original position in the surface structure and moves to the specifier position of ForceP in the logic form (Huang 1982). The specifier position of ForceP is occupied by a covert interrogative or imperative operator, and TopP still follows ForceP in the logic form. Though the linear order of these phrases on the CP layer is flexible in the surface structure, they still follow the ForceP>TopP>FocP>TP in the logic form.

3.2.3.3.6 The compatibility of TopP in conditional clauses in Chinese

It is shown that TopP and ForceP can co-occur in the Chinese clauses when CP is split. Now, I will further test whether the world operator is compatible with ForceP. As (57a-c) show in the following, the world operator carrier *ruguo* (if) is not compatible with ForceP though it is compatible with TopP.

(57)

a. *Ruguo* ni   mai le   zhe-ben   shu   ma, ...
  if   you buy ASP this-CL   book   SFP
  'If did you buy this book, ...'

b. *Ruguo* wei-shenme   ni   mai le   zhe-ben   shu, ...
  if   for-what   you buy ASP this-CL   book
  'If when did you buy this book, ...'

c. *Ruguo* fang zhe-ben   shu   zai   zhuo   shang ba, ...
  if   put   this-CL   book PREP   table   on   SFP
  'If leave this book on the table, ...'

The sentence final particle *ma* expresses the interrogative force in (57a), the wh-constituent *weishenme* (why) in (57b) expresses the interrogative force and the sentence final particle *ba* expresses the imperative force in (57c). The ungrammaticality of these sentences shows that *ruguo* (if) is not compatible with those constituents that express the illocutionary force. In other words, *ruguo* cannot co-occur with these constituents that occupy the head position of ForceP. This syntactic behavior shows that the world operator is not compatible with ForceP, and they both are in the leftmost position of the left periphery. I thus propose that the world operator carrier *ruguo* is just the head of ForceP and the real complementizer.

Then, I can go on to test whether the world operator can be compatible with TopP. As (3b=58) shows, the topicalized constituent *zhexie kaoshi* (these exams) co-occurs with the world operator carrier *ruguo*, which means it does not intervene in the movement of the world operator. Thus, the world operator can be compatible with TopP.

(58)

Ruguo *zhexie kaoshi* ni   meiyou tongguo, ni   jiu   bu neng na-dao xuewei.
if   these exam you not   pass   you then not can get-PERF degree
'If you don't pass these exams, you cannot get the degree.'

In (58), the topicalized constituent can be embedded in the conditional adverbial clause, proving that the world operator can be compatible with ForceP in Chinese.

The series of syntactic behaviors indicate that the world operator *ruguo* and ForceP should be in the leftmost position of the left periphery of the clause and compete for the same syntactic position in Chinese. However, TopP can be compatible with ForceP and world operator, respectively. Therefore, TopP is not in the leftmost position and should follow ForceP and the world operator in Chinese.

Interestingly, just like the wh-constituents in the interrogative clauses in Chinese, the world operator carrier *ruguo* does not always need to move to the initial position of the clause. Sometimes, it can stay at the original position in the surface structure though it will still move to the initial position of the clause in the logic form. See the following (59a-c):

(59)

a. *Ruguo* ni   zuotian   kan   le   zhe-ben shu, ...
    if   you yesterday read ASP this-CL   book
    'If you read this book yesterday, ...'

b. Ni   *ruguo* zuotian   kan le   zhe-ben shu, ...
you if   yesterday read ASP this-CL   book
'You, if read this book yesterday, ...'

c. Ni   zuotian   *ruguo*   kan le   zhe-ben   shu, ...
you yesterday if   read ASP this-CL   book
'You, if read this book yesterday, ...'

Because the world operator carrier *ruguo* does not move overtly to the CP layer, the surface structure of TopP and the world operator does not always follow the liner order of ForceP>TopP though they still obey this constraint in the logic form. See the following (60a-c):

(60)

a. *Ruguo* zhe-ben   shu   ni   zuotian   kan   le, ...
if   this-CL   book you yesterday read   ASP/SFP
'If this book, you read yesterday, ...'

b. Zhe-ben   shu,   *ruguo* ni   zuotian   kan   le, ...
this-CL   book if   you yesterday read   ASP/SFP
'This book, if you read yesterday, ...'

c. Zhe-ben   shu,   ni   *ruguo* zuotian   kan   le, ...
this-CL   book you if   yesterday read   ASP/SFP
'This book, if you read yesterday, ...'

In (60a), the world operator carrier *ruguo* (if) is at the initial position of the clause and occupies the [Spec, ForceP] position while the topicalized constituent *zheben shu* (this book) that occupies the [Spec, TopP] position follows the world operator carrier *ruguo*. Thus, it obeys the sequence of ForceP>TopP according to the split-CP hypothesis. On the contrary, the world operator carrier *ruguo* does not precede the topicalized constituent *zheben shu* (this book) but follows the topicalized constituent in (60b-c). Then the surface order seems to disobey the sequence of ForceP>TopP. However, the world operator carrier *ruguo* will continue to move to the leftmost position of the clause and occupies the [Spec, ForceP] position in the logic form just like the wh-operator that moves in the logic form in Chinese interrogative sentences (Huang 1982). Therefore, it will still obey the sequence of ForceP>TopP in the logic form.

3.2.3.3.7 The parametric variation in splitting CP

Based on the observation, I propose that the distinctive behaviors of English and Chinese conditionals in terms of topicalization are due to parametric variation in split-CP. Just as the split-CP hypothesis indicates, the CP layer can be further decomposed into different functional phrases. However, the specific compositions of the functional phrases can be varied among different languages, leading to parametric variation.

The conditional adverbial clauses are derived by the movement of the world operator. Based on this hypothesis, I propose that TopP in English is located at the leftmost periphery of CP and competes for the same syntactic position with ForceP and the world operator. Thus TopP is incompatible with conditional clauses and the clauses with the illocutionary force. However, TopP in Chinese will not conflict with the complementizer *ruguo* located in the head position of ForceP. When CP is split, TopP and ForceP are independent projections and do not compete for the same syntactic position. Therefore, TopP is compatible with conditional clauses in Chinese.

The whole process can be illustrated as the Table 4 in the following:

Table 4   The left periphery of English and Chinese conditional clauses

English	Chinese
ForceP TopP >FocP>FinP World Operator	ForceP >TopP>FocP>FinP World Operator
⇩	⇩
The leftmost periphery	The leftmost periphery

Ever since Rizzi (1997) puts forward the split-CP hypothesis, the CP layer has been considered to be composed of different functional phrases such as ForceP, TopP, FocP, ModP and FinP. However, just as some linguists have noticed, the compositions of these phrases can be varied in different languages. Since Rizzi (1997)'s hypothesis is mainly based on the observation of the syntactic behaviors in Italian, it can be doubtful whether these specific functional phrases in Italian can be paralleled perfectly with those in English and Chinese.

From the discussion above, one can see that in English topicalized constituents are incompatible not only with conditional adverbial clauses, but also with any clause in which the illocutionary force has been projected. TopP will compete for the same syntactic position with ForceP in English clauses no matter whether they are main clauses or embedded clauses. In other words, the CP layer has only one syntactic position to host TopP and ForceP in English. However, the situation is totally different in Chinese. Topicalized constituents are accepted in any clauses no matter whether they are main clauses or embedded clause, and no matter whether the illocutionary force has been projected or not. The opposite syntactic behaviors demonstrate that TopP and ForceP are independent phrases on the CP layer. In other words, the CP layer in Chinese has two separate and independent positions to host TopP and ForceP. In this way, the parameter of splitting CP is thus set as the binary branch in English and Chinese.

3.3 A contrastive study of MCP in English and Chinese temporal adverbials

This section will make a contrastive study of MCP in temporal adverbial clauses in English and two temporal preposition phrases in Chinese. English and Chinese temporal adverbials are different in their syntactic structures and syntactic behaviors. English temporals are clauses, while Chinese temporals are in fact preposition phrases (the *zai*-X structure and the *dang*-X structure). As for the MCP distributions, English temporal clauses do not allow topicalization and high modal markers, while Chinese temporals show very complicated syntactic behaviors to these MCP. On the one hand, the temporal preposition phrases *zai*-X structure and *dang*-X structure show sharp differences with respect to the availability of topicalization; on the other hand, they both do not allow high modal markers. This section will analyze the similarities and differences of MCP between English and Chinese temporal adverbials and the differences between the *zai*-X structure and the *dang*-X structure in Chinese. Finally, the section attempts to give a convincing account of the series of syntactic behaviors.

3.3.1 MCP in English temporal adverbial clauses

MCP in temporal adverbial clauses in English are mainly argument fronting (topicalization) and high modal markers. See the following (61) and (62):

(61)
a. When she started to write *his column* last year, I thought she would be fine.
b. *When *this column* she started to write last year, I thought she would be fine.

(Haegeman 2009: 393)

(62)
a. John will do it when he has time.
b. *John will do it when he *may/must* have time.

(Declerck and Depraetere 1995: 278)

As (61b) shows, the sentence will be ungrammatical when the argument *this column* moves to the initial position of the temporal adverbial clause. In (62b), the existence of the high modal marker *may/must* also leads to ungrammaticality. Haegeman (2009) (following Geis 1970, 1975; Enç 1987; Larson 1987, 1990; Dubinsky and Williams 1995; Declerck 1997; Demirdache and Uribe-Etexbarria 2004) proposes that the temporal adverbial clause is derived by the movement of an operator (*when*) to the left periphery (the earlier version of the movement of the temporal operator) and is a headless relative clause. Like the movement account of conditional clauses, the property of being a relative clause implies that temporal clauses will be incompatible with the argument fronting and the high modal marker because of the intervention effect, that is, the argument *this column* and the high modal marker *may/must* intervene in the movement of the temporal operator.

The evidence to support the movement derivation of a temporal clause is mainly from the following observation (Larson 1990: 170-171), which shows that a temporal adverbial clause is ambiguous when the temporal operator moves to the different positions in the process of the derivation.

(63)

I saw Mary in New York when she claimed that she would leave.

a. high construal: I saw her at the time that she made the claim.

I saw Mary in New York [_CP when_i [_TP she claimed [_CP that [_TP she would leave]] t_i]].

b. low construal: I saw her at the time of her presumed departure.

I saw Mary in New York [_CP when_i [_TP she claimed [_CP t_i that [_TP she would leave t_i]]]].

(63) is ambiguous: the time expressed by *when* might be either that of the higher clause within the adverbial clause, giving the so-called high construal in (63a), with the corresponding derivation; or it may be that of the lower clause in the adverbial clause, giving what is referred to as the low construal in (63b), with the corresponding derivation. (63a) illustrates the long movement, with the temporal operator originating in the embedded clause targeting the higher clause of the adverbial adjunct; while (63b) illustrates the short movement, with the temporal operator originating in the embedded clause targeting the lower clause of the adverbial adjunct.

In addition, Demirdache and Uribe-Etxebarria (2004) find that the movement of the temporal operator from the lower clause to the higher clause is not available in the context in which the complex noun phrase forms the island. See the following (64):

(64)

I saw Mary in New York when she made the claim that she would leave.

a. high construal: I saw her at the time that she made the claim.

I saw Mary in New York [_CP when_i [_TP she made [_DP the claim [_CP that [_TP she would leave]] t_i]]].

b. *low construal: I saw her at the time of her presumed departure.

*I saw Mary in New York [_CP when_i [_TP she made [_DP the claim [_CP t_i that [_TP she would leave t_i]]]]]. (Demirdache and Uribe-Etxebarria 2004: 165)

Unlike (63), the temporal clause in (64) contains a complex noun phrase *the claim* which takes a *that*-clause as its complement. The low construal reading cannot be available because the temporal operator (*when*) cannot be extracted from the clausal complement of the complex noun phrase *the claim* (for complex NP is an island for extraction and thus blocks the extraction of the operator). So the sentence is not ambiguous and has only one high construal. And the temporal adverbial can only be interpreted as *at the time that she made the claim.*

Considering all these findings, Haegeman (2009) proposes that temporal adverbial clauses are represented as headless or free relative clauses derived by the movement of the temporal operator. The MCP constraints on temporal adverbials are brought about by the intervention effect, i.e., the topicalized constituents and high modal markers that have the Q-feature will intervene in the movement of the temporal operator that has the same Q-feature. The intervention effect finally makes the derivation of the temporal adverbial clauses crash.

3.3.2 MCP in Chinese temporal adverbial structures

Wei and Li (2018a) have observed that the temporal adverbials in Chinese show the same MCP constraint as those in English. As (65) shows, Chinese temporals do not allow topicalization like English ones.

(65)
*Zai Li *xiaojie* wo jian-dao   de   shihou, Mali zhenghao jingguo.
 at Li Miss   I   meet-PERF DE time   Mary just   pass.by
'When Miss Li I met, Mary just passed by.'   (Wei and Li 2018a: 177)

Wei and Li (2018a) argue that the temporal adjunct contains a relative clause derived via the movement of a time expression, i.e., the temporal clause in Chinese is derived by the movement of the temporal operator. Thus, they attribute the absence of topicalized constituents in temporal adverbials in Chinese to the intervention effect proposed by Haegeman (2009).

I also notice that high modal markers are not compatible with temporal adverbials in Chinese, as (66) shows:

(66)

*zai *dagai*　 wo ting-dao zhe-shou ge　 de shihou, wo xiangqi le　 wo-de chu-lian.

at　 probably I　 hear-PERF this-CL　 song DE time　 I　 think.of ASP my　　 first-love

'When probably I hear this song, I remember my first love.'

The earlier part of this paper (see section 3.1.1) has indicated that Chinese temporal adverbials are represented as two kinds of preposition phrases: the *zai-X* structure and the *dang-X* structure. Noticeably, these two structures show similar and different availabilities to MCP. High modals are not compatible with the *dang-X* structure, just like the *zai-X* structure, as (67) shows:

(67)

*Dang *dagai*　 wo ting-dao zhe-shou ge　 de shihou, wo xiangqi le　 wo-de chu-lian.

just.at probably I　 hear-PERF this-CL　 song DE time　 I　 think.of ASP my　　 first-love

'When probably I hear this song, I remember my first love.'

While the *zai-X* structure does not allow topicalization, the *dang-X* structure shows more tolerance to topicalized constituents. See the following (68):

(68)

?Dang　 Li xiaojie wo jian-dao　 de　 shihou, Mali zhenghao　 jingguo.[1]

just.at Li Miss　 I　 meet-PERF DE time　　 Mary just　　　 pass.by

'When Miss Li I met, Mary just passed by.'

Why does the Chinese temporal adverbial *dang-X* structure behave

---

[1]　This sentence seems a little unnatural because it is imitated from Wei & Li's (2018a) example sentence (64). In fact, the sentence will be perfectly grammatical if some vocabularies are changed while the structure is maintained. See the following:

(1) Dang *zhe-ben shu*　 ni　 kan wan　 de shihou, jiegei wo kan yi-xia　 ba.

just.at this-CL book　 you read finish DE time　　 lend　 me read one-CL SFP

'When this book you finish reading, lend it to me to have a look.'

(2) Dang *boshi wenping* ni　 na-dao　　 de　 shihou, ni　 faner　 bu　 zaihu le.

just.at doctor diploma you obtain-PERF DE time　　 you instead not　 care　 SFP

'When doctor's degree you obtain, instead you will not care anymore.'

differently from the English counterpart in terms of MCP distribution? Moreover, why do the *zai-X* structure and the *dang-X* structure show different availabilities to topicalization? These are questions worth exploring further.

3.3.3 Accounting for MCP in English and Chinese temporal adverbials

Just as I have mentioned in section 3.3.1, Haegeman (2009, 2010b) proposes that both conditional and temporal clauses are derived by the movement of the operators and the operators have the Q-feature, so the intervention effect makes conditional clauses and temporal clauses resist topicalized constituents and high modal markers that have the same Q-feature. However, it is shown that this analysis cannot apply to conditional adverbial clauses in Chinese (see section 3.2.3) and proposed that the parametric variation of the splitting CP is the reason for the different availabilities of topicalization in English and Chinese. This analysis can be extended to the temporal adverbials. And I argue that this is why the English temporal adverbial clause and the Chinese temporal *dang*-X structure are different in licensing topicalization. Besides, the different syntactic behaviors between the *zai-X* structure and the *dang-X* structure can be analyzed under the same framework. The argumentation will be built on the following three steps:

(69)

a. A temporal adverbial clause in Chinese is a preposition phrase in nature and contains a relative clause derived by the movement of a temporal operator. The intervention effect causes the incompatibility of high modal markers with temporal clauses both in English and Chinese.

b. The parametric variation between English and Chinese in CP-splitting accounts for the different distributions of topicalized constituents between temporal adverbial clauses in English and the *dang*-X structure in Chinese.

c. Because the prepositions *zai* and *dang* are located on the different layers of preposition phrase, topicalization is not compatible with the *zai*-X structure while compatible with the *dang*-X structure. This analysis can extend to other contradictory syntactic behaviors between the *zai*-X structure and the *dang*-X structure.

3.3.3.1 The intervention effect

There is ample empirical evidence to prove that the temporal adverbials in Chinese are preposition phrases and contain relative clauses with *shihou* (time) being the head noun. As (70a) shows, the temporal adverbials in Chinese are introduced by the preposition *zai* (at). This preposition should always be followed by a complement *shihou* with the modification marker *de* in between. However, the sentence will be ungrammatical when the complement *shihou* is covert, just as (70b) shows.

(70)

  a. *Zai* wo ting-dao   zhe-shou ge   de shihou, wo xiangqi le   wo-de chu-lian.
     at   I   hear-PERF this-CL song DE time   I   think.of ASP my   first-love
     'When I hear this song, I think of my first love.'

  b. *Zai wo ting-dao   zhe-shou ge,   wo xiangqi le   wo-de chu-lian.
     at   I   hear-PERF this-CL   song I   think.of ASP my   first-love
     'When I hear this song, I think of my first love.'

The temporal adverbial *zai*-X structure in (70a) is grammatical when the complement *shihou* (time) is overt. However, the temporal adverbial *zai*-X structure is unacceptable when the word *shihou* is covert in (70b). The comparison of (70a) and (70b) shows that the ellipsis of the complement *shihou* will lead to ungrammaticality. The contrastive syntactic behaviors confirm that the complement of the preposition *zai* is a nominal phrase instead of a clause, and the word *zai* is a preposition rather than a conjunction or complementizer.

The choice of the conjunction words can also confirm the nominal status of the temporal complement of *zai*. According to Aoun and Li (2003), Li (2008) and Zhang (2010), the Chinese conjunction words *he/gen* (and) and *erqie* (and) conjoin different phrases: *he* and *gen* conjoin nominal phrases while *erqie* conjoin non-nominal constituents, such as clauses. The temporal adverbials conjoined by *he* or *gen* are acceptable in (71a), while the ones conjoined by *erqie* are not in (71b). This comparison further confirms the nominal status of the temporal complement of *zai*:

(71)

a. Zai wo ting-dao   zhe-shou ge   de shihou he   wo kan-dao zhexie zhaopian
   at   I   hear-PERF this-CL   song DE time   and I   see-PERF these photo

   de Shihou, wo xiangqi le   wo-de chu-lian.
   DE time   I   think.of ASP my   first-love
   'When I hear this song and see these photos, I think of my first love.'

b. *Zai wo ting-dao   zhe-shou ge   de shihou erqie wo kandao   zhexie
    at   I   hear-PERF this-CL   song DE time   and   I   see-PERF these

   zhaopian de shihou, wo xiangqi le   wo-de chu-lian.
   photo   DE time   I   think.of ASP my   first-love
   'When I hear this song and see these photos, I think of my first love.'

In (71a), when the two *zai*-X structures are conjoined by the conjunction word *he,* the sentence is grammatical. However, the sentence becomes ungrammatical in (71b) when the two *zai*-X structures are conjoined by the conjunction word *erqie.* Because *he* generally conjoins nominal phrases while *erqie* generally conjoins clauses, the comparison between (71a) and (71b) proves again that the complement of *zai* is nominal and *zai* is a preposition instead of conjunction or complementizer.

Furthermore, the temporal complement of *zai* can also be conjoined by *dou* (all or both, the totalizing or distributive quantifier in Chinese). As a totalizing quantifier, *dou* quantifies the associated plural noun phrases (Lee 1986; Li 1997; Huang 2005). This phenomenon further proves that the temporal complement of *zai* is nominal. See the examples in (72):

(72)

Zai wo ting-dao zhe-shou ge   de shihou he   wo kandao   zhexie zhaopian
at   I   hear-PERF this-CL song DE time   and I   see-PERF these photo

de shihou, *dou* xiangqi le   wo-de chu-lian.
DE time   DOU   think.of ASP my   first-love
'When I hear this song and see these photos, I think of my first love.'

In (72), the two *zai*-X structures conjoined by the conjunction word *he* can be quantified by the totalizing quantifier *dou,* and the propositions in the two temporal adverbials are both in the scope of the quantifier. This phenomenon further proves that the complement of *zai* is a nominal phrase, and the word *zai* is a preposition.

Similar to the *zai-X* structure, the *dang-X* structure also contains a relative clause with *shihou* as the head noun,[①] as (73) shows:

(73)

Dang wo ting-dao zhe-shou ge   de shihou, wo xiangqi le   wo-de chu-lian.
just.at I   hear-PERF this-CL   song DE time   I   think.of ASP my   first-love
'When I hear this song, I think of my first love.'

From these observations, I can confirm the prepositional status of the word *zai* and *dang*. Both of them are prepositions rather than conjunctions or complementizers, and the Chinese temporal adverbials *zai*-X structure and *dang*-X structure are preposition phrases. Following Wei and Li (2018a), I propose that Chinese temporal adverbials are preposition phrases and the complements of which contain relative clauses. A temporal adverbial clause in Chinese is derived by a temporal operator (a null operator), similar to the derivation process of the temporal adverbial in English. As Haegeman (2009) points out, this kind of derivation indicates that the temporal adverbials are free relative clauses. Chinese temporal adverbial, like the English one, has the ambiguity of high and low construals, and this is the main evidence to illustrate the movement of the temporal operator (Wei and Li, 2018a: 179):

(74)

Zai Mali shuo ta   yao likai de shihou, Zhangsan juban le   yi-ge   juhui.
at   Mary say she will leave DE time   Zhangsan hold ASP one-CL party
'Zhangsan held a party...
(a) at the time that Mary made the claim' (high construal)
(b) at the time of Mary's alleged departure' (low construal)

---

① The conjunction words test and the quantifier test can also prove the prepositional status of *dang*. This book will not detail the issue due to space limitations. The similar tests for the preposition *zai* can be found earlier in this section for reference.

(74) is ambiguous and has two construals: the temporal operator is moved to the higher clause for the high construal, with the corresponding derivation, and the time expressed in (74a) is when Mary says (*Mali shuo*); the temporal operator can also be in the base position in the lower clause for the low construal, with the corresponding derivation, and the time expressed in (74b) is when she will leave (*ta yao likai*). (74a) illustrates the long movement with the temporal operator targeting the higher clause of the adverbial adjunct, while (74b) illustrates the short movement with the temporal operator targeting the lower clause of the adverbial adjunct. The ambiguity of (74) proves that the temporal adverbial *zai*-X structure contains a relative clause derived by the temporal operator.[①]

The temporal adverbial clause is a free relative clause derived by the temporal operator in English, and the temporal adverbial contains a relative clause in Chinese. The temporal operator carries the Q-feature that is also carried by the high modal markers. Thus, the intervention effect arises, and the sentences (62b), (66) and (67) are ungrammatical, repeated as (75a-c) for convenience:

(75)

a. *John will do it when he *may/must* have time.

b. *Zai *dagai*   wo ting-dao   zhe-shou   ge   de shihou, wo xiangqi le
   at   probably I   hear-PERF this-CL   song DE time   I   think.of ASP

   wo-de chu-lian.
   my   first-love

   'When probably I hear this song, I remember my first love.'

c. *Dang *dagai*   wo ting-dao   zhe-shou ge   de shihou, wo xiangqi le
   just.at probably I   hear-PERF this-CL   song DE time   I   think.of ASP

   wo-de chu-lian.
   my   first-love.

   'When probably I hear this song, I remember my first love.'

---

① Although the *zai*-X structure has the ambiguity of high and low construals, the *dang*-X structure does not have this ambiguity. I will leave aside this problem here and illustrate it in the following sections.

In (75a), the high modal marker *may/must* is not compatible with the temporal adverbial clause introduced by *when* in English. And in (75b-c), the high modal marker *dagai* (probably) is not compatible with Chinese temporal adverbials *zai*-X structure and *dang*-X structure. These syntactic behaviors show that these high modals carry the Q-feature and block the movement of the temporal operator that derives the temporal adverbials. Therefore, the intervention effect causes the incompatibility of high modal markers with temporal clauses both in English and Chinese.

3.3.3.2 The parametric variation in CP-splitting

I have shown that there is a parametric variation between English and Chinese in CP-splitting (see section 3.2.3.3.7). When CP is split into ForceP, TopP, FocP and FinP, the former two phrases will compete for the same syntactic position in English, while they will not compete for the same position in Chinese because they are independent phrases. Thus, topicalized constituents are not compatible with conditional clauses in English, while they are compatible in Chinese. The parametric variation accounts for the different distributions of topicalized constituents in English and Chinese conditional clauses. This account can apply to temporal adverbial clauses.

When CP is split, ForceP and TopP will compete for the same syntactic position in temporal adverbial clauses in English. As the following (76=61b) shows, topicalized constituents cannot be compatible with temporal adverbial clauses:

(76)

*When *this column* she started to write last year, I thought she would be fine.

In (76), the topicalized constituent *this column* occupies the [Spec, TopP] position, and the temporal operator carrier *when* occupies the [Spec, ForceP] position. Because TopP and ForceP will compete for the same position and cannot co-occur on the CP layer in English, this sentence is ungrammatical.

However, there is no such competition in Chinese. TopP and ForceP can co-occur with each other. Based on this hypothesis, I predict that Chinese temporals should tolerate topicalization. (77), equivalent to (65), shows that the temporal adverbial is not compatible with topicalization, which is out of expectation:

(77)

*Zai	*Li xiaojie*	wo	jian-dao		de	shihou,	Mali	zhenghao	jingguo.
at	Li Miss	I	meet-PERF		DE	time	Mary	just	pass.by

'When Miss Li I met, Mary just passed by.'

As (77) shows, the topicalized constituent *Li xiaojie* (Miss Li) cannot be embedded in the Chinese temporal adverbial *zai*-X structure. Considering that there is no competition between TopP and ForceP in Chinese, the result is confusing.

While the *zai*-X structure cannot host topicalized constituents, the *dang*-X structure shows more tolerance to such constituents, as (78=68) shows:

(78)

?Dang	Li xiaojie	wo	jian-dao		de	shihou,	Mali	zhenghao	jingguo.
just.at	Li Miss	I	meet-PERF		DE	time	Mary	just	pass.by

'When Miss Li I met, Mary just passed by.'

(78) is acceptable though it is slightly unnatural when the topicalized constituent *Li xiaojie* appears in the *dang*-X structure. Because Force and Top can project independently and there is no conflict between ForceP and TopP in Chinese, the *dang*-X structure, a preposition phrase containing a relative clause derived by the temporal operator, can host the topicalized constituent. Nevertheless, why is not the *zai*-X structure compatible with the topicalized constituent? This sharp difference is worth exploring and I will leave it aside now.[1]

---

[1]   In section 3.3.3.3, I will give a unified account for the series of different syntactic behaviors between the *zai*-X structure and the *dang*-X structure.

3.3.3.3 The cartographic analysis for the *zai*-X structure and the *dang*-X structure

The argumentation will begin with the cartographic analysis for spatial preposition phrases. Inspired by Zhang and Lin (2021), I believe that the cartographic analysis for spatial preposition phrases can apply to temporal adverbial phrases because temporal adverbials in Chinese are preposition phrases.[①] Then, the section makes a cartographic analysis of the syntactic structures of the *zai*-X structure and the *dang*-X structure and argues that the two prepositions *zai* and *dang* are different types of prepositions. Being different types of preposition phrases, the *zai*-X structure and the *dang*-X structure have different syntactic derivational processes and thus have differences in resisting topicalized constituents and licensing high/low construals. Finally, the section proposes that the two prepositions' being on the different cartographic layers leads to a series of different syntactic behaviors between the *zai*-X structure and the *dang*-X structure.

3.3.3.3.1 The cartographic analysis for spatial preposition phrase

The discussion in the last section shows that the *zai*-X structure and the *dang*-X structure are both preposition phrases. Accordingly, I will review the research of preposition phrases before further analyzing the internal syntax of the two structures.

A preposition phrase is first regarded as a combination of a preposition and a DP, and the DP is the complement of the preposition (Jackendoff 1977). Since this analysis cannot cover the syntactic phenomenon that the preposition and postposition can co-occur in some languages like Chinese [e.g., *zai* zhuozi *shang* (on the table)], Greenberg (1995) puts forward the concept of circumposition. This concept illustrates the related phenomena in Chinese to some extent (Liu 2002), but it also meets some challenges. For example, this analysis still cannot put the preposition and postposition in the correct syntactic positions with the binary branch structure and cannot define the syntactic status of the DP.

---

① Special thanks go to Professor Qingwen Zhang for providing me with this new way of thinking.

Ever since Rizzi (1997) puts forward the cartographic program, more and more linguists (Koopman 2000; Svenonius 2006, 2007, 2008, 2010; den Dikken 2010; Cinque 2010a) realize that this proposal can apply to the analysis of preposition phrases. They argue that a preposition phrase also has full-fledged cartographic layers, and it can be decomposed into different functional phrases. These linguists reach the consensus on the cartographic approach though they have some minor discrepancies on the details of the cartographic layers. Take Cinque's analysis (2010a: 10) as an example, he states that the preposition phrase *from at two miles diagonally north up in here under the mountain* is composed of the following functional phrases:

(79)

[$_{PPdir}$ from [$_{PPstat}$ at AT [$_{DPplace}$ [$_{DegP}$ two miles [$_{ModeDirP}$ diagonally [$_{AbsViewP}$ north [$_{RelViewP}$ up [$_{RelViewP}$ in [$_{DeicticP}$ here [$_{AxPartP}$ under X [$_{PP}$ P [$_{NPplace}$ the mountain [PLACE]]]]]]]]]]]]]]

According to Cinque (2010a), a spatial preposition phrase has three basic functional phrases: the directional preposition phrase PPdir, the stative preposition phrase PPstat and the determiner phrase DPplace. The function of PPdir is to indicate the source or the goal of the preposition, which is phonologically realized as *from* when it is the source and *to* when it is the goal; the function of PPstat is to identify the region in space and it is generally phonologically realized as *at*; DPplace is the complement of PPstat. Noticeably, PPdir will not be projected if there is no directional meaning for the preposition phrase. Thus, the maximal projection of a spatial preposition phrase will be a PPstat, in this case, and it will take DPplace as its complement. The head of DPplace is an unpronounced abstract noun PLACE (Kayne 2004, 2007a).

There are a series of modifiers before DPplace. Among them, degree phrase DegP indicates the distance; mode of direction phrase ModeDirP indicates the mode of direction; absolute viewpoint phrase AbsViewP and relative viewpoint phrase RelViewP indicate the speaker's viewpoint; deictic phrase DeicticP indicates the relationship between the speaker and DPplace; axial part phrase AxPartP, which is also called the complex preposition phrase, through projecting vectors onto one of the possible axes that depart from the object that provides the reference point (Cinque 2010a: 4), indicates the specific location. In actual language, not all of the above phrases will be spelled out all the time. A simple preposition phrase has a relatively simple syntactic structure. For example, an English spatial preposition phrase *under the table* will be decomposed into different functional phrases like the following:

(80)

$[_{PPstat}$ (at) AT $[_{DPplace}$ $[_{AxPartP}$ under $[_{PP}$ P $[_{NPplace}$ the table [PLACE]]]]]]^{①}

(Cinque 2010: 5)

At first, the object *the table* indicates the reference point of PLACE (*the table* is in a possessor relation to the head noun PLACE). And then, the axial part preposition or the complex preposition *under* indicates the specific location of *the table* PLACE. At last, the stative preposition *AT* takes *the table* PLACE as the complement and identifies the region in space on the basis of the vectors. Finally, a fine-grained structure of a spatial preposition phrase is formed. Note, the stative preposition *AT* is not spelled out in the phonetic form in this phrase though it has the syntactic position.

It can be seen that the stative preposition and the axial part preposition [*at* in (79) and *under* in (80)] are the critical prepositions in the spatial preposition phrase. They are different types of prepositions and on the different cartographic layers, playing different roles in indicating the spatial location.

---

① In some languages, there are functional prepositions after the axial part (complex) prepositions. These functional prepositions assign case to the following arguments (most of them are noun phrases). In Italian, most complex prepositions can (and in certain cases must) be followed by one of the functional prepositions *a* (at/to) and di (of) (Cinque 2010: 3). Because Chinese preposition phrases do not have these functional prepositions, the related phrases will be not in the the subsequent discussion about the cartographic layers of Chinese preposition phrases.

3.3.3.3.2 The syntactic analysis of the *zai-X* structure and the *dang*-X structure

The last section introduces the cartographic analysis of the spatial preposition phrase. Although this analysis is for the syntactic structure of the preposition phrase, I believe that it will apply to temporal adverbials in Chinese because temporal adverbials in Chinese are in fact preposition phrases (see section 3.3.3.1). Besides, our human's cognition of time comes from the cognition of space, and the linguistic expressions of space and time are closely related (Lakoff 1993; Chilton 2014; Shen 1995; Wang 2013; among others). The syntactic similarity of the expressions of space and time is just the representation of the similarity of human's cognitive approaches.

Therefore, I propose that Chinese temporal preposition phrases and English spatial preposition phrases have similar internal structures and cartographic layers. Of course, the specific functional projections may not be paralleled with each other.[①] This hypothesis can be initially proved by the linguistic fact that there is a pair of preposition and postposition both in the spatial preposition phrase and the temporal preposition phrase like the following (81) and (82):

(81)

a. *zai*   zhuozi   *shang*
   at   table   up
   'on the table'

---

① There is a similar syntactic analysis for the temporal adverbial clause in English, which proves my hypothesis from another perspective. Demirdache and Uribe-Etxebarria (2004: 169) argue that the time adjuncts are concealed PPs, that is, phrases headed by a silent predicate of spatio-temporal ordering. A null preposition (can be spelled out as *at*) selects a null temporal noun phrase ZeitP (can be spelled out as *the time*) as its complement. The clause introduced by *when* can be seen as the relative clause with *the time* as the head noun. So the temporal syntax of the subordinate clause is transparently reflected in the overt syntax of temporal adjunct clauses as:

(1) a. [PP at [$_{ZeitP}$ the time [$_{CP}$ when Zooey arrived]]] Demirdache and Uribe-Etxebarria (2004: 170)

b. [PP Ø [$_{ZeitP}$ Ø [$_{CP}$ when Zooey arrived]]] Demirdache and Uribe-Etxebarria (2004: 177, n. 12)

  b. *zai* zhuozi *xia*
     at table down
     'under the table'

(82)

  a. *zai* zhe-ci kaoshi *zhiqian*
     at this-CL exam   before
     'before this exam'

  b. *zai* zhe-ci kaoshi *zhihou*
     at this-CL exam   after
     'after this exam'

In (81a-b), both the preposition *zai* (at) and the postposition *shang* (up) or *xia* (down) appear in the spatial preposition phrases. Then, in the temporal preposition phrases (82a-b), the preposition *zai* (at) and the postposition *zhiqian* (before) or *zhihou* (after) co-occur in the clause. The co-occurrence of preposition and postposition in the temporal proposition phrases can be well illustrated under the cartographic framework. Apparently, preposition and postposition are on the different cartographic layers, just like the spatial preposition phrases.

If the hypothesis above is right, I can utilize the cartographic account of the spatial preposition phrases for reference to study the internal structure of the temporal preposition phrases in Chinese. Here I propose that a temporal preposition phrase can be decomposed into different functional phrases. The reason why the *zai*-X structure and the *dang*-X structure demonstrate different syntactic behaviors is that they are different functional phrases, and the prepositions *zai* and *dang* are on the different cartographic layers of the preposition phrase.

A full-fledged temporal preposition phrase includes directional preposition phrase PP_{dir}, stative preposition phrase PP_{stat} and determiner phrase DP_{time}. Among them, PP_{dir} indicates the starting point and the ending point of the time, which can be phonologically realized as *cong* (from) and *dao* (to) respectively; PP_{stat} identify the region of the time range and is phonologically realized as *zai* (at); DP_{time} is the complement of PP_{stat}.

Similar to the spatial preposition phrase, not all functional phrases in the temporal preposition phrase will be projected. PP_{dir} will not be projected if there is no directional meaning for the preposition phrase. The maximal projection of the temporal preposition phrase will be PP_{stat} if there is no PP_{dir}, and the DP_{time} will be its complement. So the *zai*-X structure is actually a PP_{stat}, and the preposition *zai* is the head of the stative preposition phrase PP_{stat}.

Different from the English spatial preposition phrase, the head of DP_{time} is not an unpronounced abstract noun. Instead, the head noun is spelled out as *shihou* (time) in Chinese temporal preposition phrases. *Shihou* is identified as the head of DP_{time}. The following concrete linguistic behaviors can prove this.

Firstly, *shihou* cannot be used as the subject or object in the clause, which is different from other ordinary words that express time, as (83) and (84) show:

(83)

a. *Shijian*   chong-zu/   bu-zu.
   time   enough   not-enough
   'The time is enough/not enough.'

b. *Shihou   chongzu/   bu-zu.
   time   enough   not-enough
   'The time is enough/not enough.'

(84)

a. Tamen   liyong/   langfei   *shijian*.
   they   utilize   waste   time
   'They utilize/waste the time.'

b. *Tamen   liyong/   langfei   *shihou*.
   they   utilize   waste   time
   'They utilize/waste the time.'

In (83a) and (84a), *shijian* (time) is an ordinary word that expresses time, and it can be used as the subject in (83a) and the object in (84a), while *shihou* cannot be used as the subject or the object.[①] Both (83b) and (84b) are not grammatical, showing that *shihou* is not an ordinary word that expresses time.

Secondly, *shihou* cannot be modified by a numeral or quantitive phrase, which is different from other real temporal words.[②] See the following contrast between (85) and (86):

(85)

liang-ge	xiaoshi/	yue/	jidu
two-CL	hour	month	season

'two hours/months/seasons'

(86)

*liang-ge	*shihou*
two-CL	time

'two time'

In (85), *xiaoshi* (hour), *yue* (month) and *jidu* (season) are real temporal words and can be modified by the numeral and quantitive phrases. In contrast, *shihou* cannot be modified like this in (86), which shows that *shihou* is not a temporal word.

Thirdly, from the semantic perspective, the phrases or clauses which take *shihou* as the head noun can only express the location of time. See the

---

① The anonymous expert points out that sometimes *shihou* can be used as the subject, as the following shows:

(1) Shihou bu   zao le.
    time   not early ASP
    'It is not early.'

However, *shihou* in this clause indicates the location of time and just shows that it is connected with a fixed time point in the temporal axis.

② According to Lu (1991), the words that related to time can be divided into the ordinary words that express time and the real temporal words. He proposes that the words like *shijian* (time) or *shihou* (time) are ordinary words that express time instead of real temporal word. The real temporal words are the ones like *xiaoshi* (hour), *shangwu* (morning), *jintian* (today), etc. I agree with Lu's (1991) viewpoint about *shihou*'s not being the real temporal word. However, I propose that *shihou* is not the ordinary word that expresses time, either. Instead, *shihou* is the locative word that expresses the location of time.

following (87a-d):

(87)

a. na-ge   shihou
   that-CL   time
   'that time'

b. shenme-shihou
   what-time
   'when'

c. wo   nianqing   de   shihou
   I   young   DE   time
   'When I was young, ...'

d. wo   kaoshang   daxue   de   shihou
   I   be.admitted.to   university   DE   time
   'When I am admitted to the university, ...'

Lastly, from the syntactic perspective, *shihou* can co-occur with the axial part preposition phrases like *zhiqian* (before) or *zhihou* (after), see the following (88a-b):

(88)

a. Zai wo lai   zhiqian de shihou, ba yiqie   xiang de dou tai hao le.
   at I   come before DE time   BA everything think DE DOU too good SFP
   'Before I come, I think too well of everything.'

b. (zai) zhihou de shihou, changjing   hao pingjing, xiang meng   yiyang.
   (at) after DE time   scene   very tranquil like   dream same
   'After that, the scene is tranquil, just like in the dream.'

(Center for Chinese Linguistics of Peking University)

From (83) to (88), one can see that *shihou* is different from the ordinary word that expresses time or the real temporal word. It cannot be used as an argument and cannot be modified by the numeral or quantitive phrases like the ordinary word or the temporal word. It can only express the location of time and can co-occur with the axial part prepositions. All these linguistic facts show that *shihou* is just the locative word that expresses the location of time. It is the head of DP_{time} and the overt expression of the abstract noun

DP_{time}.

Actually, early Chinese linguists (Zhu 1982; Lu 1991; Lang 1997; Li 1997) have already realized that *shihou* is not a temporal word though it does express time. Lang (1997: 52) argues that *shihou* is a word that expresses the location of time. These observations are just consistent with our judgment and confirm our argumentation.

Except for these basic functional phrases, there are also a series of other functional phrases in the temporal preposition phrase, some of which are modifiers of DP_{time}. Among them, the preposition phrase with *dang* as the head is the most frequently used one. I propose that the preposition *dang* is the axial part preposition just like *under* in the spatial preposition phrase. Its function is to indicate the specific location of the event TIME (the location of the event in the time axis), similar to *under*'s indicating the specific location of the object PLACE (see section 3.3.3.3.1). It should be noted that the reference point of time is not an object that occupies a specific space on the spatial axis but an event that occupies a period of time on the temporal axis. So, the axial part preposition *dang* is not related to a concrete object like a *table* but to an abstract event, indicating the time when the event happens. In other words, the preposition *dang* is to indicate the specific location of the event on the temporal axis. This hypothesis can be proved by the following linguistic behaviors:

Firstly, *dang* can only collocate with the syntactic structures that are related to the event like the clause or the predicate structure, not just the syntactic constituents like the temporal words. See the following (89):

(89)

a. *dang*   wo zuotian   tongguo le   kaoshi de shihou
   just.at I   yesterday pass   ASP exam DE time
   'When I passed the exam yesterday, ...'

b. *dang*   tongue le   kaoshi de shihou
   just.at pass   ASP   exam   DE time
   'at the moment of passing the exam'

c. *dang   jiu-dian   de   shihou
   just.at nine   DE   time
   'at nine o'clock'

When the preposition *dang* collocates with a clause *wo zuotian tongguo le kaoshi* (I passed the exam yesterday) and a predicate structure *tongguo le kaoshi* (pass the exam) that express event, the clauses are grammatical in (89a-b). However, it becomes ungrammatical when *dang* collocates with a pure temporal word *jiudian* (nine) in (89c). The contrast between (89a-b) and (89c) shows that the preposition *dang* is related directly to the event, not to the time. It is an axial part preposition.

Secondly, *dang* does not necessarily take the head noun *shihou* (TIME) as its complement. This situation is paralleled to the usage of axial part preposition *under* in the spatial preposition phrase, which does not necessarily take the abstract head noun PLACE.

(90)

a. *dang*   wo tongguo le   kaoshi
   just.at I   pass   ASP exam
   'When I passed the exam, ...'

b. *dang*   wo   kaoshang   daxue
   just.at I   be.admitted.to   university
   'When I am admitted to the university, ...'

As (90a-b) show, the preposition *dang* does not take the head noun *shihou* as its complement, the clauses are still grammatical. The performance also show that *dang* is just the axial part preposition in the temporal preposition phrase.

Lastly, *dang* cannot co-occur with other axial part prepositions like *zhiqian* (before) or *zhihou* (after). Early Chinese linguists (Lü and Zhu 1952/2013: 99) have argued that there are no usages such as "*dang*-X *zhiqian*" or "*dang*-X *zhihou*".[①] Their argumentation is just consistent with our judgment. The corpus shows that *dang* cannot co-occur with other axial part prepositions, especially *zhiqian*.[②] This linguistic phenomenon proves that the preposition *dang* itself has the axis elements and is just the axial part preposition.

From these syntactic behaviors of the preposition *dang* (it can only collocate with the clause or the predication, its usage is similar to the axial part preposition like *under* in spatial preposition phrase, and it cannot co-occurs with other axial part prepositions like *zhiqian* or *zhihou*), I can safely conclude that *dang* is just the axial part preposition, and its function is to indicate the location of the event on the temporal axis.

According to the discussion, I propose that the prepositions *zai* and *dang* are on the different cartographic layers though they both can introduce temporal phrases. *Zai* is a stative preposition and on the PP_{stat} layer, while *dang* is an axial part preposition and on the AxPartP layer. *Zai* is above

---

①   Lü and Zhu (1952/2013) list some sentences in which *dang* co-occurs with *zhiqian* or *zhihou*:

    (1) Dang   tu-gai   jiu   yao   shixian   zhiqian,

        just.at agrarian-reform just will realize   before

        'Before the realization of the agrarian reform,'

    (2) Keshi *dang* ta yi   ting-dao   Shi Dehui deng shi-ji ren   bei fandongpai zhuazhu

        but   just.at he once hear-PERF Shi Dehui etc. dozen people BEI reactionaries arrest

        guan   zai   an-ku   li   de   xiaoxi zhihou

        imprison PREP hidden-cave in   DE   news   after

        'But after he heard the news that a dozen of people including Shi Dehui are arrested by

        the reactionaries and imprisoned in the hidden cave,'   (Lü and Zhu 1952/2013: 99)

    They argue that when *dang* co-occurs with such words as *zhiqian* or *zhihou*, these sentences are not natural, and the words *zhiqian* or *zhihou* should be eliminated. I agree with their opinion and infer that such usages are the results of the mixture of *dang* and *zai*.

②   According to the statistics from CCL and BCC, *dang* rarely co-occurs with *zhiqian*, but sometimes can co-occur with *zhihou*. I believe that, on the one hand, *dang* gradually has some properties of *zai* with the process of grammaticalization, and this makes *dang* can be used in this way (strictly speking, this is a misusage of the preposition *dang*). On the other hand, *dang* in these clauses possibly introduces the conditional adverbial clause, not temporal adverbial. It is out of the discussion in this dissertation for the study of *dang* in conditional clauses and the relationship between the conditional clause and the temporal clause. As for these issues, the related research can be done in the future.

the phrase DP_{time} while *dang* is under the phrase DP_{time} in the cartographic structure. The preposition *zai* selects the phrase DP_{time} as its complement, while dang selects the phrase NP_{time} as its complement. The *dang*-X structure together with NP_{time} is contained in the phrase DP_{time}. In other words, the preposition phrase *dang*-X structure is just one part of the phrase DP_{time}. The following evidence can support the proposal.

Firstly, the complement of the preposition *zai* can be modified by the determiners *zhege* (this) or *nage* (that), while the complement of the preposition *dang* cannot be modified by these determiners, as the following (91-92) show:

(91)

a. *zai* renmen   benzou   xianggao   de   shihou
   at   people   run   tell   DE   time
   'When people run around spreading the news, ...'

b. *zai* zhe-ge   renmen   benzou   xianggao   de   shihou
   at   this-CL   people   run   tell   DE   time
   'When people run around spreading the news, ...'

(92)

a. *dang*   renmen   benzou   xianggao   de   shihou
   just.at   people   run   tell   DE   time
   'When people run around spreading the news, ...'

b. **dang*   zhe-ge   renmen   benzou   xianggao   de   shihou
   just.at   this-CL   people   run   tell   DE   time
   'When people run around spreading the news, ...'

The complement of the preposition *zai* can be modified by the determiner *zhege* (this) in (91b). However, when the complement of the preposition *dang* is modified by *zhege* in (92b), the sentence becomes ungrammatical. The comparison between (91) and (92) shows that the complement of the preposition *zai* is a DP in (91), while the complement of the preposition *dang* is an NP in (92).

Secondly, the prepositions *zai* and *dang* can co-occur in one temporal phrase, and *zai* must precede *dang*, as (93) and (94) show:

(93)

a. *zai* na-ge *dang* chi-fan dou cheng wenti de shihou

   at that-CL just.at eat DOU be problem DE time

   'When even eating is a problem, ...'

b. **dang* na-ge *zai* chifan dou cheng wenti de shihou

   just.at that-CL at eating DOU be problem DE time

   'When even eating is a problem, ...'

(94)

a. Zhexie shigu jiu fasheng *zai dang* ni diaoyiqinxing de shihou.

   these accident just happen at just.at you let.down.the.guard DE time

   'These accidents just happen when you let down your guard.'

b. *Zhexie shigu jiu fasheng *dang zai* ni diaoyiqinxing de shihou.

   these accident just happen just.at at you let.down.the.guard DE time

   'These accidents just happen when you let down your guard.'

As (93-94a) show, when the prepositions *zai* and *dang* appear in one phrase, *zai* must precede *dang*. The opposite word order in (93-94b) will make the sentences ungrammatical. The co-occurrence of *zai* and *dang* in (93-94) illustrates that they are different types of prepositions and on the different cartographic layers. The preceding preposition *zai* is higher than the following preposition *dang* in the cartographic structure.

Thirdly, the subject in the *zai*-X structure can move to the initial position of the structure, which is before the preposition *zai*, while the subject in the *dang*-X structure cannot do so.

(95)

a. *zai* wo kaoshang daxue de shihou

   at I be.admitted.to university DE time

   'When I am admitted to the university, ...'

b. wo *zai* kaoshang daxue de shihou

   I at be.admitted.to university DE time

   'When I am admitted to the university, ...'

(96)

a. *dang* wo kaoshang   daxue   de shihou

   just.at I   be.admitted.to university DE time

   'When I am admitted to the university, ...'

b. *wo *dang*   kaoshang   daxue   de shihou

   I   just.at be.admitted.to university   DE time

   'When I am admitted to the university, ...'

It can be seen that the subject *wo* (I) in the *zai*-X structure in (95b) can move from the original position (after the preposition *zai*) to the targeting position (before the preposition *zai*). However, the similar movement in (96b) makes the sentence ungrammatical. As the head of the phrase, the stative preposition *zai* allows the subject of its complement to move to the initial position of the phrase in (95b). In contrast, the axial part preposition *dang* on the lower cartographic layer cannot license this movement in (96b) because it will disobey the Phase Impenetrability Condition (PIC) (Chomsky 2000, 2001, 2004).

All these syntactic performances confirm the hypothesis that the prepositions *zai* and *dang* are different types of prepositions, and the syntactic position of *zai* is higher than that of *dang* in the cartographic structure of the preposition phrase. Based on these findings, the cartographic structure of a temporal preposition phrase in Chinese should be like this:

(97)

[$_{PPdir}$ cong/dao [$_{PPstat}$ zai [$_{DPtime}$ [$_{AxPartP}$ dang [$_{NPtime}$ shihou TIME]]]]]

Except for the axial part preposition phrase with *dang* as the head, some other phrases can also modify the head noun TIME (*shihou*) in the temporal preposition phrase. These phrases can provide the reference point for the temporal axis and can be divided into two types: the simple DP and the complex DP or NP, i.e., the DP or NP modified by a relative clause. Compared with the *dang*-X structure, the *zai*-X structure shows more tolerance to the two types of phrases as its complements. See the following (98a-d):

(98)

a. *zai zhe-ge* shihou
   at   this-CL   time
   'at this time'

b. *zai* wo tongguo le   kaoshi de shihou
   at I   pass   ASP exam DE time
   'When I passed the exam, ...'

c. *zai* wo tongguo le   kaoshi de zhe-ge shihou
   at I   pass   ASP exam DE this-CL time
   'When I passed the exam, ...'

d. *zai zhe-ge* wo tongguo le   kaoshi de shihou
   at this-CL I   pass   ASP exam DE time
   'When I passed the exam, ...'

In (98a-b), the simple DP *zhege shihou* (this time) and the complex DP or NP *wo tongguo le kaoshi de shihou* (the time that I passed the exam) can be embedded in the *zai*-X structure, and the sentences are grammatical. Noticeably, when the complements of the preposition *zai* are DPs [*wo tongguo le kaoshi de zhege shihou* (the time that I passed the exam) or *zhege wo tongguo le kaoshi de shihou* (the time that I passed the exam)] in (98c-d), the phrases will still be acceptable. The complex DP or NP can both be hosted in the *zai*-X structure.

However, only the complex NP can be embedded in the *dang*-X structure. Besides, when the complements of the preposition *dang* are DPs (whether they are simple or complex DPs), the phrases will be unacceptable, as the following (99a-d) show:

(99)

a. **dang zhe-ge* shihou
   just.at this-CL time
   'at this time'

b. *dang* wo tonguo le   kaoshi de shihou
   just.at I   pass   ASP exam DE time
   'When I passed the exam, ...'

c. *dang wo tongguo le kaoshi de zhe-ge shihou
   just.at I pass ASP exam DE this-CL time
   'When I passed the exam, ...'

d. *dang zhe-ge wo tongguo le kaoshi de shihou
   just.at this-CL I pass ASP exam DE time
   'When I passed the exam, ...'

In (99a), the simple DP *zhege shihou* (this time) is embedded in the *dang*-X structure, and the phrase is ungrammatical. As (99b) shows, only the complex NP *wo tongguo le kaoshi de shihou* (the time when I passed the exam) can be embedded in the *dang*-X structure. In this structure, the relative clause (the CP structure) *wo tongguo le kaoshi* (I passed the exam) modifies the head noun *shihou*. It is worth noticing that the phrases will be unacceptable when the complements of the preposition *dang* are DPs [*wo tongguo le kaoshi de zhege shihou* (the time that I passed the exam) or *zhege wo tongguo le kaoshi de shihou* (the time that I passed the exam] in (99c-d). [1]

As the modifier of the head noun *shihou*, the relative clause should be analyzed as the adjunct of the noun phrase with *shihou* as the head. Just as (97) and (98a-d) show, as the complement of the preposition *zai*, the maximal projection of the abstract noun TIME (*shihou*) is a DP_{time}. Besides, in the process of derivation, the abstract noun TIME can project an NP_{time} in between. Thus, the relative clause forms a left-adjoined temporal determiner phrase $[_{CP} X (DE)]$ $[_{DPtime} [_{AxPartP} \emptyset [_{NPtime} [_{CP} X (DE)] [_{NPtime} shihou TIME]]]]$. The relative clause in the *zai*-X structure can be adjoined to DP_{time} or NP_{time}, i.e., the *zai*-X structure provides two sites for the relative clause to be adjoined. The preposition *zai* is out of DP_{time} and DP_{time} is the complement of the preposition *zai*. Using X to refer to the relative clause, the full-fledged temporal preposition *zai*-phrase in Chinese is like (100a-b) in the following:

---

[1]   The anonymous expert points out that only the DP can be the argument of the preposition but not the NP. I believe that the preposition *dang* can take NP as the argument because the maximal projection of a noun phrase can either be an NP or a DP in Chinese (Bošković 2012, 2014).

(100)

a. [$_{PPstat}$ zai [$_{DPtime}$ [$_{CP}$ X (DE)] [$_{DPtime}$ [$_{AxPartP}$ Ø [$_{NPtime}$ shihou TIME]]]]]

b. [$_{PPstat}$ zai [$_{DPtime}$ [$_{AxPartP}$ Ø [$_{NPtime}$ [$_{CP}$ X (DE)] [$_{NPtime}$ shihou TIME]]]]]

However, the cartographic structure of (97) and the syntactic behaviors in (99a-d) show that the internal structure of the *dang*-X structure is different. As the complement of the preposition *dang*, the maximal projection of the abstract noun TIME (*shihou*) can only be an NP$_{time}$ instead of a DP$_{time}$. So the relative clause should be adjoined to NP$_{time}$ and forms a left-adjoined temporal noun phrase [$_{NPtime}$ [$_{CP}$ X (DE) [$_{NPtime}$ shihou TIME]]]. The preposition *dang* is within DP$_{time}$ and the *dang*-X structure is just a part of DP$_{time}$. The detailed cartographic hierarchy of the *dang*-X structure should be like the following (101):

(101)

[$_{AxPartP}$ dang [$_{NPtime}$ [$_{CP}$ X (DE)] [$_{NPtime}$ shihou TIME]]]

Finally, a temporal preposition phrase in Chinese has a full-fledged cartographic structure:

(102)

[$_{PPdir}$ cong/dao [$_{PPstat}$ zai [$_{DPtime}$ [$_{CP}$ X (DE)] [$_{DPtime}$ [$_{AxPartP}$ dang [$_{NPtime}$ [$_{CP}$ X (DE)] [$_{NPtime}$ shihou TIME]]]]]]]]][1]

(102) shows that the temporal adverbial clause in Chinese is a preposition phrase with various functional projections, being on the different cartographic layers and playing different roles. A full-fledged temporal preposition phrase includes the directional preposition phrase PP$_{dir}$, the stative preposition phrase PP$_{stat}$, the axial part preposition phrase AxPartP and the determiner phrase DP$_{time}$ with *shihou* as the head noun.

As the most important prepositions in this temporal phrase, *zai* and *dang* are obviously different types of prepositions. The former is a stative preposition and is on the PP$_{stat}$ layer, while the latter is an axial part

---

[1]   Because not all the functional phrases will be projected in the temporal preposition phrase, some of the unrelated phrases are omitted here.

preposition and is on the AxPartP. The function of the preposition *zai* is to identify the region of the time range, while the function of preposition *dang* is to indicate the location of the event on the temporal axis. The preposition phrase with *zai* as the head is out of DP_{time}, while the preposition with *dang* as the head is within DP_{time}. Therefore, they have different syntactic structures and different derivation patterns though they seem the same for they both take a head noun *shihou* modified by a relative clause.

Note that not all the functional phrases will be projected in the actual language utterance, just like the spatial preposition phrase. If there is no particular directional meaning, the directional preposition *cong/dao* (from/to) does not often project the independent phrases. And the stative preposition *zai* and the axial part preposition *dang* do not necessarily co-occur with each other in the same phrase.[①]

3.3.3.3.3 The syntactic derivation of the *zai*-X strucure and the *dang*-X structure

The last section discusses the syntactic behaviors of the *zai*-X structure and the *dang*-X structure. Under the cartographic framework, I propose that *zai* is a stative preposition while *dang* is an axial part preposition. They are two types of prepositions and on the different layers of the temporal preposition phrase. Different from the preposition *zai* that is out of DP_{time}, the preposition *dang* is within DP_{time}. The prepositions *zai* and *dang* both

---

①   In most cases, the preposition *zai* and *dang* do not co-occur, but that does not mean that they cannot co-occur. In fact, sometimes they can appear in the same phrase, as the following sentence shows:

Zhexie canju   jiu fasheng zai dang   daren-men bu zai shen-bian de shihou.

these   tragedy just happen   at just.at adult-PL not at side   DE time

'These tragedies just happened when the adults were not by the side of the children.'

I believe that they do not co-occur very often due to the semantic factors and economic principle. Semantically, it is known that indefinite nouns can be used for definite meaning in Chinese. So, the maximal projection of a noun phrase in Chinese can be an NP or a DP (Bošković 2012, 2014). This specific linguistic behavior in Chinese will bring about a problem that *zai* and *dang* can be adjacent very often, but two adjacent prepositions are not normal in actual utterance. For economic reasons, both *zai* and *dang* can take the head noun *shihou* as the complement and express the similar meaning, they do not need to appear together in the same phrase. It is just like the English spatial preposition phrase in which the stative preposition *at* seldom co-occurs with the axial part preposition *under* though actually they are different types of prepositions.

can contain a relative clause with *shihou* as the head noun. The relative clause modifies the head noun *shihou*, and the relative clause, together with the head noun *shihou*, is the complement of the two prepositions. Based on these findings, this section will discuss the syntactic derivations of the *zai*-X structure and the *dang*-X structure.

Because the *zai*-X structure and the *dang*-X structure both contain a relative clause, it is necessary to analyze the syntactic structure and derivational pattern of relative clauses. Generally speaking, there are two streams of analysis for the derivation of the relative clauses. Some linguists (Schachter 1973; Vergnaud 1974) argue that the relative clause is the adjunct of the head noun, while others (Kayne 1994) argue that the relative clause is the complement of the head noun. Huang, Li and Li (2009) believe that the latter does not apply to Chinese relative clauses and argue that the relative clause is the adjunct of the head noun. I agree with Huang et al. (2009) and believe that the relative clause contained in the *zai*-X structure and the *dang*-X structure should be the adjunct of the head noun *shihou*.

Being the complement of the preposition *dang*, the maximal projection of the head noun *shihou* can only be NP_{time} [see (101)]. Note that the relative clause is connected to the head noun *shihou* with a particular word *de* (DE). Chinese linguists have two different opinions on the syntactic structure of this DE phrase. One group of linguists argue that the word *de* is the head of the noun phrase, and the noun phrase embedding the word *de* forms a DeP phrase (Simpson2002; Si 2002, 2004, 2006; Lu 2003; Xiong 2005, among others). Other linguists (Li 2008; Shi 2008; Pan and Lu 2013; among others) argue that the word *de* is the head of the adjunct that modifies the noun phrase and forms a DeP phrase to modify the noun phrase. In other words, *de* selects a complement to modify the noun phrase, and the noun phrase itself will ultimately form a DP. Considering the theoretical and actual linguistic behavior, I prefer the latter analysis.[①]

Unlike the *dang*-X structure, the maximal projection of the head noun

---

① For the specific syntactic operations of DeP phrase, interested readers can go to Pan and Lu (2013) for reference.

shihou selected by the preposition *zai* is DP_{time} [see (102)]. And DP_{time} includes NP_{time} in this temporal preposition phrase. In other words, the relative clause CP in the *zai*-X structure, as an adjunct of the head noun *shihou*, can either be adjoined to the domains of DP_{time} or NP_{time}. The following (103a-b) can prove this hypothesis:

(103)

a. *zai zhe-ge renmen benzou xianggao de shihou*
   at   this-CL people   run   tell   DE time
   'When people run around spreading the news, ...'

b. *zai renmen benzou xianggao de zhe-ge shihou*
   at   people   run   tell   DE this-CL time
   'When people run around spreading the news, ... '

However, because the head noun *shihou* can only project NP_{time} in the *dang*-X structure, the relative clause X can only be adjoined to NP_{time}. So the determiner *zhege* cannot appear in the *dang*-X structure, which again proves my hypothesis:

(104)

a. **dang zhe-ge renmen benzou xianggao de shihou*
    just.at this-CL people   run   tell   DE time
   'When people run around spreading the news, ...'

b. **dang renmen benzou xianggao de zhe-ge shihou*
    just.at people   run   tell   DE this-CL time
   'When people run around spreading the news, ...'

As for the derivation of the relative clause, there are two patterns of movements-the head noun movement and the operator movement-according to different types of clauses (Huang 1982; Ning 1993; Simpson 2002; Aoun and Li 2003; del Gobbo 2003; Xiong 2005; Chen 2007; Hsu 2008; among others). In the temporal preposition phrase, because the head noun *shihou* does not move from the argument position to the initial position of the relative clause but generates in the base position, I propose that the relative clause is derived by the operator movement (Aoun and Li 2003; Huang et al. 2009).

A null temporal operator moves from the [Spec, AspP] position to the [Spec, CP] position and derives the relative clause with *shihou* as the head noun. And the moved temporal operator in the [Spec, CP] position is construed through feature matching with the head noun *shihou* in the relative clause.[①]

The *Zai*-X structure and the *dang*-X structure have some similarities and differences in their derivation patterns. In the *zai*-X structure, the relative clause used as the adjunct together with the head noun *shihou* becomes the complement of the stative preposition *zai* after the movement of the temporal operator, and the temporal operator should be co-indexed with the head noun *shihou* to be construed (Chen 2007, Hsu 2008). The whole structure is a stative preposition phrase after the process of derivation. Just as (99a-b) show, the relative clause X can either be adjoined to DP_{time} or to NP_{time}, and the phrase has two different syntactic structures. See the following (105a-b):

(105)

   a. $[_{PPstat}$ zai $[_{DPtime} [_{CP} Op_i [_{TP}$ wo kaoshang daxue $t_i]$ (de)$]$ $[_{DPtime} [_{AxPartP} \emptyset [_{NPtime}$ shihou$_i]]]]]$
     'When I am admitted to the university, ...'

   b. $[_{PPstat}$ zai $[_{DPtime} [_{AxPartP} \emptyset [_{NPtime} [_{CP} Op_i [_{TP}$ wo kaoshang daxue $t_i]$ (de)$]$ $[_{NPtime}$ shihou$_i]]]]]$
     'When I am admitted to the university, ...'

Similar to the *zai*-X structure, the relative clause in the *dang*-X structure is also derived by the temporal operator. However, different from the *zai*-X structure, the relative clause X in the *dang*-X structure is adjoined to NP_{time} [see (101)], and the whole structure is an axial part preposition phrase after the process of the derivation, as (106) shows:

(106)

$[_{AxPartP}$ dang $[_{NPtime} [_{CP} Op_i [_{TP}$ wo kaoshang daxue $t_i]$ (de)$]$ $[_{NPtime}$ shihou$_i]]]$
'When I am admitted to the university, ...'

[①] According to Huang et al. (2009), the relative clause can be licensed by the feature matching between the relative operator and the head noun. These features include not only the Phi-features like person, gender and number, but also the substantive features like human, place, time, etc. In the temporal preposition phrase, the feature matching is fulfilled by the substantive feature matching of [time] between the temporal operator and the head noun *shihou*.

After the syntactic derivation, the structure of the temporal preposition phrase can be demonstrated like the following, (70) is repeated here as (107-108) for convenience:

(107)

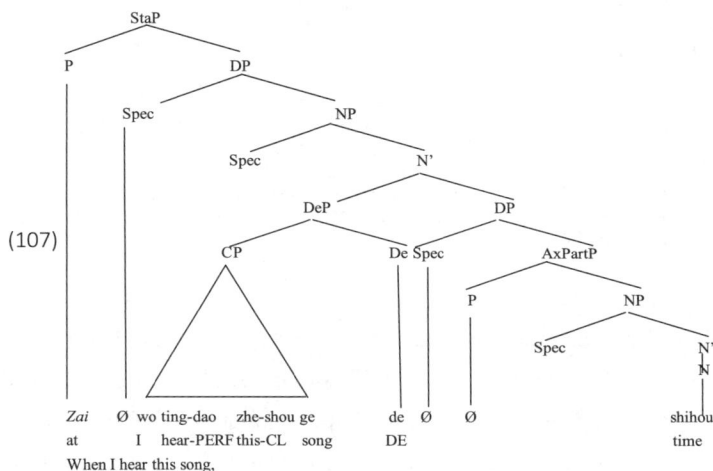

Zai	Ø wo ting-dao	zhe-shou ge	de	Ø	Ø	shihou
at	I hear-PERF	this-CL song	DE			time
When I hear this song,						

(107) is a *zai*-X structure, the relative clause *wo tingdao zheshou ge* (I hear this song) is adjoined to the outer DP$_{time}$, which is above the preposition *dang*.

In contrast, (108) can either be a *zai*-X structure or a *dang*-X structure, the relative clause *wo tingdao zheshou ge* is adjoined to the inner NP$_{time}$, which is below the preposition *dang*.

(108)

```
                              StaP
              ┌────────────────┴──────┐
              P                       DP
              │                ┌──────┴──────┐
             Spec            AxPartP
                          ┌────┴───────────┐
                          P                NP
                          │          ┌─────┴──────┐
                        Spec               N'
                                     ┌─────────┴──────┐
                                    DeP               N'
                               ┌─────┴─────┐           │
                              CP          De           N
                            ┌──┴──┐        │           │
```

Zai	Ø	Dang	wo	ting-dao	zhe-shou ge	de	shihou
at		just.at	I	hear-PERF	this-CL song	DE	time

When I hear this song,

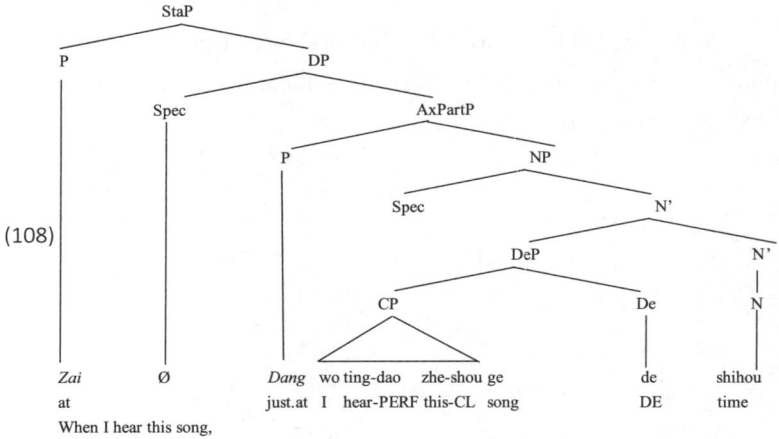

These two diagrams show that both the *zai*-X structure and the *dang*-X structure contain a relative clause with *shihou* as the head noun, and this relative clause is derived by a null temporal operator. After the syntactic derivation, the prepositions *zai* and *dang* are on the different cartographic layers. The preposition *zai* is above DP_{time} and is the head of the stative preposition phrase, while the preposition *dang* is within DP_{time} and is the head of the axial part preposition phrase. Therefore, I argue that the syntactic differences between the *zai*-X structure and the *dang*-X structure are just because the prepositions *zai* and *dang* are on different cartographic layers in the temporal preposition phrase.

3.3.3.3.4 Different cartographic layers

If the analysis is on the right track, I can give a reasonable explanation of the different syntactic behaviors between the *zai*-X structure and the *dang*-X structure.

Firstly, I will concentrate on the different availabilities of high and low construals between the *zai*-X structure and the *dang*-X structure. Both the *zai*-X structure and the *dang*-X structure contain relative clauses derived by the movement of the temporal operator. The temporal operator moves to different landing sites and thus causes high and low construals. Because *shihou* is the head of the phrase DP_{time}, the temporal operator should co-index with the head noun *shihou* and then obtain the construal (Chen 2007, Hsu 2008).

In the *zai*-X structure, the relative clause can be adjoined to three different positions when the relative clause is composed of a main clause and an embedded clause. Firstly, the main clause of the relative clause (main clause for abbreviation in the following) and the embedded clause together are adjoined to the outer DP_{time}; secondly, the main clause and the embedded clause together are adjoined to the inner NP_{time}; lastly, the main clause and the embedded clause are adjoined to the outer DP_{time} and the inner NP_{time}, respectively.

The three possibilities can be demonstrated in the following (109-111). When the main clause *Mali shuo* (Mary says) and the embedded clause *ta yao likai* (she will leave) together are adjoined to the outer DP_{time}, the temporal operator can move from the TP of the relative clause to the edge position of CP of the main clause or from the TP of the embedded clause to the edge position of the CP of the embedded clause. Because the temporal operator is a null operator, it should be antecedent-governed according to Empty Category Principle (Chomsky 1986). In (109a), when the temporal operator moves from the TP of the relative clause *Mali shuo ta yao likai* to the edge position of CP of the main clause, the moved temporal operator is antecedent-governed by the head noun *shihou* and co-indexed with the head noun to be construed. Thus, the phrase obtains the high construal. However, when the temporal operator moves from the TP of the embedded clause *ta yao likai* to the edge position of the CP of the embedded clause in (109b), there will be two bounding nodes CP and DP between the temporal operator and the antecedent *shihou*. The temporal operator cannot be antecedent-governed by the head noun *shihou* because crossing two bounding nodes will disobey the subjacency condition proposed by Chomsky (1973), which requires that one movement should not cross more than one bounding node at one time. Therefore, the phrase cannot obtain the low construal.

(109)

a. [PPstat zai [DPtime [CP OP_i [TP Mali shuo [CP [TP ta yao likai]] t_i] DE] [DPtime (nage) [NPtime shihou_i]]]]

b. *[PPstat zai [DPtime [CP [TP Mali shuo [CP OP_i [TP ta yao likai t_i]]]] DE] [DPtime (nage) [NPtime shihou_i]]]]

Then, when the main clause *Mali shuo* and the embedded clause *ta yao likai* together are adjoined to the inner NP_time, only the temporal operator that moves to the edge position of the CP of the relative clause *Mali shuo ta yao likai* can be co-indexed with the head noun *shihou*, the phrase can still get the high construal but not the low construal for the same reason. See the following (110a-b):

(110)

a. [PPstat zai [DPtime (nage) [AxPartP Ø [NPtime [CP OP_i [TP Mali shuo [CP [TP ta yao likai]] t_i] DE] [NPtime shihou_i]]]]]

b. *[PPstat zai [DPtime (nage) [AxPartP Ø [NPtime [CP [TP Mali shuo [CP OP_i [TP ta yao likai t_i]]]] DE] [NPtime shihou_i]]]]]

Lastly, when the main clause *Mali shuo* and the embedded clause *ta yao likai* are adjoined to the outer DP_time and the inner NP_time respectively, the temporal operator can move from the TP of the main clause to the edge position of CP of the main clause in the outer DP_time or from the TP of the embedded clause to the edge position of the CP of the embedded clause in the inner NP_time. When the temporal operator moves from the TP of the main clause *Mali shuo* to the edge position of CP of the main clause in (111a), it should be antecedent-governed by the head noun *shihou*. However, the head noun *shihou* is embedded in DP_time and modified by the inner CP. If the temporal operator moves to the edge position of CP of the main clause, it cannot be antecedent-governed according to subjacency condition because there are two bounding nodes DP_time and inner CP between the temporal operator and the head noun *shihou*. The temporal operator cannot move to the edge position of CP of the main clause, and the high construal cannot be obtained. In contrast, when the temporal operator moves from the TP of the embedded clause to the edge position of the CP of the embedded clause in the inner NP_{time} in (111b), the moved temporal operator is antecedent-governed by the head noun *shihou* and co-indexed with the head noun to be construed. Thus, the low construal is obtained.

(111)

a.*[$_{PPstat}$ zai [$_{DPtime}$ [$_{CP}$ OP$_i$ [$_{TP}$ Mali shuo t$_i$]] [$_{DPtime}$ [$_{AxPartP}$ Ø [$_{NPtime}$ [$_{CP}$ [$_{TP}$ ta yao likai] DE] [$_{NPtime}$ shihou$_i$]]]]]]

b. [$_{PPstat}$ zai [$_{DPtime}$ [$_{CP}$ [$_{TP}$ Mali shuo]] [$_{DPtime}$ [$_{AxPartP}$ Ø [$_{NPtime}$ [$_{CP}$ OP$_i$ [$_{TP}$ ta yao likai t$_i$] DE] [$_{NPtime}$ shihou$_i$]]]]]]

In the *dang*-X structure, because there is only one landing site for the relative clause to be adjoined, the main clause *Mali shuo* and the embedded clause *ta yao likai* can only be adjoined together to the inner NP_{time}. In order to be co-indexed with the head noun *shihou* to be construed, the temporal operator can only move to the edge position of the CP of the main clause *mali shuo* in (112a), and the clause obtains the high construal. If the temporal operator moves to the edge position of the CP of the embedded clause in (112b), the operator cannot co-index with the head noun *shihou* and then cannot obtain the low construal. If the clause wants to obtain the low construal, the main clause *Mali shuo* must be out of DP_{time}. The temporal operator is then can be co-indexed with the head noun *shihou* and can be construed, as (112c) shows:

(112)

a. [$_{AxPartP}$ dang [$_{NPtime}$ [$_{CP}$ OP$_i$ [$_{TP}$ Mali shuo [$_{CP}$ [$_{TP}$ ta yao likai]] t$_i$] DE] [$_{NPtime}$ shihou$_i$]]]

b. *[$_{AxPartP}$ dang [$_{NPtime}$ [$_{CP}$ [$_{TP}$ Mali shuo [$_{CP}$ OP$_i$ [$_{TP}$ ta yao likai t$_i$]]] DE] [$_{NPtime}$ shihou$_i$]]]

c. [$_{CP}$ Mali shuo [$_{DPtime}$ [$_{AxPartP}$ dang [$_{NPtime}$ [$_{CP}$ OP$_i$ [$_{TP}$ ta yao likai t$_i$] DE] [$_{NPtime}$ shihou$_i$]]]]]

The syntactic behaviors from (109-112) demonstrate that the *zai*-X structure can obtain the high construal when the main clause and the embedded clause together are adjoined to the outer DP_{time} or the inner NP_{time}. And it can obtain the low construal when the main clause and the embedded clause are adjoined to the outer DP_{time} and the inner NP_{time}, respectively. On the contrary, the *dang*-X structure can only obtain the high construal because the main clause and the embedded clause can only be adjoined to the inner NP_{time} together.

Following this line, I can explain the different syntactic behaviors in terms of MCP between the *zai*-X structure and the *dang*-X structure. (100) shows that the preposition *zai* is out of DP_{time} in the hierarchy of the temporal phrase. As (113) shows, when the topicalized constituent *Li xiaojie* (Miss Li) moves [whether it moves from the outer DP_{time} (113a) or the inner NP_{time} (113b)], it will cross two bounding nodes, i.e., the CP and the DP_{time}. And this will go against the subjacency condition.

(113)

*Zai Li xiaojie wo jian-dao   de shihou, Mali zhenghao jingguo.
at Li Miss I   meet-PERF DE time   Mary just   pass.by
a. $[_{PPstat}$ zai li xiaojie$_i$ $[_{DPtime}$ $[_{CP}$ wo jiandao t$_i$ de $[_{DPtime}$ $[_{AxPartP}$ Ø $[_{NPtime}$ shihou]]]]]
b. $[_{PPstat}$ zai li xiaojie$_i$ $[_{DPtime}$ $[_{AxPartP}$ Ø $[_{NPtime}$ $[_{CP}$ wo jiandao t$_i$ de $[_{NPtime}$ shihou]]]]]
'When Miss Li I met, Mary just passed by.'

In (113a-b), the topicalized constituent *Li xiaojie* moves to the initial position of the clause. No matter it moves from the outer DP_{time} or the inner NP_{time}, it will cross the bounding node CP [*wo jiandao (Li xiaojie)*] (I meet Miss Li) and the bounding node DP_{time} [*wo jiandao (Li xiaojie) de shihou*] (the time that I meet Miss Li), the sentence is then ungrammatical.

However, in the *dang*-X structure, the preposition *dang* is within DP_{time} [see (101)]. Thus, when the topicalized constituent *Li xiaojie* moves, it will cross only one bounding node, i.e., the CP [*wo jiandao (Li xiaojie)*]. So the sentence is grammatical, as (114) shows:

(114)

?Dang Li xiaojie wo jian-dao   de shihou, Mali zhenghao jingguo.
just.at Li Miss I   meet-PERF DE time   Mary just   pass.by
$[_{PPstat}$ $[_{DPtime}$ $[_{AxPartP}$ dang li xiaojie$_i$ $[_{CP}$ wo jiandao t$_i$ de $[_{NPtime}$ shihou]]]]]
'When Miss Li I met, Mary just passed by.'

In (114), the topicalized constituent *Li xiaojie* will cross only one bounding node CP, and the derivation converges. The sentence is then grammatical.

Besides, the current analysis can apply to other issues about temporal adverbials in Chinese. The first issue is the property of the complements of the prepositions *zai* and *dang*. According to Lü (2016/1980: 149), when *zai* and *dang* introduce temporal adverbials, *dang* must take clause or the predicate phrase as the complement but not the simple temporal words, while *zai* is not confined to this rule. In other words, the complement of *zai* can be predicative or nominal, while the complement of *dang* can only be predicative not nominal. See the following (115a-d):

(115)

a. Zai wo ting-dao   na-shou ge   de shihou, wo xiangqi le   wo-de chu-lian.
   at I   hear-PERF that-CL song DE time   I   think.of ASP my   first-love
   'When I hear that song, I think of my first love.'

b. Zai na-ge   shihou, wo xiangqi le   wo-de   chu-lian.
   at that-CL time   I   think.of ASP my   first-love
   'At that time, I think of my first love.'

c. Dang wo ting-dao   na-shou ge   de shihou, wo xiangqi le   wo-de chu-lian.
   just.at I   hear-PERF that-CL song DE time   I   think.of ASP my   first-love
   'When I hear that song, I think of my first love.'

d. *dang   na-ge   shihou, wo xiangqi le   wo-de   chu-lian.
   just.at that-CL time   I   think.of ASP my   first-love
   'At that time, I think of my first love.'

As (115a-d) show, Lü's (2016/1980) description is indeed accurate, but he does not explain why there is such a discrepancy between the *zai*-X structure and the *dang*-X structure. Under the cartographic framework, this problem can be tackled properly. The prepositions *zai* and *dang* are on the different layers of the temporal preposition phrase. *Zai* is a stative preposition, and its function is to identify the region of the time range. *Dang* is an axial part preposition, and its function is to indicate the location of the event on the temporal axis. This requires that the complement of *zai* be a simple DP [*nage shihou* (that time) in (115b)] or a DP modified by a relative clause [*wo tingdao nashou ge de shihou* (when I hear that song) in (115a)]. On the contrary, the cartographic layer of *dang* requires that the complement of *dang* be an NP modified by a relative clause [*wo tingdao nashou ge de shihou* in (115c)], but not a simple DP [*nage shihou* (that time) in (115d)]. This is because *dang* is directly related to the event not the time, and its function is to indicate the location of the event. As a result, *dang* cannot be associated with simple temporal words. This is just the reason why the complement of *zai* can be predicative or nominal while the complement of *dang* can only be predicative rather than nominal.

The second issue is the covertness of the head noun *shihou*. Chen (2016), Pan and Paul (2018) observe that the head noun *shihou* sometimes can be covert in the temporal adverbials, but they do not generalize the conditions for the covertness. In fact, the preposition *zai* and the preposition *dang* sometimes can also be covert in the temporal adverbials. Whether the covertness of these constituents follow from some regularities? The previous literature does not provide a reasonable solution to this problem. However, the current cartographic analysis can uncover the truth of the issue. See the following (116):

(116)

a. Wo ting-dao zhe-shou ge de shihou, xiangqi le wo-de chu-lian.
   I hear-PERF this-CL song DE time think.of ASP my first-love
   'When I hear this song, I think of my first love.'

b. Wo ting-dao zhe-shou ge, xiangqi le wo-de chu-lian.
   I hear-PERF this-CL song think.of ASP my first-love
   'I hear this song and I think of my first love.'

c. *Zai wo ting-dao zhe-shou ge, xiangqi le wo-de chu-lian.
   at I hear-PERF this-CL song think.of ASP my first-love
   'When I hear this song, I think of my first love.'

d. Dang wo ting-dao zhe-shou ge, xiangqi le wo-de chu-lian.
   just.at I hear-PERF this-CL song think.of ASP my first-love
   'When I hear this song, I think of my first love.'

As (116a) shows, the sentence is grammatical when the head noun *shihou* is overt and the prepositions *zai* and *dang* are both covert. This is because the function of the head noun *shihou* is to express the location of time, and the word itself (without the prepositions) can indicate the time when the event happens in the main clause. In (116b), the sentence is grammatical when the head noun *shihou*, the prepositions *zai* and *dang* are all covert. This clause expresses the event but not the time. The preceding clause is not a temporal adverbial and not a subordinate clause of the subsequent one. These two clauses form a coordinate relationship and are in fact two independent clauses. (116c) is ungrammatical when the head noun is covert while the preposition *zai* is overt. This is because *zai* is a stative preposition, and its complement is DP instead of CP. So the covertness of the head noun *shihou* goes against the requirement of collocation of the preposition *zai*. Lastly, (116d) is grammatical when the head noun *shihou* is covert while the preposition *dang* is overt. This is because *dang* is an axial part preposition, its function is to locate the event on the temporal axis. Without the head noun *shihou*, the preposition *dang* can still indicate the event on the temporal axis, and the clause can still express the time. Therefore, whether the head noun *shihou* exists or not does not influence the grammaticality of the clause.

The syntactic structures and the derivation patterns of temporal adverbials in English and Chinese are different. The temporal in English is a free relative clause derived by a temporal operator (when). In contrast, the temporal in Chinese is a preposition phrase and contains a relative clause derived by a null operator. In Chinese, the *zai*-X structure and the *dang*-X structure are the most frequently used temporal adverbials. *Zai* is a stative preposition, and its function is to identify the region of the time range, while *dang* is an axial part preposition, and its function is to indicate the specific location of the event on the temporal axis. Because these two prepositions are on the different layers of the cartographic hierarchy, they have different syntactic behaviors regarding the availability of high and low construals, MCP, the property of the complements and the covertness of the head noun *shihou*, and the series of differences.

The analysis of the syntactic structures and the derivation patterns of temporal adverbials in Chinese is under the cartographic framework. It deepens the understanding of the syntactic structures of the temporal adverbials both in English and Chinese, and sheds light on the syntactic differences between the *zai*-X structure and the *dang*-X structure, which are not analyzed clearly by previous linguists.

3.4 Summary

In this chapter, I have analyzed the distribution and restriction of MCP in English and Chinese conditional adverbial clauses, English temporal adverbial clauses and Chinese temporal preposition phrases.

After classifying CAC and PAC, I chose conditional and temporal adverbial clauses to analyze since these two types are central adverbial clauses. At the same time, I demonstrated that the conjunctions in Chinese adverbials are complementizers instead of adverbs. The preliminary work in this section has removed some theoretical and practical obstacles and make full preparations for further analysis.

The first type of adverbial clause that I have chosen to analyze is the conditional adverbial clause. The previous literature has shown that MCP in English conditional clauses are topics and high modal markers. According to Haegeman (2010b), conditional clauses in English are derived by the movement of the world operator and thus they are relative clauses. Topics and high modal markers share the Q-feature with the world operator and intervene in the movement. So they are not compatible with conditional clauses.

However, MCP in Chinese conditional clauses are just high modals, topics are not MCP in Chinese conditionals.

Observing the differences, I launched the contrastive study of MCP in English and Chinese conditional clauses. Firstly, I have shown that high modals have Q-feature. Intervention effect results in the incompatibility of high modals with English and Chinese conditionals adverbial clauses.

Then, I showed that topicalized constituents do not have Q-feature. So intervention effect does not arise, and the movement and intervention proposal is not the reason for the incompatibility of topics with conditional clauses in English.

Lastly, I illustrated that there is a competition of TopP and ForceP in English. Topics are not only incompatible with conditional adverbial clauses, they are also incompatible with any clauses in which the illocutionary force has been projected. That means TopP will compete for the same syntactic position with ForceP in English clauses no matter they are main clauses or embedded clauses. In English, TopP, ForceP and the world operator compete for the same syntactic position, they can never be compatible with each other. Because the world operator also moves to the specifier position of ForceP and thus bring about the competition, topics cannot be compatible with conditional clauses in English

However, the situation is totally different in Chinese. Topics in all the corresponding clauses are accepted. That means TopP and ForceP can co-occur with each in any type of clause in Chinese. Because TopP and ForceP project their own phrases independently and topics as well as the world operator thus move to different syntactic positions, topics can be compatible with Chinese conditional clauses.

When CP is split, it can be further decomposed into different functional phrases. But the specific compositions of the functional phrases can be varied among different languages, leading to parametric variation. In English, Topic and illocutionary force project only one phrase, while in Chinese, TopP and ForceP are independent projections. Therefore, the parametric variation in splitting CP is the primary cause for the different distributions of topics in English and Chinese conditional clauses.

The second type I chose to analyze is the temporal adverbial. MCP in English temporal clauses are topics and high modal markers. Similar to conditional clauses, temporal adverbial clauses cannot hold topics and high modal markers. According to Haegeman, temporal clauses in English are derived by the movement of the temporal operator. For the same intervention effect, topics and high modal markers are not compatible with temporal clauses.

The distribution of MCP in Chinese temporals is very complicated.

Generally speaking, on the one hand, the Chinese temporal *zai*-X structure does not tolerate topicalized constituents. But the *dang*-X structure shows enough tolerance to these fronted constituents. On the other hand, they both resist high modal markers.

Then, I accounted for the differences of MCP distributions between English and Chinese temporals and also between the *zai*-X structure and the *dang*-X structure. Firstly, I showed that Chinese temporals are preposition phrases and contain relative clauses. Being relatives implies that the intervention effect will bring about the incompatibility of high modals.

And then, I argued that the parametric variation in splitting CP results in different distributions of topics in English and Chinese temporal adverbials.

Lastly, I analyzed the *zai*-X structure and the *dang*-X structure by referring to the cartographic analysis of spatial preposition phrases. Because temporal adverbials in Chinese are also preposition phrases, I believe this cartographic analysis can apply to temporal preposition phrases. Similar to the spatial preposition phrase that can be decomposed into different functional phrases, a full-fledged temporal preposition phrase in Chinese also has different functional phrases. I thus hypothesized that the preposition *zai* is the stative preposition and the preposition *dang* is the axial part preposition. To distinguish the prepositions *zai* and *dang* is the critical step in the analysis of Chinese temporal preposition phrases because the prepositions' being on different cartographic layers in the temporal preposition phrase is just the reason for their different syntactic behaviors in licensing high and low construals and resisting MCP.

Through the contrastive study of the similarities and differences of MCP, I offered a panorama of MCP distribution in English and Chinese adverbial clauses and phrases in this chapter. Moreover, I provided a reasonable account for the restriction of MCP in these clauses after detailed analyses. All these outcomes can be seen as supplements to the current MCP research because rare literature is involved with these MCP in Chinese. Meanwhile, my research about the parametric variation in splitting CP between English and Chinese contributed to the cartographic proposal, especially to the split-CP hypothesis.

Chapter Four
MCP in Complement Clauses

This chapter will discuss MCP in two types of complement clauses, i.e., the complement clause of the factive predicate (mainly the verb, sometimes the adjective) and the complement clause of the noun phrase in English and Chinese.[①] The former can also be called factive complement clause and the latter noun complement clause.[②] The discussion starts with the re-classification of Chinese complement clauses. The goal of this discussion is to establish the status of the complement clause and form the comparison with the English corresponding clauses. The chapter then concentrates on the property of factivity that brings about MCP in factive complement clauses in English. Following Haegeman and Ürögdi (2010a, 2010b), I argue that referentiality is better than factivity to account for the MCP restriction. After the preliminary work, the chapter continues to analyze MCP in factive complement clauses and noun complement clauses in Chinese and contrasts them with the related phenomena in English. Finally, the chapter shows that the left periphery of these two types of complement clauses in Chinese does not pattern with that of the English ones. This accounts for the different distributions of topicalization in English and Chinese complement clauses. As the other typical kind of MCP, the compatibility of high modal markers is quite complicated. While some complement clauses resist high modals, others

---

① The term "complement clause" generally refers to the clause that is the complement of the predicate or noun.

② In this book, the term "factive complement clause" is used loosely, which refers to the clause that is associated with factive complement (Haegeman 2012a: Preface).

tolerate their existence. I argue that the semantic factors determine whether high modals can be compatible with complement clauses.

4.1 Re-cognition of Chinese complement clauses

At the very beginning of this chapter, it is necessary to illustrate the syntactic status of complement clauses in Chinese. The traditional grammarians once argued that the clausal complement in Chinese is a predicative or a noun phrase but not a clause. The observation shows that the complement is a clause embedded in the complex sentence in the formal syntactic standard. And then, the discussion extends to the property of factivity. I propose that referentiality rather than factivity determines the MCP distribution, but the operator movement does not derive the complement clauses of factive predicates or noun phrases.

4.1.1 Re-classifying Chinese complement clauses

The classification of the complement clause in Chinese is not the same as that of English. In English, the complement clause is regarded as a part of a complex sentence (Foley and van Valin 1984; Haiman and Thompson 1988; Payne 1997; Lyons 1995; Croft 2001). The complement clause is the argument of the main clause in which it is embedded. Together with the main clause, they form a complex sentence, as the following (117a-b) show:

(117)
a. I told her *that I was writing a book.*   (Croft 2001: 326)
b. The announcement *that the king's new residence was beyond the next hill* surprised the tourists.   (Haegeman 2012: 94, rev.)

However, a complement clause in Chinese is generally considered as a part of a simple sentence (li 1924/2007; Wang 1943/1985; Chao 1968; Zhu 1982; Liu 2005, 2008). The complement clause is regarded as an embedded predicative phrase (VP or AP), functioning as the subject or object of the simple sentence. For example, Liu (2005) indicates that some traditional grammarians argue that the nominative clauses in (118a-b) should not be regarded as complement clauses related to the matrix clauses but as phrases of predicative structures embedded in the matrix clause, functioning as the object and subject. See the following (118a-b) from Liu (2005: 193-194):

(118)
a. Ta gaosu wo *Xiaozhang chuan le jian xin yifu.*
   he   tell   me Xiaozhang   wear   ASP CL   new clothes
   'He tells me that Xiaozhang wears new clothes.'
b. *Women qu lüyou de jihua quxiao le.*
   we   go   travel DE plan   cancel   SFP
   'The plan that we go traveling cancled.'

According to traditional grammarians, the embedded constituents *Xiaozhang chuan le jian xin yifu* (Xiaozhang wears new clothes) in (118a) and *women qu lüyou* (we go traveling) in (118b) are predicative phrases instead of clauses. Unlike this argumentation, I will classify the constituent *xiaozhang chuan le jian xin yifu* in (118a) as a complement clause of the predicate and *women qu lüyou* (we go traveling) in (118b) as a complement clause with *jihua* (plan) as the head noun.

The classification is supported by the syntactic structures. The syntactic constituents *xiaozhang chuan le jian xin yifu* in (118a) and *women qu lüyou* in (118b) are embedded in the matrix clause. Syntactically, they all have complete predicative structures, external arguments and tense (or aspect) systems. That means these constituents are finite clauses (finite CPs) rather than non-finite phrases (VPs or APs). In the formal syntax schema, finite CPs are clauses. Thus, it is not reasonable to classify these constituents as predicative phrases.

After classifying the Chinese complement clauses, this chapter will concentrate on the embedded constituents like *xiaozhang chuan le jian xin yifu* in (118a) and *women qu lüyou* in (118b), since they are complement clauses of the predicate and the noun phrase, respectively. Thus, these two types of complement clauses (especially the complement clauses of factive predicates and factive nouns) are the foci in the following discussion.

4.1.2 Re-defining factivity in complement clauses

The research about factive complement clauses and the related MCP brought about by the factive predicates can be dated back to Kiparsky and Kiparsky (1970). They believe that the distinctive semantic property that sets apart the embedded propositions in (119a-b) and (119c) is factivity. More specifically, the truth of the embedded propositions in (119a-b) is taken to be presupposed by the factive verb *regret* and *realize*. In contrast, the truth of the embedded proposition in (119c) is not presupposed by the non-factive verb *think*. Thus, the property of factivity is thought to determine the distribution of topicalized constituents in the complement clauses. The property of factivity blocks the movement of the topicalized constituent *this book* in (119a) and (119b). Therefore, (119a-b) are ungrammatical. However, (119c) is grammatical because the verb of the main clause is not factive and not involved with the blocking.

(119)
a. *John regrets that *this book* Mary read.   (Maki, Kaiser and Ochi 1993: 3)
b. *Mary realizes that *this book*, John read.   (Hegarty 1992: 52)
c. John thinks that *this book* Mary read.   (Haegeman and Ürögdi 2010a: 112)

Except for the property of factivity, Hegarty (1992) argues that the ungrammaticality of sentences like (119a-b) depends on the familiarity of embedded clauses. In particular, the movement of the topic from a clause with the property of being discourse bound will make the sentence ungrammatical. Thus, for him, familiarity replaces factivity as the determining property. Other linguists also give some other terms (d-linking, givenness, presupposition, etc.) to characterize the property of information status in these complement clauses.

One more point should be noted here. MCP in factive complement clauses are not only topicalization; high modal markers are also forbidden. See the following (120) from Haegeman (2006b: 1664):

(120)

*John regrets that Mary *probably/obviously/unfortunately* did not attend the meeting.

As (120) shows, the high modals *probably*, *obviously* and *unfortunately* are not compatible with the factive complement clause.

On the basis of these observations, Haegeman and Ürögdi (2010a) explore a new way to define this property. Following de Cuba and Ürögdi (2009, 2010), Haegeman and Ürögdi (2010a) argue that the clauses like (119a-b) are defined not by the factivity of the selecting predicate, but rather by the referentiality of the CP of the embedded clause itself. Such clauses are derived by event relativization, which is the movement of an event operator. Hence, their resistance to MCP is also from the intervention effect. They give the definition of referentiality and referential CP as follows (Haegeman and Ürögdi 2010a: 137):

(121)

Referential: XP is referential if XP has the potential for referring.

Referential CP (RCP): a referential entity that denotes a proposition without illocutionary force (a sentence radical in the sense of Krifka 2001); a semantic object encoding a proposition/question which the complex sentence (the embedding context) positions in the dynamics of conversation. As such, an RCP in itself does not constitute a speech act and cannot be used as an utterance. RCPs can be embedded under both factives and non-factives.

Non-referential CP (NCP): a non-referential semantic object denoting a speech act with illocutionary force, i.e., one which involves a conversational move. An NCP can thus be a matrix sentence, or an embedded clause subject to various restrictions. Factive verbs cannot embed speech acts due to conflicting semantic requirements.[1]

The definitions show that complement clauses are not divided by the

---

[1]   Though the term "referential" is adopted by Haegeman and Ürögdi (2010a) as the property of the CP of the complement clause, the referential property is closely related to the predicate that selects the CP complement. The predicates that select the complements (RCP or NCP) can also be divided into referential predicates and non-referential predicates. I will address the classification in section 4.2.3.3.3.

property of factivity or familiarity, but are differentiated by referentiality. In this way, non-factive predicates have two complementation options (RCP and NCP), while factives are restricted to one (RCP). The referentiality is a precondition of familiarity or givenness, D-linking and presupposition. That means the referential propositions-just like referring expressions in general-may be used as given or D-linked, and their truth may be presupposed if they are subordinated to a factive predicate. Factivity is a lexico-semantic property of the predicate and enforces truth-conditional presupposition on the complement of the predicate. Referentiality, unlike givenness or D-linking, is not contextually defined but syntactically derived through operator movement.

Instead of factivity, referentiality is then regarded as the key point to be involved in MCP restriction. I agree with this argumentation because sometimes the proposition in the complement clause of the so-called factive predicates is not true or factive but is only referential.[①] And the property of truth presupposed by factive predicates cannot illustrate certain syntactic behaviors in these complement clauses.

However, I do not think that the factive complement clause is derived through the operator movement. There is empirical evidence supporting that these complement clauses do not experience the operator movement.[②] My viewpoint is that referentiality is the decisive factor that influences the MCP distribution, but the operator movement does not derive the complement clauses of factive predicates or noun phrases.[③]

The property of factivity and the related syntactic phenomena in English are always hot topics for linguistic study. However, it is very difficult to find related syntactic research in Chinese. The publications about the research of factivity (Yuan 2014; Zhang 2015; Li 2014, 2015, 2016, 2018; Li and Yuan 2016, 2017; Chen and Zhen 2017; Yuan and Kou 2018; Guo and Chen 2019)

---

① I will illustrate this in section 4.2.3.3.2.

② I will demonstrate this in section 4.2.3.1.

③ For convenience and consistency, the book will still use the terms *factivity* and *factive* in the rest of this section.

concerns more about the semantic properties of the factive predicates. In these works, linguists seldom concentrate on the syntactic behaviors in these factive complement clauses, needless to say the different MCP distributions between English and Chinese.

There is no doubt that the factivity of the selecting predicates in the main clauses influences the distribution of MCP in complement clauses in English. While in Chinese, it seems that the constraint of topicalization does not apply to factive clauses though the constraint of high modals does. See the following (122a-b):

(122)

a. Yuehan   gan-dao   yihan   *zhe-ben   shu*   Mali   du   guo   le.
   John   feel-PERF   regretful   this-CL   book   Mary   read   ASP   SFP
   'John regrets that this book Mary read.'

b. Mali   yishi-dao   *zhe-ben   shu*   Yuehan   duo   guo   le.
   Mary   realize-PERF   this-CL   book   John   read   ASP   SFP
   'Mary realized that this book John read.'

c. *Yuehan   gan-dao   yihan   Mali   *dagai/   mingxian/   buxing*   meiyou
   John   feel-PERF   regretful   Mary   probably   obviously   unfortunately   not

   canjia   huiyi.
   attend   meeting
   'John regrets that Mary probably/obviously/unfortunately did not attend the meeting.'

In (122a-b), the topicalized constituent *zheben shu* (this book) moves from the original position to the [Spec, CP] position of the complement clauses of the factive verbs *yihan* (regret) and *yishidao* (realize), respectively. And the sentences are grammatical. While in (122c), all the high modal markers *dagai* (probably), *mingxian* (obviously) and *buxing* (unfortunately) are not allowed to exist in the complement clause of the factive verb *yihan*. One can see that the Chinese factive complement clauses show different tolerance to topicalization and high modal markers from their English counterparts.

From factivity, familiarity to referentiality, linguists provide many hypotheses to illustrate the MCP constraints. However, these hypotheses cannot apply accurately and entirely to the Chinese associated clauses. It seems that factivity is not a determining factor in these complement clauses in Chinese. The observations show that the property of factivity and its relationship with MCP should be analyzed further.

4.2 A contrastive study of MCP in English and Chinese factive complement clauses

This section will make a contrastive study of MCP in English and Chinese complement clauses of factive predicates. There are similarities and differences in terms of MCP distribution in English and Chinese factive complement clauses. English factive complement clauses do not allow topicalization and high modal markers, while Chinese factives allow topicalized constituents but disallow high modals. The following parts of this section will analyze the similarities and differences between English and Chinese factive complement clauses and attempt to find the reasons behind these phenomena.

4.2.1 MCP in English factive complement clauses

MCP in English factive complement clauses are mainly topicalization and high modal markers, as the following (123a-b) show, (120) is repeated here as (123b):

(123)
a. *John regretted that *Gone with the Wind* he never went to see.

(Haegeman and Ürögdi 2010a: 113)

b.*John regrets that Mary *probably/obviously/unfortunately* did not attend the meeting.

In (123a), the fronted topic *Gone with the Wind* is not allowed in the complement clause introduced by the factive verb *regretted*. In (123b), the high modal markers *probably*, *obviously* and *unfortunately* exist in the complement clause of the factive verb *regret*, resulting in the ungrammaticality of the sentence.

Since the beginning of MCP research, such particular syntactic phenomena have been noticed. Some linguists (Hooper and Thompson 1973; Green 1976; Krifka 2001) attempt to characterize these complement clauses from the semantic side. For those clauses where MCP are allowed, they define them as non-factive, novel or asserted; while for those where MCP are banned, they argue that they are factive, given or non-asserted.

From the syntactic side, some other linguists (Haegeman 2003a, 2006a, 2006b; Emonds 2004; de Cuba 2007) propose that these complement clauses are truncated (or reduced) and cannot accommodate these MCP like topics or high modals. Thus, MCP are excluded from these complement clauses.

Haegeman and Ürögdi (2010a, 2010b) try to account for the MCP restriction in the factive complement clauses from a cartographic perspective. They propose that the absence of MCP in such clauses is not from the truncated syntactic structures. Instead, they argue that the incompatibility of factive complement clauses with MCP is defined by the referentiality of the CP of the embedded clause. That means they deny the possibilities of semantic factors or the factivity of the selecting predicates being the reasons for MCP restriction.

Their argumentation is built on the following steps. Firstly, they propose that the so-called referential clause (i.e., a term used in their papers to replace the factive complement clause) is derived by the operator movement to the left periphery, and it is a free relative clause. To be specific, the clause is derived by event relativization, which is an event operator movement from the original position to the [Spec, CP] position. Then, they argue that the operator chain results in the intervention effect in the clause. The moving left-peripheral elements such as topicalized constituents and high modals block the movement of the event operator. However, the non-referential clause that is not derived by the operator movement is thus more liberal to the moving operation. Finally, MCP are incompatible with the referential clause because of the intervention effect, but the non-referential clause will not be influenced by the effect and allow MCP. The process of the derivation can be illustrated in the following (124a-b):

(124)

a. [$_{CP}$ John regrets [$_{RP}$ that [$_{CP}$ OP$_i$ *this book* [$_{FP}$ t$_i$ [$_{TP}$ Mary read t$_j$]]]]]

b. [$_{CP}$ John regrets [$_{RP}$ that [$_{CP}$ OP$_i$ Mary *probably* [$_{FP}$ t$_i$ [$_{TP}$ did not attend the meeting]]]]]

As (124a-b) show, the topicalized constituent *this book* and the high modal marker *probably* block the movement of the event operator that derives the factive complement clauses, and the sentences are then ungrammatical.

Apparently, Haegeman and Ürögdi's (2010a, 2010b) movement account follows from Haegeman's (2009, 2010b) analysis of conditional and temporal adverbial clauses. Their argumentation is from the following observation:

(125)

a. **Why$_i$* did you notice that Mary had fixed the car t$_i$?

b. ??*What$_i$* did you notice that Mary had fixed t$_i$?

c. *Which car$_i$* did you notice that Mary had fixed t$_i$?

(Haegeman and Ürögdi 2010a: 120)

Referential clauses are weak islands and result in the ungrammaticality of (125a) and degradation of (125b) because the extraction of the wh-constituents *why* and *what* is blocked. However, if the moved constituents are D-linked wh-phrases like *which car* in (125c), the extraction will become easy. To account for this, they propose that such D-linked wh-phrases are featurally richer than the event operator in the left periphery of the referential clauses.

Because the event operator needs to move to the left periphery to derive the referential clause, the features carried by the operator and the topicalized constituents and high modal markers are the critical characteristics involved in MCP distribution. Haegeman and Ürögdi (2010a, 2010b) argue that all these three constituents share Q-feature. Thus, the unavailability of topicalization and high modals in referential clauses can be attributed to the intervention effect.

At last, they give a reasonable illustration for the counter-examples proposed by Bianchi and Frascarelli (2009: 69) in the following:

(126)
He tried to conceal from his parents that *the maths exam* he had not passed, and *the biology exam* he had not even taken.

In (126), the topicalized constituents *the maths exam* and *the biology exam* are compatible with the complement clause introduced by the factive verb *conceal*. If the analysis above is right, this result is unexpected. To explain the unexpected syntactic behavior, they argue that (126) involves a contrast between two events. The entire event of *not passing the maths exam* is contrasted with the other event *not even taking the biology exam*. By virtue of being contrasted with the other event, the event itself is relativized in the referential clause and is a part of a reference set, and is thus D-linked (endowed with δ-feature). So the contrast is actually not encoded on the fronted argument but rather on the event operator and the entire clause. However, the fronted argument only has Q-feature, so it will not intervene in the movement of the event operator that carries both δ-feature and Q-feature, according to the feature-based locality condition (Strake 2001; Rizzi 2004; 2013; Friedmann et al. 2009).

It can be seen that the core thinking of this argumentation is that any constituent that expresses speech acts (whether matrix or embedded) will run counter to the requirement of truth-conditional presupposition imposed on the complement clauses by the lexical semantics of factive predicates. Thus, MCP, which are involved in the conversational move, are not compatible with the complement clauses selected by the factive predicates. Their incompatibility comes from the semantic conflict between MCP and factive predicates. From the syntactic perspective, the fronted elements (topicalized constituent and high modal markers) are not compatible with referential clauses because the fronted elements intervene in the movement of the event operator that derives these referential clauses. So, referentiality, instead of factivity, is the determining factor leading to MCP in the factive complement clauses.

4.2.2 MCP in Chinese factive complement clauses

Generally speaking, the factive predicates in Chinese include but are not limited to: *aitan* (lament), *aohui* (regret), *baoyuan* (complain), *beiai* (mourn), *chayi* (be surprised), *ganxin* (be reconciled), *ganyuan* (be willing), *gaoxing* (feel happy), *manyuan* (complain), *mingbai* (be clear), *piping* (criticize), *qingchu* (be clear), *qingxing* (rejoice), *shuluo* (reprove), *wangji* (forget), *xianmu* (envy), *xiaode* (know), *zhidao* (know), etc. (Li 2016: 93).[①] In the corpus, I find some sentences in which the complement clauses of these factive predicates are compatible with the topicalized constituents, see the following (127) and (128):

(127)

a. Zhushou   Heifengkou   judian   de ri-jun   aitan   *zhe-zhong*
garrison   Heifengkou   stronghold DE Japanese-army lament this-kind

beidong ai-da   que bu *neng* *huan-shou* *de* *zhandou,* congwei
passive   beaten yet not can   strike-back DE battle   never

yu-dao   guo.
meet-PERF ASP

'The Japanese army garrisoned at Heifengkou stronghold lamented that they had never met this kind of battle in which they are passive and beaten yet cannot strike back.'

(Center for Chinese Linguistics of Peking University)

b. Wo aohui wo *naxie* *jiang* meiyou dai   zai   shen-bian.
I   regret my those award not   bring PREP side
'I regret that I have not brought those awards by my side.'   (ibid.)

c. Wo zhidao *zhe* *liang-ge* *yaoqiu*   ni jiben   mei zuo-dao   guo.
I   know these two-CL requirement you basically not fulfill-PERF ASP
'I know that you have not basically fulfill these two requirements.'

(Beijing Language and Culture University Corpus of Chinese)

[①]   In fact, not all the predicates on this list are factive predicates. Some predicates (*zhidao* for instance) are just referential but not factive. They cannot presuppose the property of factivity in the complement clauses. I will illustrate this point in detail in section 4.2.3.3.3.

In (127a-c), the topicalized constituents *zhezhong beidong aida que bu neng huanshou de zhandou* (this kind of battle in which they are passive and beaten yet cannot strike back), *wo naxie jiang* (my awards) and *zhe liangge yaoqiu* (these two requirements) are allowed to appear in the complement clauses of the factive predicates *aitan* (lament), *aohui* (regret) and *zhidao* (know), respectively. (127a-c) show that topicalization in factive complement clauses in Chinese is allowed. The so-called factivity or referentiality does not result in the absence of these topicalized constituents in Chinese factive complement clauses.

Factive complement clauses are compatible with topicalization in Chinese, while they are not always compatible with high modals. According to Hooper (1975), Li (2014, 2016) and Chen and Zhen (2017), factive verbs can be classified into several types. Among them, the classical and well-accepted two types are subjective factive verbs (*yihan* (regret) is the representative) and objective factive verbs (*zhidao* (know) is the representative). As (122c) (repeated here as (128a) for convenience) shows, the former is not compatible with high modals, while the latter seems not constrained by the rule:

(128)

a. *Yuehan　gan-dao　yihan　　Mali　*dagai/　　mingxian/　buxing*
　　John　　feel-PERF　regretful　Mary　probably　obviously　unfortunately

　　meiyou　canjia　huiyi.
　　not　　attend　meeting
　　'John regrets that Mary probably/obviously/unfortunately did not attend the meeting.'

b. Zhangchu　zaici　yishi-dao　　*dagai*　　zhiyou　zhe-ge　chengshi　de
　　Zhangchu　again　realize-PERF　probably　only　　this-CL　city　　DE

　　mou-ge　　bianyuan　cai hui gei ta　tigong　"gudu"　de yi-yu.
　　certain-CL　margin　　just can give him　provide　"longely"　DE one-corner
　　'Zhangchu again realized that probably only a certain margin of this city could give him a lonely corner.'

(Center for Chinese Linguistics of Peking University)

In (128a), the high modals *dagai* (probably), *mingxian* (obviously) and *buxing* (unfortunately) are not compatible with the complement clause of the verb *yihan* (regret), which is a subjective factive verb. However, the high modal *dagai* is compatible with the complement clause of the verb *yishidao* (realize) in (128b), an objective factive verb.

Similar syntactic behaviors can be found in English factive complement clauses. See the following (129a-b) from Corpus of Contemporary American English:

(129)

a. She realized that he *probably* lied to the insurance company to get the money ASAP.

b. I realized that he *probably* had no more money to buy alcohol.

As (129a-b) show, the high modal *probably* is compatible with the English factive complement clause when the verb is objective factive like *realize*. So the natural result of this parallel between English and Chinese is that the high modal markers are just incompatible with the subjective factive complement clauses but not the objective factive ones.

The observations above show that the properties of these factive verbs are not completely involved in MCP restrictions in Chinese. The series of contrastive syntactic behaviors bring about a bunch of questions. Why do factive complement clauses behave differently from non-factive complement clauses? Why do factive complement clauses show different availabilities to topicalized constituents in English and Chinese? And why do the subjective factive complement clause and the objective factive complement clause demonstrate different compatibilities with high modals? The previous linguists do not answer these questions properly. A new account is needed to illustrate the different MCP distributions between English and Chinese in factive complement clauses. In the next section, I will provide a possible account of these differences.

4.2.3 Accounting for MCP in English and Chinese factive complement clauses

The syntactic behaviors of factive complement clauses show that MCP restrictions in English and Chinese are varied. Specifically, topicalization is not compatible with English factives, while Chinese factives show enough tolerance to these topicalized constituents. As for the high modal markers, the situation is more intricate. When subjective factive predicates introduce the complement clause in English and Chinese, the high modals cannot be embedded. However, the high modals can be permitted in the complement clauses introduced by objective factive predicates. I propose that the different distributions of topicalization between English and Chinese are also due to the parametric variation of CP-splitting, and the absence of high modals in the subjective factive complement clauses is because of the semantic factors. The argumentation will be built on the following three steps:

(130)
a. The complement clauses of factive predicates in English and Chinese are not derived by the movement of the event operator.
b. The different syntactic behaviors of topicalization in English and Chinese in factive clauses are due to the parametric variation of CP-splitting. The incompatibility of ForceP and TopP leads to the absence of topicalization in English, but there is no such incompatibility in the corresponding clauses in Chinese.
c. Because factive and referential (but not factive) predicates require different semantic contexts, the semantic mismatch results in the incompatibility of high modals with factive complement clauses but not referential complement clauses.

4.2.3.1 The movement of the event operator

Haegeman and Ürögdi (2010a, 2010b) argue that the referential clause is derived by the movement of an event operator to the position [Spec, CP] and is a free relative clause. The incompatibility of the clause with MCP is defined by the referentiality of the CP of the complement clause instead of the factivity of the predicate of the main clause. In the process of derivation, the fronted topics and high modal markers intervene in the movement of the event operator that derives the factive complement clause. Thus, the argumentation captures the lack of MCP in the factive complement clauses and attributes it to the intervention effect.

However, as Lipták (2010) indicates, the strongest empirical evidence for the existence of the operator movement in the factive complement clause (and the treatment of this movement as a case of the event relativization) comes from the observation of Kwa Language, where factive complements are headed relative clauses formally and involve event relativization. However, one particular case in Kwa language cannot reveal thoroughly the universal syntax of factive complements. Another interesting case study by Caponigro and Polinsky (2011) shows that Circassian Adyghe language uses relative clauses to express a whole range of clauses usually expressed by embedded clauses in other languages (embedded declarative clauses, embedded yes-or-no interrogative clauses and embedded wh-interrogative clauses). Of course, one cannot conclude that all the embedded clauses are relatives just because it is the case in Circassian Adyghe language. According to Caponigro and Polinsky (2011), the lack of ordinary embeddings can be tracked back to lexical properties of embedding (verbs in Circassian Adyghe language can embed DPs but not CPs) or accidental lexical gaps (the language lacks non-relative complementizer).

Besides, the more serious problem about Haegeman and Ürögdi's (2010a, 2010b) intervention account is from the counter-evidence in the factive interrogative complements in English. According to Haegeman and Ürögdi (2010a, 2010b), the landing site of the event operator is taken to be [Spec, CP] of the complement clause, which is standardly assumed to accommodate operator material in the left periphery in English. Thus, if the [Spec, CP] position were already occupied by some other element like overt wh-constituent (a wh-operator by itself), the sentence should be ungrammatical because the wh-constituent should intervene in the movement of the event operator. Out of expectation, this prediction is not correct. See the following (129) from Lipták (2010: 227):

(131)

a. I still remember *how* John looked when he heard the news.

b. Jane has found out *where* John lives.

In (131a), the [Spec, CP] position of the complement clause is already occupied by the wh-constituent *how*, the intervention effect will arise because the wh-constituent *how* (which is a wh-operator itself) fully matches the feature of the event operator that derives the factive complement clause according to the feature-based locality condition. However, the sentence is grammatical. Similar to (131a), the wh-constituent *where* should intervene in the movement of the event operator that derives the factive complement clause in (131b), and the sentence should be ungrammatical. Nevertheless, the result is on the contrary.

The wh-exclamative in factive clause is another potential problem for Haegeman and Ürögdi's (2010a, 2010b) intervention analysis. The wh-exclamative can also exist in the factive complement clauses, as (132) shows:

(132)

a. It's amazing *what* a large house John lives in.

b. I'm surprised at *how* fast John can run.   (Lipták 2010: 227)

In (132a-b), the factive predicates are not verbs but adjectives, and this will not alternate or cancel the factivity of the predicates. Of course, the syntax of wh-exclamatives is distinct from that of wh-questions, but there seems no reason to assume that wh-exclamatives occupy a position different from [Spec, CP]. If the wh-exclamatives *what* in (132a) and *how* in (132b) occupy the position [Spec, CP], they will intervene in the movement of the event operator that derives the factive complement clauses and make the sentences ungrammatical. However, this prediction is not correct, either. (132a-b) are both grammatical sentences in English.

Moreover, I find that the distribution of negative constituents also goes against this movement and intervention proposal. As (133a-b) show, factive complement clauses can be compatible with negative fronting:

(133)

a. I realized that *never* since I'd known him had Vernor gone out of town, or spoke of visiting "home". (Corpus of Contemporary American English)

b. In that moment Step realized that *never, never* would Glass be left alone with any of his children, even for a moment. (ibid.)

According to Rizzi (2004), negation is quantificational, just as the operator in the typology of the specifiers. So the negative fronting should belong to the same structural type as operators and share the same Q-feature. If this were the case, the negative constituent should also be the intervener to the movement of the event operator, and then the sentence should be ungrammatical. (133a-b) show that this is not borne out. In (133a-b), the fronted negative constituent *never* appears in the factive complement clauses, and the sentences are still grammatical.

The corresponding Chinese factive complement clauses show similar syntactic behaviors to their English counterparts. All the wh-interrogative, wh-exclamative and negative fronting are allowed in the factive complement clauses. Firstly, wh-interrogative can be embedded in the factive complement clauses. See the following (134a-b) from Center for Chinese Linguistics of Peking University:

(134)

a. Zhuanye   gongcheng-dui   gan   le   san   tian san   ye,   jing
professional engineering-team work ASP three day three night unexpectedly

meiyou faxian   wenti   chu   zai   *nali*.
not   find.out problem from PREP where

'The professional engineering team worked all along for three days, unexpectedly, they did not find out what went wrong.'

b. Wo jiaojin-naozhi nuli   shi   ta xianzai jiu neng wanquan   yishi-dao,   ta
I   exhaust-mind try.hard make her now   just can   completely realize-PERF she

yihou   jiang shenghuo zai   yi-ge   shenmeyang de huanjing   zhizhong.
afterwards will live   PREP one-CL what   DE environment   in

'I exhausted my mind, trying hard to make her realize now what kind of environment she will live in afterwards.'

In (134a), the wh-interrogative *nali* (where) exists in the complement clause of the factive verb *faxian* (find out), and the sentence is grammatical. Although the wh-phrase *nali* does not move to the [Spec, CP] position in the overt syntax, it moves to the position in the logical form (Huang 1982). That is to say, the wh-operator will still occupy the [Spec, CP] position of the factive complement clause in the covert syntax. If the factive clause were involved with an event operator movement to this position, the intervention effect should arise, and the sentence should be ungrammatical. However, (134a) is a well-accepted sentence, which is out of expectation. (134b) is almost the same situation as (134a). The wh-constituent *shenmeyang* (what) has already occupied the [Spec, CP] position of the complement clause introduced by the factive verb *yishidao* (realize), and the wh-operator should block the movement of the event operator that derives the factive clause. Nevertheless, (134b) is also grammatical. The syntactic behaviors in (134a-b) show that the movement of the wh-constituents is not influenced by the factive predicates, proving that the operator movement account is not on the right track.

Secondly, wh-exclamative is also allowed in the factive complement clauses. See the following (135a-b):

(135)

a. Ta ceng   bu-wu   wanxi de shuo,   duome   xiwang you   shijian jingjing de
   he once not-not regret DE say   how   hope   have time   quietly DE

   duo   shendu   yixie shugao,   ke xianzai nande you jihui
   more read.and.approve some manuscript but now   seldom have opportunity

   xiangshou   zhe-fen   lequ.
   enjoy   this-CL   pleasure

   'He once regretted to say how much he hopes that he can have more time to read and approve more manuscripts quietly, but now he seldom has the opportunity to enjoy this pleasure.'

   (Center for Chinese Linguistics of Peking University)

b. Zai wo-de yantaohui shang, tingzhong-men chijing-de faxian, ziji yu
in my seminar up audience-PL surprisingly find.out oneself with

xiashu de gongming shi duome shao, er duo yidian zhudongxing
subordinate DE empathy be how little while more a.little initiative

jing neng rang ziji beitian keai.
unexpectedly can let oneself add loveliness

'In my seminar, the audiences surprisingly found out that how little empathy they shared with their subordinates, while a little more initiative can make them more lovable unexpectedly.' (ibid.)

In (135a), the wh-exclamative *duome* (how) can exist in the complement clause introduced by the factive verb *wanxi* (regret). According to the movement account, the event operator will move to the [Spec, CP] position of the factive complement clause, while the wh-exclamative *duome* has already occupied this position. Thus, the wh-exclamative will intervene in the movement of the event operator, and the clause should be ungrammatical. However, the grammaticality of (135a) shows that the intervention effect does not arise. Like (135a), the wh-exclamative *duome* in (135b) is also compatible with the complement clause introduced by the factive verb *faxian* (find out). If the movement account were correct, this clause should also be ill-formed. But (135b) is a well-accepted clause. The result again casts doubt on the movement and intervention account proposed by Haegeman and Ürögdi (2010a, 2010b).

Lastly, negative fronting is permitted in the factive complement clauses. See the following (136a-b) from Center for Chinese Linguistics of Peking University:

(136)

a. Yinwei ta-ziji mingbai, ta conglai-meiyou kuanshu-guo yi-ge ren, ye
because he-oneself be.clear he ever-not forgive-ASP one-CL person also

jiu conglai bu gan sheqiu bie-ren kuanshu ta.
then ever not dare demand other-people forgive him

'Because he himself is clear that never in his life did he forgive anyone, and then he can never demand too much other people's forgiveness for him.'

b. Hong Xingguo kan-kan zhouwei yijing yishi-dao, qi lian
   Hong Xingguo look-look around already realize-PERF seventh company

conglai-meiyou shou-guo zheme da de cuozhe.
   ever-not suffer-ASP this big DE setback
   'Hong Xingguo looked around and already realized that never did the seventh
   company suffer from such a big setback.'

In (136a), the negative word *conglai meiyou* (never) appears in the complement clause introduced by the factive predicate *mingbai* (be clear). Because negation is quantificational (Rizzi 2004), it should intervene in the movement of the operator that is also quantificational. However, the intervention effect does not arise, and (136a) is grammatical. In (136b), the same negative word exists in the complement clause introduced by the factive verb *yishidao* (realize), and the sentence is well-accepted. The grammaticality of (136a-b) proves that the intervention effect does not work in these factive clauses. Therefore, there is no event operator movement to derive the factive complement clauses. These factive complement clauses are not relative clauses and their being lack of MCP is not from intervention effects but instead from other factors.

4.2.3.2 The parametric variation of CP-splitting

The last section illustrates that the factive complement clause is not derived by the event operator and is not a relative clause. This section will discuss the problem of MCP distribution in these clauses. Factive complements are not compatible with topicalization in English, while they are compatible in Chinese. See the following sentences, (123a) is repeated here as (137a) and (127b) is repeated here as (137b), respectively:

(137)
a. *John regretted that *Gone with the Wind* he never went to see.
b. Wo aohui *wo naxie jiang* meiyou dai zai shen-bian.
   I regret my those award not bring PREP side
   'I regret that I have not brought those awards by my side.'

In (137a), the topicalized constituent *Gone with the Wind* is not compatible with the complement clause introduced by the factive verb *regret* in English. While in Chinese, the paralleled topicalized constituent *naxie jiang* (those awards) can be compatible with the complement clause introduced by the factive verb *aohui* (regret). The contrast between (137a) and (137b) shows that English and Chinese factive complement clauses differ with respect to the availability of topicalization.

I have shown that both English and Chinese factive complement clauses are not derived by the movement of the event operator and thus not relative clauses. The earlier discussion of this book (see section 3.2.3.2) has also shown that topicalized constituents do not share Q-feature with the operator and do not intervene in the movement of the operator. So the intervention effect will not be involved with the incompatibility of topics with factive complements. The incompatibility must stem from other factors.

Van Gelderen (2004), McCloskey (2006) and Haegeman (2006b) once proposed that the truncated structure of the factive complement clause in English is the reason for the incompatibility. Haegeman (2006b: 1666) points out that the left periphery of the factive complement clause is a truncated CP structure. (17) is repeated here as (138) for convenience:

(138)
Complements of factive predicates: that ModP FinP

As (138) shows, the topicalized constituent cannot exist in the factive complement clause because there is no ForceP, TopP or FocP in the CP structure. As for the absence of these phrases, she argues that the factive complement clause in English lacks the feature of speaker-deixis. Thus it cannot accommodate the topicalized or focalized constituents that are speaker-oriented.

This proposal is not without controversy. Firstly, it is noticeable that the factivity of the complement clause is presupposed as true by the speaker, not by the subject of the clause. This is particularly salient in the case of negation.

Consider the following (139):

(139)
a. John *knows* that Mary was late.
b. John does not *know* that Mary was late.   (Basse 2008: 56)

In (139a), both the speaker and the matrix subject *John* presuppose the truth of Mary's being late. In (139b), however, it cannot be the case that *John* presupposes the truth of the complement clause as he is not cognizant of the event. The speaker of (139b), on the other hand, does presuppose that *Mary* was late and states that *John* is not aware of this fact. Thus, it is evident that the factive complement clause has the feature of speaker-deixis and is speaker-oriented.

Besides, as (131) and (132) demonstrate, the [Spec, CP] position of the factive complement clause can be occupied by the wh-interrogatives and wh-exclamatives. And these wh-constituents definitely are the specifiers of ForceP. Therefore, it is not accurate to claim that there is no ForceP in the CP structure of the factive complements in English.

I hereby modify this proposal for a better solution to the problem. Following the analysis of conditional adverbial clauses, I argue that the competition between ForceP and TopP leads to the absence of topicalization in English factive complement clauses. However, there is no such competition in the corresponding Chinese clauses. The different syntactic behaviors of topicalization in factive clauses in English and Chinese are also due to the parametric variation in CP-splitting.

Compared with ordinary predicates, factive predicates do have some special properties, resulting in the incompatibility of topicalization with factive complements in English. In the previous sections, I have mentioned that this special property should be referentiality instead of factivity (see section 4.1.2). The factive complement clause has the property of referentiality. When the factive complement clause has a null ForceP, it will inherit the referential force from the factive predicate in the main clause. In other words, the factive predicate in the main clause can percolate the referential feature [+Ref] to the ForceP of the complement clause. Then the ForceP of the complement clause has the referential feature. And this ForceP will compete for the same syntactic position with the topicalized constituents, leading to incompatibility. The detailed derivational process can be demonstrated in the following, (123a) is repeated here as (140):

(140)

*$[_{CP}$ $[_C$ $[_{TP}$ John regretted $[_R$ that $[_{CP}$ $[_C$ [+Ref] $[_{TopP}$ Gone with the Wind$_i$ [+TOP] $[_{TP}$ he never went to see t$_i$]]]]]]]].

In (140), the linking word *that* connects the main clause and the complement clause. There is a null constituent that expresses force (a null ForceP) after the word *that*. The factive verb *regretted* in the main clause percolates its referential feature [+Ref] to the null ForceP in the complement clause and indicates that the edge feature is [+Ref]. This null constituent inherits the force from the factive verb in the main clause. Therefore, the topicalized constituent *Gone with the Wind* of the complement clause that carries the [+TOP] feature will mismatch the [+Ref] feature inherited by the null ForceP. The sentence is then ungrammatical.

If this analysis is on the right track, a natural prediction is that the co-occurrence of overt ForceP and TopP in the factive complement clause in English should be ungrammatical. The following (141) shows that this prediction is correct. An overt ForceP cannot be compatible with TopP in factive complements in English:

(141)

*Robin knows where *the birdseed* you are going to put.　　　(Culicover 1991: 5)

As (141) shows, the topicalized constituent *the birdseed* that occupies the specifier position of TopP is not compatible with the wh-constituent *where* that occupies the specifier position of ForceP in the complement clause introduced by the factive verb *know*. The ungrammaticality of (141) shows that ForceP and TopP cannot co-occur in the factive complements, and they will compete for the same syntactic position. I propose that the competition of ForceP with TopP in English (see section 3.2.3) is the reason behind the absence of topicalized constituents in factive complement clauses.

However, in the corresponding Chinese factive complements, ForceP can be compatible with TopP, as (142) shows:

(142)

Luobin	zhidao	zhexie	niaoshi	ni	hui		fang	zai	nali.
Robin	know	these	birdseed	you	are.going.to		put	PREP	where.

'Robin knows where *the birdseed* you are going to put.'

In (142), the topicalized constituent *zhexie niaoshi* (these birdseed) can be embedded in the complement clause of the factive verb *zhidao* (know), showing that there is no competition between TopP and ForceP in Chinese factive complements.

More similar syntactic behaviors can be found in the Chinese factive complement clauses:

(143)

a.
Zaichang	de	hai	bu-zhi	wo	yi-ge	bu	zhidao	wei-shenme	*zhe*	*guangcai*
present	DE	yet	not-only	I	one-CL	not	know	for-what		this glory

ta	turan	bu	yao	le.
he	suddenly	not	accept	ASP

'More than one person present including me did not yet know why he suddenly did not accept this glory.'

(Center for Chinese Linguistics of Peking University)

b.
Ta	dacong	xin-li	qiguai	*zhe-ge*	*mingzi*	zenme	ye	hui	wangdiao	ne.
he	from	heart-in	be.surprised	this-CL	name	how.come	also	able	forget	SFP

'He was surprised from his heart how come he was able to also forget this name.'

(Beijing Language and Culture University Corpus of Chinese)

In (143a), the topicalized constituent *zhe guangcai* (this glory) that occupies the specifier position of TopP is compatible with the wh-constituent *weishenme* (why) that occupies the specifier position of ForceP in the complement clause introduced by the factive verb *zhidao* (know). The grammaticality of (143a) proves that TopP and ForceP can co-occur in the factive complement clause in Chinese. Under the framework of Split-CP hypothesis, TopP and ForceP occupy different positions in the CP structure and do not compete for the same position. In (143b), a similar syntactic behavior appears again in the factive complement clause in which the topic *zhege mingzi* (this name) is compatible with the wh-constituent *zenme* (how).

The observations demonstrate that the co-occurrence of TopP and ForceP in the factive complement clauses is a well-accepted syntactic behavior in Chinese, which is different from the corresponding English factive complement clauses. Just because the CP structure is split into different phrases, and there is a parametric variation in CP-splitting among different languages, the factive complement clauses show different tolerance to topicalized constituents between English and Chinese.

Besides, I also notice that focalized constituents are not easily embedded in the factive complement clauses in English while they are in Chinese factive complement clauses. See the following contrastive pairs (144a-b), (a) from Haegeman and Ürögdi (2010: 131); (b) from Zhang (2018: 63):

(144)
a. ??What John regrets is that *the pension fund* Mary chose.
b. Hanyu hai dei   ganji shi *ta na bazhang* da xing le ta.
   Hanyu yet have.to thank be her that slap   hit awake ASP him
   'Hanyu has to be thankful that it is her slap that makes him awake.'

(144a) is a pseudo-cleft structure, and the phrase *the pension fund* has been focalized in this structure. However, the sentence is degraded a lot when the predicate is factive, i.e., *regret*. When a similar syntactic operation happens in the Chinese factive clause, the sentence is without any problem. In (144b), *shi* (be) is a focus-sensitive marker and *ta na bazhang* (her slap) is the focalized constituent. The sentence is grammatical when the focalization happens in the complement clause introduced by the factive predicate *ganji* (be thankful).[①]

4.2.3.3 The semantic mismatch

The argumentation starts from the discussion of possible worlds semantics and the distinction between realis and irrealis. Based on the discussion, the section will draw a clear demarcation line between the subjective and objective factive predicates. The section will show that the events in the complement clause of subjective and objective factive predicates are different. So the predicates in the main clauses can be further classified into four types. With this new classification, the section proposes that the factivity of predicates is not determined by the traditional standard. Instead, it is determined by the semantic connotation. Moreover, the properties of referentiality and factivity can be easily distinguished. At last, the section shows that the semantic mismatch results in the incompatibility of high modals with subjective factive complement clauses.

4.2.3.3.1 The notion of possible world and the distinction between realis and irrealis

Before I make a specific analysis of MCP restrictions in these factive complement clauses, I will first discuss the possible worlds semantics and the distinction between realis and irrealis. According to Portner (2009: 21), a possible world is a complete way that the universe could be throughout its history. The possible worlds semantics indicate that our world (the actual world) is also a possible world by nature. However, because this possible world is consistent with the world in which the speaker exists, it can be called the actual world semantically. Apart from this actual world, other possible worlds are similar to our world, but things in these worlds may be altered. For example, if I define a world in terms of someone's knowledge, a possible world can be formed in an epistemic frame. In this world, it is even true that the sun is rising from the west only if this is consistent with one's knowledge. The notion of the possible world plays a vital role in modern logic and

---

① Here, I will not explore further the compatibility of focalization with the factive complement clause due to space limitations.

semantics. It provides us with a new way to analyze the property of factivity brought about by these factive predicates.

Strictly speaking, the world in which the speaker exists and the world in which the subject of the main clause exists are also different. In front of every sentence, there should be a declarative clause *I say,* as the following (145) shows:

(145)
(I say) he knows this thing.

In (145), the speaker *I* is in the actual world, and the subject *he* is in the same actual world as the speaker. Thus the two worlds overlap with each other. However, although the two worlds are shared by the speaker and the subject in most cases, there are also exceptions. For instance, in the following sentence, the subject in the main clause is not in the same actual world as the speaker:

(146)
Zhu Bajie shiyong jiu chi dingpa zuo wuqi.
Zhu Bajie use nine tooth rake as weapon
'Zhu Bajie uses the nine-tooth rake as the weapon.'

In (146), *Zhu Bajie* is a fictional character in the novel *The Journey to the West*, and this figure cannot be in the same actual world as the speaker. So the information in the clause (*Zhu Bajie uses the nine-tooth rake as the weapon*) cannot be tested as true or false in the actual world. If one wants to discuss the truth value of *Zhu Bajie's using the nine-tooth rake as the weapon*, it is necessary to form a possible world in which *Zhu Bajie* exists in advance. Obviously, this world cannot be the actual world.

Under the framework of possible worlds semantics, linguists' attention is mainly on the former situation, i.e., the speaker and the subject are in the same actual world. Therefore, in the rest of this book, I will concentrate on this situation and ignore the situation where the speaker and the subject are in different possible worlds.

Generally speaking, the event that happens in the main clause is in the actual world, while the event in the complement clause is in the possible world (not actual) in most cases. Interestingly, the factive predicate in the main clause has the ability to transfer its factivity to the complement clause. That means the factive predicate can presuppose the truth value of the event in the complement clause. According to possible worlds semantics, a proposition is true if and only if it is true in the actual world and all the other possible worlds accessible to the actual world. However, the property of factivity brought about by the factive predicate cannot always guarantee the truth value of the proposition in the complement clause. Just as Norrick (1976), de Cuba (2006), Li (2015) and Li and Yuan (2017) indicate, the factive predicate suggests that the speaker accepts the information in the complement clause as factual according to the speaker's own knowledge and judgment. In other words, it is the speaker himself who presupposes the factive complement. So, the term factivity is a speaker-oriented grammatical category. Being speaker-oriented, the factivity of the predicate cannot always presuppose the truth value of the event in the complement clause because the world formed by the speaker's knowledge is epistemic or cognitive in nature, but not actual. The property of factivity in this case is clearly demonstrated in the following (147):

(147)

Ta zhidao Zhu Bajie shiyong   jiu   chi dingpa zuo wuqi.
he know   Zhu Bajie use   nine tooth rake   as   weapon
'He knows that Zhu Bajie uses the nine-tooth rake as the weapon.'

In (147), the verb *zhidao* (know) is a classic factive verb, and the information *Zhu Bajie uses the nine-tooth rake as the weapon* in the complement clause is true according to the speaker's knowledge or imagination. However, the event of *Zhu Bajie's using the nine-tooth rake as the weapon* in the complement clause is obviously cannot be factual or true in the actual world. So, factivity cannot be defined just by the truth value when the notion of possible worlds semantics is involved.

Observing this, Coates (1983: 235) argues that presupposition is not involved in the complement clauses like (147) though the factive verb *know* clearly suggests that the speaker accepts the information as factual. Specifically, the factive verb *know* does not suggest that the addressee equally accepts the factuality of the information in the complements, and the complements of *know* are not factive in the presuppositional sense. Therefore, the term of factive predicates can be misleading to some extent.

Aware of this, the chapter then introduces the concepts of realis and irrealis to further illustrate the property of factivity. According to Comrie (1985: 39-40), Chafe (1995: 350), Mithun (1999: 173) and Palmer (2001: 1),[①] The notion of realis portrays situations as actualized, as having occurred or actually occurring, knowable through direct perception. In contrast, the notion of irrealis portrays situations as purely within the realm of thought, knowable only through imagination.

For a long time, realis is regarded as a grammatical term equivalent to indicative, factual or real, while irrealis is equivalent to subjunctive, non-factual or unreal. However, this tradition is also misleading to a certain degree. Palmer (2001) investigates many languages and finds that the realis/ irrealis marker can co-occur with other functional categories related to indicative/subjunctive mood in some languages. Observing this, Palmer (2001: 145) indicates that: although the distinction between realis and irrealis is basically the same as that between indicative and subjunctive, ... there are still sufficient differences between them.

In addition, languages can be described in terms of the grammatical markers of realis and irrealis. For those languages with the clear-cut distinction between realis and irrealis grammatical markers, Roberts (1990: 375) lists the grammatical categories that they are associated with:

(148)
Realis: habitual past, remote past, yesterday's past, today's past, present tense;

---

① Palmer (2001) quotes the definition of Mithun (1999) in his book.

Irrealis: future, imperative, hortative, prohibitive, counter-factual/prescriptive, apprehensive.

The contrast shows that present, immediate past and remote past are marked as realis, while future, imperative, and counter-factual are marked as irrealis in these languages. In the languages with the grammatical distinction between realis and irrealis, the realis mainly concentrates on the objective reality (Chafe 1995), which means on the timeline, the event has already been factual. In other words, the category of time is the essential property that distinguishes realis from irrealis.

4.2.3.3.2 The differences between subjective and objective factive predicates

Introducing the possible worlds semantics and the distinction between realis and irrealis, the discussion then goes back to the factive complement clauses.

Firstly, the section will discuss the differences between subjective and objective factive predicates. According to Hooper (1975), Li (2014, 2016) and Chen and Zhen (2017), factive verbs can be classified into subjective factive verbs (yihan (regret) is the representative) and objective factive verbs (zhidao (know) is the representative).Take Chinese factive predicates as examples, Chen and Zhen (2017: 11-12) point out that the subjective and objective factive predicates in Chinese mainly contain the following ones:

(149)
Subjective factive predicates: *houhui* (regret), *yuanhen* (resent), *aonao* (be annoyed), *aitan* (lament), *qiguai* (be surprised), *chayi* (be surprised), *kangyi* (protest), *qingxing* (rejoice), *gaoxing* (be happy), *zihao* (be proud), *biaoyang* (praise), *xinshang* (appreciate), *ganxie* (thank), etc.
Objective factive predicatess: *zhidao* (know), *renshidao* (realize), *qingchu* (be clear), *xiaode,* (know), *mingbai* (be clear), *jide* (remember), *xiangqilai* (think of), etc.

The differences between subjective and objective factive predicates are self-evident with the notion of possible worlds semantics and the distinction between realis and irrealis. The event that happens in the complement clause of subjective factive predicates is in the actual world and is realis. In contrast, the event that happens in the complement clause of objective factive predicates can have two options, that is, it can be either in the actual world or in the possible world and can be either realis or irrealis. In other words, a subjective factive predicate like *regret* can only refer to an already-existing event that is also true, while an objective factive predicate like *know* does not need to satisfy these two requirements at the same time.

Then, I will illustrate the different types of factive predicates with the corresponding sentences. The different types of factives are connected to different types of events in the complement clauses. Firstly, see the event in the complement clause of subjective factive predicates in (150):

(150)

Ta *houhui* mei ting tongshi jia-ren de quangao, pinbo de tai
he regret not listen colleague family-member DE advice struggle DE too

hen le, jianzhi na shenti zuo du-zhu.
hard ASP simply use body as gambling-stake

'He regretted that he did not listen to the advice of his colleagues' family members, struggling too hard, simply taking the body health as the gambling stake.' (Center for Chinese Linguistics of Peking University)

Houhui (regret) is a classic subjective factive verb, and the subjective factive verb can guarantee that the event in the complement clause is in the actual world and is also realis. In (150), the event *mei ting tongshi jiaren de quangao* (he did not listen to the advice of his colleagues' family members) is in the actual world and realis. That means this event has already happened in the actual world. In other words, the event in the complement clause of the subjective factive predicate is factual. The event that has not happened or not happened in the actual world cannot be embedded in the complement clause introduced by the factive verb *houhui,* as (151a-b) show:

(151)

a. *Ta *houhui*   yao   qu   Beijing.

   he   regret   will   go   Beijing

   'He regrets that he will go to Beijing.'

b. *Ta *houhui*   Zhu Bajie shiyong   jiu   chi   dingpa   zuo   wuqi.[①]

   he   regret   Zhu Bajie use   nine tooth rake   as   weapon

   'He regrets that Zhu Bajie uses the nine-tooth rake as the weapon.'

In (151a), the event *yao qu Beijing* (will go to Beijing) in the complement clause of the subjective factive verb *houhui* (regret) has not happened (irrealis). Because the predicates of subjective factive types require that the event in the complement clause be realis, the sentence is ungrammatical. In (151b), the event *Zhu Bajie shiyong jiu chi dingpa zuo wuqi* (Zhu Bajie uses the nine-tooth rake as the weapon) in the complement clause is not in the actual world (the event that *Zhu Bajie uses the nine-tooth rake as the weapon* is in the novel, so it is in a possible world). Because the predicates of subjective factive types require that the event in the complement clause be in the actual world, and the sentence is then ungrammatical.

The event that happens in the complement clause of objective factive predicates has not always been in the actual world. On the one hand, objective factive predicates can indeed presuppose that the event in the complement clause is in the actual world and also realis. I will label the predicates in this situation as type 1 objective factive predicates. See the following (152) from Center for Chinese Linguistics of Peking University:

---

① If the subject of the main clause is not in the same actual world as the speaker, the following sentences can be acceptable:

Zhu Bajie houhui shiyong jiu   chi   dingpa zuo wuqi.

Zhu Bajie regret   use   nine tooth rake   as   weapon.

'Zhu Bajie regrets that he uses the nine-tooth rake as the weapon.'

In the main clause, the subject *Zhu Bajie* is a fictional character in the novel and not in the same actual world as the speaker. Thus, the sentence seems grammatical. However, this situation is not the main concern of possible worlds semantics (see section 4.2.3.3.1). So this book will not go further in this field.

(152)

Women	zhidao	minguo		yilai	de	Beiyang-junfa		liyong	siyou	de
we	know	the.Republic.of.China	since	DE	northern-warlord			exploit	private	DE

jundui,	geju			guojia,	zuai	tongyi.
army	set.up.the.separatist.regime			country	hinder	unification

'We know that since the formation of the Republic of China, the Northern Warlords exploited the private armies, set up the separatist regimes and hindered the unification of the country.'

In (152), *zhidao* (know) is an objective factive verb, and the events (all the things that the Northern Warlords had done since the formation of the Republic of China) in the complement clause are in the actual world and also have happened (realis). In this case, the objective predicate presupposes that the event is in the actual world and also realis. The objective factive predicate has the property of presupposition, but this is just one situation out of many.

On the other hand, the events in the complement clauses of the objective factive predicates are not always in the actual world. For example, the event in the complement clause of the objective predicates sometimes is not in the actual world but realis. I will label the predicates in this situation as type 2 objective factive predicates. See the following (153) from Center for Chinese Linguistics of Peking University:

(153)

Ta	zhidao	nüer		keneng	yijing	zhui-ru	qing-wang.
he	know	daughter	probably	already	fall-PREP	love-net	

'He knows that probably his daughter has already fallen in love.'

In (153), the event in the complement clause of the objective factive verb *zhidao* (know) is in the imaginary world of the subject *ta* (he) in the main clause (this subject *ta* of the main clause should be the father of the subject nüer (daughter) of the complement clause). Thus, the event should be in the possible world instead of the actual world. At the same time, the event (his daughter has already fallen in love) has happened in the possible world, and it should be realis. The grammaticality of (153) shows that the verb *zhidao* in this case cannot presuppose that the event in the complement clause is in the actual world, i.e., not factive.

There is also the situation in which the event is not in the actual world and also not realis, and I will label the predicates in this situation as type 3 objective factive predicates.[1]

(154)

Wo yao rang dajia   zhidao wo zai zhe-zhong qingkuang   xia   budan   bu
I   will make everyone know   I   at this-kind   situation   under not.only not

hui duoluo, faner   hui chuhu tamen yiliao   de chongfen biaoxian
will deprave instead will out.of their expectation DE fully   show

chu wo-de youxiu pinzhi.
out my   good   quality

'I will make everyone know that in this situation I will not deprave myself,
instead, I will fully show my good quality out of their expectation.'

(Center for Chinese Linguistics of Peking University)

In (154), the events *bu hui duoluo* (will not deprave myself) and *hui chuhu tamen yiliao de chongfen biaoxian chu wode youxiu pinzhi* (will fully show my good quality out of their expectation) in the complement clause are under a specific condition (*zai zhezhong qingkuang xia,* (in this situation)), which means that these two events are in a possible world. Besides, the auxiliary verb *hui* (will) indicates that these two events have not happened. Therefore, the information in the complement clause is not in the actual world and not realis. Again, the grammaticality of (154) shows that the verb *zhidao* in this case cannot presuppose that the event in the complement clause is in the actual world.

From the discussion, it can be seen that the events that happen in the complement clauses of factive predicates are not always in the actual world and realis. Subjective and objective factive predicates do have some

---

[1]   Theoretically speaking, there is no situation in which the event is in the actual world but not realis because the future world is not the actual world by nature but one kind of possible world.

differences in presupposing the factivity of the events. The complicated relationships can be demonstrated in the following Table 5:

Table 5   Subjective factive complement and objective factive complement

Event	Actual world	Realis
Subjective factive complement	+	+
Objective factive complement (type 1)	+	+
Objective factive complement (type 2)	-	+
Objective factive complement (type 3)	-	-

4.2.3.3.3 The relationship between factivity and referentiality

As table 5 shows above, it is clear that the event in the subjective factive complement clause is in the actual world and also realis, which means that the subjective factive predicate can presuppose the factivity of the event in the complement clause. However, only one type of objective factive predicate, i.e., type 1, can presuppose the factivity of the proposition in the complement clause. For the rest types of objective factive complement clauses, the events are in fact not always in the actual world or realis. In other words, the propositions in these objective factive complement clauses are not factive at all. They are just referential, and their property should be referentiality instead of factivity.

This classification is essential for the following discussion. It breaks the traditional classification between factive and non-factive predicates and builds up a new systematic classification between referential and non-referential predicates.[①] Under this framework, the factivity of predicates is not determined by the traditional standard. Instead, it will be determined by the semantic connotation. The traditional factive predicates are included in the group of referential predicates. Only subjective factive and type 1 objective factive predicates are true factive predicates, while type 2 and

---

① The discussion in this chapter is mainly associated with factive verbs. The classification of the factive adjectives is similar to the verbs. For space limitation, the book will not illustrate the factivity of the adjectives further.

type 3 objective factive predicates are actually referential but not factive. Subjective predicates and some objective predicates (type 1) can presuppose the factivity of the propositions in the complement clauses. Other factive predicates (type 2 and type 3) do not have this property and thus should not be regarded as factive predicates. The former is closely related to the speaker's attitude, while the latter does not directly relate to the speaker. The relationship between factivity and referentiality is listed in Table 6:

Table 6   Referential predicates and factive predicates

Referential predicates	Factive verbs
Subjective factive predicates	+
Objective factive predicates (type 1)	+
Objective factive predicates (type 2)	-
Objective factive predicates (type 3)	-

Notice, according to Haegeman and Ürögdi's (2010a) terminology, referentiality actually includes factivity. That is to say, factivity is only one special subset of referentiality. For the purpose of convenience, I henceforth will use factive predicates to refer to the subjective factive predicates and type 1 objective factive predicates and use referential predicates to refer to type 2 and type 3 objective factive predicates in the rest of this book. The alteration of the terminology here implies that the property of referentiality is not always factive.

4.2.3.3.4 The semantic mismatch between high modals and factive predicates

Based on the classification of factive predicates and referential predicates, I propose that the semantic mismatch brings about the incompatibility of high modals with factive complement clauses. I have shown that factive predicates (subjective factive predicates and type 1 objective factive predicates) can presuppose the factivity of the propositions in the complement clauses. In contrast, referential predicates (type 2 and type 3 objective factive predicates) are actually not factive predicates. The former is closely related to the speaker's attitude, while the latter does not directly relate to the speaker. Logically, the factivity of the event in the factive complement is the precondition of the event in the main clause, and thus the event in the complement is closely related to the speaker. However, the event in the referential complement clause is not constrained by this rule. The referentiality of the event in the complement is not directly connected with the event in the main clause or the speaker. Its property is autonomous. Whether the speaker realizes it or not, the referentiality is unchanged and external to the speaker's knowledge or cognition.

According to Palmer (2001: 1), Peng (2005: 46) and Potner (2009: 45), high modal markers (or propositional modal markers in Palmer's (2001) terminology), generally are associated with the non-factual or unreal propositions. This is because these high modals are used to judge, evaluate the truth value or the factual status of the proposition and not to state or claim the proposition. In other words, the speaker uses these high modals to change the truth value or the factual status of the proposition but not to describe it. The event modified by these high modals is in the speaker's knowledge, cognition or even imagination, but not in the actual world. Thus, the requirement for the event in the complement clause introduced by the factive predicates (the event should be in the actual world and realis) will conflict with the requirement for the event modified by the high modals (the event should be non-factual or unreal). The semantic mismatch is likely to lead to the incompatibility of high modals with factive complement clauses. See the following (155a-b), (123b) is repeated here as (155a) and (128a) is repeated here as (155b) respectively:

(155)
a. *John *regrets* (actual and realis) that Mary *probably/obviously/unfortunately* (non-factual and unreal) did not attend the meeting.

b. *Yuehan gan-dao   *yihan* (actual and realis) Mali *dagai/*   *mingxian/buxing* (non-factual

John   feel-PERF regretful   Mary probably obviously unfortunately

and unreal) meiyou canjia   huiyi.

         not   attend   meeting

'John regrets that Mary *probably/obviously/unfortunately* did not attend the meeting.'

As (155a) shows, the factive verb *regrets* requires that the event in the complement clause be in the actual world and realis, i.e., factive or factual. However, the high modals *probably*, *obviously* and *unfortunately* are generally associated with the non-factual or unreal propositions. That means the event modified by these high modals in the complement clause cannot be factual. Therefore, the semantic mismatch brings about the incompatibility of high modals and factive complement clauses in (155a). The same analysis can apply to (155b).

I have proposed that the semantic mismatch between the information in the factive complements and the high modals results in their incompatibility. The event in the factive complement clause should be in the actual world and realis. And this will go against the semantic connotation of high modals that are more inclined to be related to the non-factual or unreal events. However, I have also found that high modals can be embedded in the complement clause introduced by the factive predicates both in English and Chinese. Consider the following (156a-b):

(156)

a. John hates that Mary *obviously* doesn't like him.   (Basse 2008: 57)

b. Meiguo   quanguo   guangbo   gongsi   bu xiang gongji renhe ren,   dan
   American national   broadcast company not want   attack any   person but

women gan-dao   yihan de shi zhe-zhong   gongji *xianran*   fasheng le.
we   feel-PERF regret DE be this-kind   attack clearly   happen ASP/SFP

'National Broadcasting Company of the United States does not want to attack anyone, but what we regret is that clearly this kind of attack has already happened.'   (Center for Chinese Linguistics of Peking University)

At first sight, these sentences are out of expectation. However, these sentences are just evidence supporting my hypothesis. In (156a), *hates* is a factive verb, and the high modal marker *obviously* can be embedded in the complement clause introduced by it. Because the modal *obviously* is not associated with the non-factual or unreal propositions, instead, it indicates that the proposition is easily noticed, recognized or understood. Semantically, there is no mismatch between the requirement of factive predicates and the high modal marker *obviously*. So, (156a) is grammatical. It proves that the semantic mismatch results in the incompatibility of high modals with factive complement clauses instead of the syntactic factors. In (156b), *yihan* (regret) is a factive verb, and the high modal marker *xianran* (clearly) occurs in the complement clause. *Xianran* is also a high modal that is not associated with the non-factual or unreal propositions; instead, it indicates that the proposition is seen or recognized in an easily perceptible manner. There is no semantic mismatch between the requirement of the factive verb *yihan* and the modal *xianran*. (156b) is also a well-accepted sentence, and its grammaticality again proves that it is the semantic mismatch that results in the incompatibility of high modals with factive complement clauses.

In the modal system, a small number of high modals like *obviously* in (156a) and *xianran* (clearly) in (156b) are related to the propositions that are factual and real though most of them are not. Just because these particular modals are associated with the factual and real propositions, they are compatible with factive complements. This linguistic phenomenon proves that the incompatibility of high modal markers with factive complement clauses is not from syntactic factors, instead, it is from semantic elements.

4.3 A contrastive study of MCP in English and Chinese noun complement clauses

This section will explore MCP in English and Chinese noun complement clauses. Similar to the factive complement clauses, there are still similarities and differences in terms of MCP distribution in English and Chinese noun complement clauses. English noun complement clauses do not allow topicalization and show different availabilities to high modal markers according to the property of the head nouns. In contrast, Chinese noun complements allow topicalization and show similar availability to high modals with their English counterparts. The following parts of this section will analyze the similarities and differences between English and Chinese noun complement clauses. Following the analysis of the factive complement clauses, this section provides a reasonable solution to the problem of the MCP distribution in these noun complement clauses.

4.3.1 MCP in English noun complement clauses

MCP in noun complement clauses in English mainly refer to topicalization. Following Stowell (1981), Nichols (2003), Kayne (2008, 2010a), Arsenijević (2009), Haegeman (2014a) adopts a similar relativization approach for the derivation of noun complement clauses. She extends the operator movement analysis to these clauses and argues that the movement of the event operator derives the noun complement clauses. Thus, the noun complement clauses are relative clauses and referential. The absence of MCP in these clauses is then attributed to the intervention effect. In (157a-b), the topicalized constituents *each part* and *flights to Chicago* intervene in the movement of the event operator, and the sentences are ungrammatical.

(157)
a. *I resent the fact that *each part* he had to examine carefully.
(Hooper and Thompson 1973: 479)
b. *A warning that *flights to Chicago* travelers should avoid will soon be posted.
(Emonds 2004: 77)

However, de Cuba (2017) argues that this analysis is on the wrong track. First, he presents cross-linguistic evidence showing that the syntactic behaviors of the noun complement clause do not pattern with the relative clause. Patterns of complementizer choice and complementizer drop as well as patterns involving MCP differ in the two constructions, which is unexpected under a relative clause analysis that involves the operator movement. Then, he proposes that the referentiality of noun complement clauses is linked to their syntactic behavior. In particular, the referential clause has a syntactically truncated left-periphery, and the truncation can account for the lack of MCP in the noun complement clause. In this way, MCP restriction in the noun complement clause can be captured by the lack of cP structure (a term adopted by de Cuba, which is an extra structural position to provide a landing site for MCP).

The essential difference between the analyses of Haegeman (2014a) and de Cuba (2017) is that for Haegeman, referentiality is the result of the event operator movement, and thus the noun complement clause is a relative clause. However, for de Cuba, the noun complement clause is referential by default, and thus not a relative clause but a truncated CP structure. As for MCP, Haegeman argues that they are blocked through the intervention effect caused by the operator movement, while de Cuba proposes that they are disallowed because of the truncated structure.

Both Haegeman (2014a) and de Cuba (2017) do not discuss the issue of compatibility of high modal markers with the complement clauses. Topicalization is a typical kind of MCP in noun complement clauses, while the high modal marker is not that representative in these clauses. The following (158a-b) show that high modals can be compatible with noun complement clauses.

(158)
a. President Pervez Musharraf's meticulously managed political stage was jolted this week by the news that he *may* face challenges to his power from not one, but two. (Corpus of Contemporary American English)
b. He does acknowledge at one point that he *probably* is biased in his selection of bands on which to focus. (ibid.)

As (158a-b) show, the high modals *may* and *probably* are compatible with the complement clauses of NP with *the news* and *the point* as the head nouns.

However, some other noun complement clauses are not compatible with high modal markers. The corpus shows that high modals cannot be embedded in the noun complement clauses with the head nouns such as the fact, the claim, the clarification, the statement, the good news, the bad news, etc.[①] Why do the different noun complement clauses show different tolerance to the high modals? The previous linguists do not yet pay attention to this problem. And this problem needs to be studied further since high modals are also one type of typical MCP in almost all kinds of embedded clauses.

4.3.2 MCP in Chinese noun complement clauses

The English noun complement clauses in (157a-b) can be translated into the corresponding Chinese ones in (159a-b). The grammaticality of (159a-b) shows that noun complement clauses in Chinese allow topicalization, which is different from the syntactic behaviors in English noun complements.

(159)

a. Wo yuanhen *mei-ge bufen* ta fei   dei   renzhen jiancha zhe-jian shi.
   I   resent   every-CL part he must have. to carefully examine this-CL   thing
   'I resent the fact that *each part* he had to examine carefully.'

b. *Qu wang Zhijiage de hangban* lüke   yingdang bimian chengzuo de
   go to   Chicago DE flight   traveler should   avoid   take   DE

   jinggao   hen kuai hui zhangtie   chulai.
   warning   very soon will post   out
   'A warning that *flights to Chicago* travelers should avoid will soon be posted.'

In (159a-b), the topicalized constituents *meige bufen* (each part) and *qu wang Zhijiage de hangban* (flights to Chicago) exist in the noun complement clauses, and the sentences are grammatical.

In Chinese, topicalization is allowed in noun complement clauses, as the following (160a) shows. Moreover, in the corpus, I find more sentences in which the topicalized constituent is embedded in noun complement clause, as the following (160b) shows:

(160)

a. *Na-ci kaoshi* ta meiyou tongguo de xiaoxi rang wo hen jingya.
   that-CL exam   he not   pass   DE news make me very surprised
   'The news that he has not passed that exam makes me very surprised.'

---

① The following section 4.3.3.2 will discuss the issue of the incompatibility of high modals with some noun complement clauses.

b. Qin-liugan   qijian,   *jidan haizi* chi le   hui si   de   chuanyan   rang ta

   bird-flu   period   egg   child   eat ASP   will die DE rumor   make her

gan-dao   kongju.

feel-PERF   terrified

'In the period of the bird flu spreading, the rumor that the child will die after eating eggs makes her terrified.'

(Center for Chinese Linguistics of Peking University, rev.)

In (160a-b), the topicalized constituents *naci kaoshi* (that exam) and *jidan* (eggs) are allowed to be embedded in noun complement clauses. The grammaticality of (160a-b) shows that topicalization is not a kind of MCP in noun complement clauses in Chinese, which is different from the situation in English noun complement clauses.

Chinese noun complement clauses show similar compatibility with high modal markers as the English corresponding clauses do. Some nouns introduce complement clauses in which high modal markers can be embedded. See the following (161a) from Zhang (2008: 1010) and (161b) from Center for Chinese Linguistics of Peking University:

(161)

a. Wo tingshuo   le   Lulu *juran*   qiang   le   yinhang   de   baodao.

  I   hear   ASP Lulu unexpectedly rob   ASP   bank   DE   report

  'I heard the report that Lulu unexpectedly robbed a bank.'

b. Ta hai   dui   guanyu   ta *keneng*   cizhi   de   chuanyan   yuyi   fouding.

  he also against about   he may   resign DE   rumor   give   negation

  'He also denies the rumor that he may resign.'

In (161a-b), the high modal markers *juran* (unexpectedly) and *keneng* (may) are compatible with complement clauses introduced by the noun phrases *baodao* (the report) and *chuanyan* (the rumor).

Other nouns introduce complement clauses in which high modal markers are prohibited. See the following (162a-c):

(162)

a. *Xuduo lao   yi-bei   wuchan-jieji geming-jia   he   guangda
   many older one-generation proletariat   revolutionist and broad

   renmin-qunzhong   mengshou de pohai   he   tamen *dagai/   juran/*
   people   suffer   DE persecutio and they   probably unexpectedly

   keneng jinxing kangzheng de shishi ye cai deyi wei dajia   zhidao
   may   conduct resistance DE fact   yet just able for everyone know
   'The facts that many older generation proletariat revolutionists and the broad
   masses of the people suffered from the persecutions and they probably/
   unexpectedly/may fought/fight against these persecutions are just known by
   everyone.'

   (Center for Chinese Linguistics of Peking University, rev.)

b. *Guo Shuqiang   de fumu   dezhi   erzi *dagai/juran/ keneng*   siwang
   Guo Shuqiang   DE parents   receive son   probably/unexpectedly/may die

   de e-hao   beitong-yujue.
   DE sad-news   be.extremely.grieved
   'Guo Shuqiang's parents are extremely grieved at the sad news that their son
   probably/unexpectedly/may die.'   (ibid.)

c. *Guowuyuan *dagai/juran/keneng*   zhengshi pizhun   jianli   Dalian
   Sate.Council probably/unexpectedly/may   formally approve establish Dalian

   baoshui-qu   de xi-xun,   jida   de guwu   le   baoshui-qu   de
   bonded-area   DE good-news   greatly DE inspire ASP bonded-area DE

   jianshe-zhe-men.
   builder-PLU
   'The good news that the State Council probably/unexpectedly/may formally
   approve of establishing Dalian bonded area greatly inspire the builders of the
   bonded area.'   (ibid.)

In (162a-c), the high modal markers *dagai* (probably), *juran* (unexpectedly), *and keneng* (may) cannot be embedded in the noun complement clauses with the head nouns *shishi* (the facts), *ehao* (the bad news) or *xixun* (the good news). These observations show that high modals are not always incompatible with noun complement clauses. I believe that the property of the head noun plays a crucial role in determining whether the high modals can be allowed in the clausal complements. The property of the head noun should be the primary focus to analyze the issue of compatibility of high modals with noun complement clauses.

By and large, the constraint of MCP in the noun complement clauses is still a relatively less popular research topic. Moreover, because the previous linguists seldom concentrate on the issue, there are no satisfactory solutions to the related problems. Thus, the following sections will discuss MCP in the noun complement clauses both in English and Chinese and attempt to give a feasible proposal.

4.3.3 Accounting for MCP in English and Chinese noun complement clauses

English and Chinese noun complement clauses show different tolerance to topicalization. English noun complement clauses are not compatible with topicalized constituents, while the paralleled clauses in Chinese are indeed compatible with topicalized constituents. Contrary to this, English and Chinese noun complement clauses demonstrate similar availability to high-modal markers. Some of the noun complement clauses are compatible with high modals, while others are not. And the compatibility depends on the property of the head nouns. The differences and the similarities between English and Chinese noun complement clauses regarding MCP distribution can be accounted for in the following three steps:

(163)

a. English noun complement clauses disallow topicalization. This is not because of the intervention effect (Haegeman 2014a) or the truncated structure of CP (de Cuba 2017), but because of the competition between ForceP and TopP. Different from English noun complement clauses, there is no competition between ForceP and TopP in Chinese. The parametric variation in CP-splitting leads to the differences.

b. The head nouns of the complement clauses can be divided into factive and non-factive types. The noun complement clauses show different tolerance to the high modal markers in English and Chinese because there is a distinction between factive and non-factive types of nouns.

c. The semantic factors determine the distribution of the high modal markers in the noun complement clauses.

4.3.3.1 The parametric variation in CP-splitting

Haegeman (2014a) argues that topicalized constituents are not allowed in the noun complement clause because of the intervention effect caused by the operator movement, while de Cuba (2017) proposes that topicalized constituents are banned due to the truncated structure of the noun complement clause in which there is no TopP to accommodate these constituents. Both of them pay attention to the distribution of topics while neglecting high modal markers. As an important and classical type of MCP, the high modal is not mentioned in their works.

I have shown that some noun complement clauses also resist high modal markers while others do not. Haegeman (2014a) first proposes that the noun complement clauses should be analyzed as a type of relative clauses and derived by the movement of the event operator. Then she argues that the topicalized constituent intervenes in the movement of the event operator since the topicalized constituent shares the same Q-feature with the event operator. Following this movement and intervention proposal, the absence of the high modals in some noun complement clauses can be accounted for. Because both the high modal and the event operator carry the Q-feature, the intervention effect arises and makes the sentences ungrammatical. However, this account has some obvious shortcomings. Firstly, it is hard to believe that the topics share the same features with high modal markers because these two constituents apparently belong to different syntactic categories. In the previous section (3.2.3.2), I have shown that topics do not carry Q-feature. Compared with the operator and the high modal marker that are naturally quantificational, topics are not of the same structural type as quantificational specifiers (Cinque 2004).

Secondly and more importantly, this movement and intervention account goes against the feature-based locality condition. The high modals that carry the Q-feature intervene in the movement of the world operator and the temporal operator in the conditional and the temporal adverbial clauses but do not intervene in the movement of the event operator in some noun complement clauses {see [158 (a-b)]}. This selective intervention effect disobeys the feature-based locality condition because both the world operator, the temporal operator and the event operator should share the same Q-feature. It is not likely that the high modals block the movement of the world operator and the temporal operator while allowing the movement of the event operator. Consider the following (164a-c), (30b) is repeated here as (164a), (62b) is repeated here as (164b), and (158a) is repeated here as (164c) respectively:

(164)

a. *[$_{CP}$ If$_i$ George *probably* t$_i$ [$_{TP}$ comes]], the party will be a disaster.

b. *John will do it [$_{CP}$ when$_i$ he [$_{TP}$ *may/must* have time t$_i$]].

c. President Pervez Musharraf's meticulously managed political stage was jolted this week by the news [$_{RP}$ that [$_{CP}$ OP$_i$ he *may* t$_i$ [$_{TP}$ face challenges to his power from not one, but two]]].

In (164a-b), the high modals *probably* and *may/must* block the movement of the world operator and the temporal operator that derive the conditional and temporal adverbial clauses, respectively. Thus, the two sentences are ungrammatical. While in (164c), the high modal *may* should block the event operator that derives the noun complement clause, and the sentence should also be ungrammatical. However, the result is on the contrary. The grammaticality of (164c) shows that the noun complement clause is not derived by the operator movement and not a relative clause. Thus the movement and intervention account is not a reasonable solution to the problem. Based on these findings, I propose that the incompatibility of topicalized constituents with noun complement clauses is not because of the intervention effect.

De Cuba (2017) attributes the incompatibility of topics with noun complement clauses to the lack of cP structure (an extra functional phrase to host MCP in his argumentation). According to him, the syntactic behavior of noun complement clauses does not pattern with relative clauses, and the referentiality of the noun complement clause is linked to its syntactic behavior. Referential clauses have a syntactically truncated left-periphery, and this truncation can account for the lack of the topicalized constituents in noun complement clauses because there is no TopP position in the truncated CP structure. However, the cross-linguistic evidence shows that the complement clauses of NP can indeed host the topicalized constituents [see (159-160)]. Thus, the obvious counter-examples in Chinese noun complement clauses show that de Cuba's account is not a satisfactory solution to the problem.

Besides, de Cuba's (2017) analysis is on the basis of the discussion of Haegeman and Ürögdi (2010a, 2010b). He accepts that referentiality is the default property of the truncated CP structure of the noun complement clause though he denies the operator movement and the intervention effect account. For him, referentiality is the reason that the CP structure of the noun complement clause is truncated and has no illocutionary force. However, I have shown that the referential CP structure also has an illocutionary force. See the following (165a-b), (131a) is repeated here as (165a) and (132a) is repeated here as (165b) respectively:

(165)
a. I still remember *how* John looked when he heard the news.
b. It's amazing *what* a large house John lives in.

Similar to noun complement clauses, factive complement clauses are also regarded as referential. In (165a-b), the wh-constituent *how* and *what* occupy the [Spec, CP] position of the complement clause introduced by the factive predicates *remember* and *be amazing* and express interrogative and exclamative force. The grammaticality of these two sentences shows that the referential CP can host the constituents that express the illocutionary force. Based on these observations, I propose that the incompatibility of topicalized constituents with noun complement clauses is not because of the truncated structure of CP, either.

I argue that the incompatibility of topicalized constituents with noun complement clauses in English is because of the competition between ForceP and TopP. In the complement clause, the ForceP and TopP will compete for the same syntactic position, leading to incompatibility. Similar to the factive complement clause, the referential force in the CP of the noun complement clause competes for the same syntactic position with the topicalized constituents. I have shown that the CP structure of the factive complement clause will inherit the referential force from the factive predicate in the main clause (see section 4.2.3.2). Similar to this operation, the CP structure of the noun complement clause will also inherit the referential force from the head noun in the main clause. Thus, the ForceP with the feature referential [+Ref] will compete for the same syntactic position with the topicalized constituents featured as [+TOP], leading to incompatibility. See the following (166), converted from (157a):

(166)

*$[_{CP}$ $[_C$ $[_{TP}$ I resent the fact $[_{RP}$ that $[_{CP}$ $[_C$ [+Ref] $[_{TopP}$ each part$_i$ [+TOP] $[_{TP}$ he had to examine t_i carefully]]]]]]]].

In (166), the CP structure of the noun complement clause inherits the referential force from the head noun *the fact* in the main clause and indicates that the edge feature of the CP is [+Ref]. The linking word *that* connects the main clause and the complement clause. The zero constituent following the linking word *that* expresses the null Force. This zero constituent then inherits the referential force from the head noun in the main clause. Therefore, the topicalized constituent *each part* of the complement clause which carries the [+TOP] feature will mismatch the [+Ref] feature inherited by the null ForceP. The sentence is then ungrammatical.

Contrary to this competition in English, ForceP and TopP will not conflict with each other in the noun complement clauses in Chinese. I have shown that there is only one position to host TopP or ForceP in the left periphery in English when the CP is split. The co-occurrence of TopP and ForceP will make the derivation crash, and the sentence will be ungram- matical (see section 3.2.3.3.3). Thus, the noun complement clause in English cannot host the topicalized constituents. While in Chinese, ForceP and TopP will project independently when CP is split. In the noun complement clause, ForceP indicates the referential force, and the topicalized constituents are not in conflict with the referential ForceP. Therefore, the topicalized constituents can be compatible with noun complement clauses in Chinese.

4.3.3.2 Factive and non-factive types of nouns

I have shown that the noun complement clauses show different tolerance to high modal markers in English and Chinese (see sections 4.3.1 and 4.3.2). Some noun complement clauses are compatible with high modals, while others are not easily compatible with high modals. It seems that there is no regularity for the distribution of the high modal markers in noun complement clauses. Further observation shows that the distribution of these high modals in noun complement clauses is connected to the property of the head nouns. That is to say, the head noun itself determines the distribution of high modals in noun complement clauses.

Following Guchuan (1989), Yuan and Kou (2018), Kou and Yuan (2018), Fang (2018) and Lai and Zhang (2018), I argue that the head nouns in noun complement clauses can also be divided into two types, i.e., the true factive nouns and the non-factive [or referential (but not factive) in my terminology] nouns.[1]

Similar to factive predicates, factive nouns can also presuppose the factivity of the events in complement clauses.[2] That is to say, factive nouns also have the property factivity like factive predicates. According to Yuan and Kou (2018), Kou and Yuan (2018), these factive nouns in Chinese include *shishi* (fact), *shiji* (deed), *zhenxiang* (truth), *gushi* (historical fact),[3] *shishi* (historical fact), *zhenli* (truth) and *zhendi* (true essence), etc.

The following (167a-c) show that the events in these complement clauses are factive:

---

[1]   Theoretically, all the head nouns in noun complement clauses are referential by nature.

[2]   If there is no specific illustration, the term "factive nouns" refers to true factive nouns in the rest of the book.

[3]   In this word, *shi* is pronounced as the rising tone.

(167)

a. Mei-ge haizi dou zhidao diqiu weirao taiyang zhuandong de *shishi*.
   every-CL child DOU know earth surround sun turn DE fact
   'Every child knows the fact that the earth turns around the sun.'

(Kou and Yuan 2018: 3)

b. Meiti dou zai xuanchuan ta bangzhu gugua lao-ren de *shiji*.
   media DOU ASP propagate he help lonely elderly-person DE deed
   'The media all propagate the deeds that he helps the elderly persons of no families.'

(Yuan and Kou 2018: 6)

c. Quanti zhigong dou tingshuo le qiye chuyu weixian jingdi
   all staff DOU hear ASP company be dangerous situation

   de *zhenxiang*.
   DE truth
   'All the staff hears the truth that the company is in a dangerous situation.'

(ibid.)

In (167a-c), the complement clauses are introduced by the factive nouns *shishi* (the fact), *shiji* (the deeds) and *zhenxiang* (the truth). The events in these complement clauses are factive.

In the complement clauses of these factive nouns, high modal markers are not easy to be embedded. The following (168a-c) show that the existence of these high modals will make the sentences unaccepted:

(168)

a. *Mei-ge haizi dou zhidao diqiu *dagai/ juran/ keneng*
    every-CL child DOU know earth probably unexpectedly may

    weirao taiyang zhuandong de shishi.
    surround sun turn DE fact
    'Every child knows the fact that the earth probably/unexpectedly/may turn(s) around the sun.'

b.* Meiti dou zai xuanchuan ta *dagai/ juran/ keneng* bangzhu
    media DOU ASP propagate he probably unexpectedly may help

    gugua lao-ren de shiji.
    lonely elderly-person DE deed
    'The media all propagate the deeds that he probably/unexpectedly/may

help(s) the elderly persons of no families.'

c. *Quanti zhigong dou tingshuo le qiye   *dagai/*   *juran/*
  all   staff   DOU hear   ASP company probably unexpectedly

keneng chuyu weixian   jingdi   de zhenxiang.
may   be   dangerous situation DE truth

  'All the staff hear the truth that the company probably/unexpectedly/may is/
be in a dangerous situation.'

In (168a-c), the head nouns of the complement clauses are factive nouns *shishi*, *shiji* and *zhenxiang*, respectively. The sentences become ungrammatical when the high modals *dagai* (probably), *juran* (unexpectedly), or *keneng* (may) are embedded in these factive noun complement clauses. The ill-formedness of (168a-c) shows that high modal markers are not easily compatible with the complement clauses of factive nouns.

Meanwhile, there are also non-factive (referential) nouns in Chinese. According to Yuan and Kou (2018), Kou and Yuan (2018), these non-factive nouns include *panduan* (judgement), *kanfa* (opinion), *guandian* (opinion), *shuofa* (view), *jiashe* (hypothesis), *lunduan* (inference), *jiashuo* (hypothesis), *huida* (answer), *jiekou* (excuse), *gushi* (story),[1] *chuanshuo* (hearsay), *liuyan* (rumor), *xiaoxi* (news), *xinxi* (information), *xinwen* (news), *baodao* (report), *jilu* (recording), *yinxiang* (impression), xianyi (suspicion), *ganjue* (feeling), etc.

The high modals are easily embedded in the complement clauses of these non-factive nouns. See the following (169a-c):

(169)

a. Jingzhang   zuochu le sizhe   *keneng* shi zisha   shenwang
  the.police.chief make   ASP the.dead.man may   be suicide dead

de panduan.[2]
DE judgment

  'The police chief makes the judgment that the man may commit suicide.'

(Yuan and Kou 2018: 10, rev.)

---

[1]   In this word, *shi* is pronounced as the falling tone.

[2]   I test high modal markers' compatibility by adding the suitable high modal to the original example sentence quoted from Yuan and Kou (2018).

b. Zhendui xunjing   de tiwen,   Laozhang zuochu le   an-fa

aim-at   patrolman DE question Laozhang make   ASP crime-happen

shi   ziji   *keneng*   zhengzai shuijiao de   huida.

time oneself may   ASP   sleep   DE   answer

'To the question of the patrolman, Laozhang gave his answer that he may

sleep at the time of the crime.'   (ibid.)

c. Ta xie le   Wang Xiaochuan *juran*   xia   he   jiu   ren

he write ASP Wang Xiaochuan unexpectedly down river rescue person

de   xinwen.

DE   news

'He has written the news that Wang Xiaochuan unexpectedly went into the

river to rescue the persons.'   (ibid.)

In (169a-c), the head nouns of the complement clauses are non-factive nouns *panduan* (judgment), *huida* (answer) and *xinwen* (news). As these sentences show, high modals *keneng* (may) and *juran* (unexpectedly) can be embedded in these non-factive complement clauses.

A similar situation extends to English noun complement clauses. I have found that the complement clauses of factive nouns do not allow the existence of high modal markers, while the complement clauses of non-factive nouns allow these modals. In the following (170a-b), the contradictory behaviors between factive and non-factive noun complement clauses are demonstrated clearly:

(170)

a. *He also cited the facts that the incident *probably/obviously/unfortunately* occurred within the trade of illegal drugs.[①]

(Corpus of Contemporary American English, rev.)

b. Allen is innocent until proven guilty-and I am of the view that he *probably* isn't guilty of anything at all.   (Corpus of Contemporary American English)

In (170a), the head noun phrase *the facts* of the complement clause is

---

① This sentence is quoted from the Corpus of Contemporary American English and I add the high modal markers for revision. 10 native speakers are tested, and they all think that adding the high modals will make the sentence unaccepted.

factive, so it is ungrammatical when the clause embeds high modals such as *probably, obviously or unfortunately*. On the contrary, (170b) is grammatical when the high modal *probably* is embedded in the complement clause introduced by the non-factive head noun phrase *the view*. The contradictory syntactic behaviors between the factive and non-factive complement clauses show that it is the head noun itself that determines the distribution of high modal markers in noun complement clauses. The distinction of factive and non-factive nouns plays a crucial role in distributing high modals in the noun complement clauses.

4.3.3.3 The semantic mismatch

The argumentation follows from the analysis of the factive complement clauses. Because the head nouns in these clausal complements can also be classified into factive and non-factive types, the semantic mismatch is then regarded as the factor leading to the incompatibility of high modal markers with the noun complement clauses. At last, a contrast between the factive complement clause and the noun complement clause is presented.

4.3.3.3.1 The semantic mismatch between high modals and factive nouns

Following the analysis of MCP in the factive complement clauses (see section 4.2.3.3.4), I propose that the incompatibility of high modal markers with complement clauses of factive nouns is due to the semantic mismatch. I have shown that the distinction between factive and non-factive head nouns plays a part in deciding whether the high modal markers can be permitted in noun complement clauses (see section 5.3.3.2). As Palmer (2001: 1), Peng (2005: 46) and Potner (2009: 45) indicate, high modal markers generally are associated with the non-factual or unreal propositions. This property will conflict with the requirement of factive noun complement clauses in which the propositions are generally factive and real. Then, a semantic mismatch exists between the high modals and the requirements of factive noun complement clauses, and the high modals are not easily embedded in these factive noun complement clauses. Therefore, I can conclude that the semantic mismatch results in the restriction for the high modals both in factive complement clauses and noun complement clauses. In this sense, one can say that these two types of complement clauses show some similarities in MCP restrictions. The next section will discuss these similarities and also differences between the factive complement clause and the noun complement clause.

4.3.3.3.2 The contrast of MCP in factive and noun complement clauses

In this chapter, I have talked about the restriction of MCP in factive complement clauses and noun complement clauses. There are some similarities in these two types of complement clauses in terms of MCP distribution. Firstly, these two types of complement clauses both disallow topicalized constituents in English, but allow them in Chinese. Secondly, both types of clauses show different tolerance for the high modal markers in English and Chinese. I have shown that factivity is only one character for the restriction of MCP. Simultaneously, other semantic factors also contribute to the distribution of MCP in these two types of clauses. To be specific, referentiality in the factive complement clauses decides whether the topicalized constituents can be accommodated in English, but it does not do so in Chinese. I argue that this is because of the parametric variation in splitting CP between English and Chinese. ForceP and TopP cannot co-occur in English, while they can do so in Chinese. Following this line, the problem of the differences between English and Chinese noun complement clauses in terms of the distribution of topics can also be tackled easily. As for the restriction for high modals in factive and noun complement clauses, factivity will take over the business both in English and Chinese. The semantic mismatch will decide whether the high modals can be embedded in these two types of complement clauses.

The discussion shows that factivity is never the only property that decides the MCP distribution in the factive complement clauses and the noun complement clauses. In the factive and noun complement clauses, referentiality (but not factivity) is the property that goes all along with the two types of complement clauses. Factivity does play a part in determining the distribution of MCP (mainly high modal markers), but it cannot function in many other cases. In other words, factivity is not the only important factor that decides the distribution of MCP as the previous literature indicates. Instead, referentiality may be the more important property that should be studied further in future linguistic research into the factive and noun complement clauses.

4.4 Summary

In this chapter, I have talked about the MCP in complement clauses in English and Chinese. Firstly, I showed that clausal complements in Chinese are clauses (CP), not predicative phrases (VP or AP). And then, I argued that referentiality may be the decisive property in factive and noun complement clauses, rather than factivity. Again, all the work is for the detailed analyses in the following.

As usual, I began the analyses with the syntactic behaviors in English. MCP in English factive complement clauses are topics and high modal markers. I noticed that some factive complement clauses sometimes do allow high modals. Haegeman adopts the same movement and intervention proposal to account for the absence of MCP in factive complements. And this time the operator becomes the event operator. But apparently, this account cannot solve the problem of the compatibility of high modals.

MCP in Chinese factive complements are mainly high modals, topics are not MCP. Similar to English factives, Chinese factives also show different availabilities to high modals according to the property of the predicates.

Observing the differences between English and Chinese, I attempted to account for the absence of MCP in factive complements.

Firstly, I showed that factive complement clauses are not derived by the movement of the event operator.

And then, I illustrated that the parametric variation in splitting CP results in different distributions of topics in English and Chinese factive complements.

Lastly, I talked about the compatibility of high modals with factives. Through introducing possible worlds semantics and the distinction between realis and irrealis, I meticulously analyze the characteristics of the events in the subjective and objective factive complement clauses. Observation shows that only the events in the subjective factive complement clause and type 1 objective factive complement can be guaranteed as factual and also realis, or just say, factive. Thus, the factive predicates in the previous literature are in fact not always factive. Sometimes, they are just referential. Based on this finding, I defined the relationship between referential and factive predicates. Factive predicates are only one sub-type of referential predicates. Only the subjective and type 1 objective factive complement clauses are true factives and thus resist high modals. With this clear-cut distinction, I can argue that the semantic mismatch results in the incompatibility of high modals with some factive complements but not others. Specifically, the true factive predicates require that the events in the complements be factive while high modals require the events be non-factive.

The next complement clause I chose to analyze is the noun complement clause. MCP in English noun complements are topics. Interestingly, Haegeman and other linguists do not extend their research into the question of the compatibility issue of high modals. But I found that some noun complements allow high modals while others do not. Haegeman adopts the same event operator movement account to explain the absence of MCP in these clauses. She deliberately ignores the issue of compatibility of high modals.

MCP in Chinese noun complement clauses are mainly high modals. Topicalization is allowed in noun complements in Chinese. Similar to English, some noun complements indeed allow high modals while others do not.

The noun complement clause is the last type of clause I chose to analyze in this book. Firstly, I showed that noun complement clauses are not derived by the movement of the event operator.

And the parametric variation in splitting CP results in different distributions of topics in English and Chinese noun complements.

Lastly, I argued that the compatibility of high modals with noun complements depends on the property of the head nouns. Although all the head nouns are referential by nature, they can also be divided into factive and non-factive types. The corpus shows that factive noun complement clauses are not easily compatible with high modal markers while non-factive types are just on the contrary. Similar to the analysis of factive complement clauses, I proposed that the semantic mismatch results in the incompatibility of high modals in some factive noun complement clauses but not in non-factive types. At the end of the chapter, I indicated that there are some similarities in these two types of complement clauses in terms of MCP distribution.

This chapter made a contrastive study of the similarities and differences of MCP in factive and noun complement clauses in English and Chinese. Except for the leaving problems of MCP in the literature, I found some other problems that are ignored by the previous linguists (the compatibility issue of high modal markers). I gave convincing illustrations to these problems through meticulous analyses. The research outcomes solve the remaining and newly found problems of MCP in complement clauses. Besides, they also contribute to the semantic study of the property factivity and related linguistic phenomena.

Chapter Five
Conclusion

The restriction of MCP is a hot topic in today's linguistic research. Many linguists engage in the research and give various accounts for it. This research tradition starts from Emonds (1970) and Hooper and Thompson (1973) and lasts till the recent publications from Haegeman (2007, 2009, 2010a, 2010b, 2012a, 2012b, 2014a, among others). Among them, some believe that the syntactic operation determines the distribution of MCP in embedded clauses (including the cartographic account from mainly Haegeman's series of works), others think that the semantic mismatch is the critical ingredient that leads to the absence of MCP in these embedded clauses. Unfortunately, all these researches cannot yet solve the problem of MCP restriction in English.

On the other hand, these analyses of MCP cannot be applied to Chinese since they mostly focus on the syntactic behaviors in English and other European languages. The distribution of MCP in Chinese embedded clauses is different from those in English. However, Chinese linguists seldom notice MCP in Chinese and the different syntactic behaviors regarding MCP between English and Chinese. Therefore, it is necessary to launch the contrastive study of MCP in English and Chinese embedded clauses.

5.1 The conclusions reached in the book

This book analyzes MCP in four types of subordinate clauses and two types of preposition phrases, including two types of adverbial clauses and two types of complement clauses in English and Chinese, and two types of temporal preposition phrases in Chinese. Firstly, I investigate the distribution of MCP in these clauses. In the adverbial clauses and complement clauses, topicalization is one kind of typical MCP in English while it is not in Chinese. Although topicalized constituents are not compatible with adverbial clauses and complement clauses in English, they are more tolerable in the corresponding clauses in Chinese. I have also noticed an exception. One kind of temporal adverbial in Chinese, the temporal preposition phrase *zai*-X structure cannot accommodate the topicalized constituents.

As for the other kind of MCP, i.e., the high modal markers, the situation is far more complicated. On the one hand, the conditional and temporal adverbial clauses in English and Chinese are not compatible with high modals. However, in factive complement clauses, high modals are just not easily allowed to exist in the subjective factive and type 1 objective factive complement clauses (the true factive complement clauses). And the type 2 and type 3 objective factive complement clauses (the referential (but not factive) complement clauses in my terminology) can indeed host high modal markers both in English and Chinese. In the noun complement clauses, high modals are not allowed in the complement clauses of factive nouns. In contrast, they can be embedded in the complement clauses of non-factive nouns in English and Chinese.

Then, I attempt to give a reasonable account of the similarities and differences of MCP distributions in English and Chinese adverbial and complement clauses through various tests and systematic argumentation. Generally speaking, Chinese adverbial clauses and complement clauses do not demonstrate the restriction for topics compared with the English ones. I propose that this is because of the parametric variations in splitting CP between these two languages.

In English and Chinese, the movement of the world operator and temporal operator derive the conditional and temporal adverbial clauses, respectively. In Chinese, the split constituents of CP can project independently, and the full-fledged CP structure can provide enough positions for these fronted constituents like topics. I believe that this is from the analytic nature of the Chinese language. In this kind of language, the syntactic constituents tend to project independently, and TopP and ForceP will not compete for the same syntactic position. However, the constituents tend to syncretize in English because of the synthetic nature of English as well as other European languages. TopP and ForceP occupy the same syntactic position and lead to the competition. When TopP occupies the only syntactic position, the adverbial clause cannot be derived by the movement of the operator in English.

In the factive and noun complement clauses, neither English nor Chinese are involved with operator movement. I have shown that the movement analysis for the complement clauses is not correct. Therefore, factive and noun complement clauses are not derived by the operator movement and not relative clauses. In English, the factive predicates and the head nouns in these complement clauses express the referential force. They will conflict with the topicalized constituents because ForceP and TopP will compete for the same syntactic position. So the sentences will be ungrammatical when the topics are embedded in these complements. While in Chinese, the co-occurrence of ForceP and TopP will not bring about the competition. Thus, the factive and noun complement clauses can host the topicalized constituents in Chinese.

The compatibility issue of high modal markers is more complicated. High modals are not allowed in the conditional and temporal adverbial clauses both in English and Chinese. Because these two types of adverbials are derived from the operator movement and the operator has the Q-feature, the movement of the operator is blocked by the high modal marker that also carries the Q-feature (Haegeman 2009, 2010b). In other words, the high modals intervene in the movement of the operators that derive the conditional and temporal adverbial clauses according to the feature-based locality condition. Thus, the intervention effect leads to the incompatibility of high modals with the conditional and temporal adverbial clauses.

Factive complement clauses are not compatible with high modals, either. Before I come to this conclusion, it is necessary to draw a clear distinction between factive and referential (but not factive) predicates in advance. In the previous literature, linguists do not distinguish factive predicates from referential predicates or just confuse factive predicates with referential predicates. Many referential (but not factive) predicates are regarded as factive ones by linguists, so they cannot give a reasonable explanation to the issue of the compatibility of high modals. Through a comprehensive contrast and careful differentiation, I re-classify the so-called factive predicates into four new types, i.e., the subjective factive predicates, type 1 objective factive predicates, type 2 and type 3 objective factive predicates. Furthermore, I indicate that the subjective factive predicates and the type 1 objective factive predicates are true factive predicates, while type 2 and type 3 objective factive predicates are not factive but just referential.

From this standpoint, I can give a more promising solution to the problem of the compatibility of high modal markers. The non-factual and unreal property of high modals will be contradictory with the requirement for the complement clauses of factive predicates. So the semantic mismatch brings about incompatibility, and the semantic factors decide the availability of the high modals in these factive complement clauses. The accurate situation is that true factive complement clauses are not easily compatible with high modals. In contrast, the referential (but not factive) complement clauses are indeed more tolerant to these high modal markers.

Following this line, it becomes clear for the issue of the compatibility of high modals with noun complement clauses. The head nouns can also be classified into factive and non-factive types. The complement clauses of the factive nouns do not accommodate these high modals easily, while the complement clauses of the non-factive nouns do allow the existence of these high modals. That is to say, the issue of compatibility of high modals with noun complement clauses is still the result of the semantic factors.

Finally, I can give a unified account for the MCP restrictions in English and Chinese adverbial clauses and structures and complement clauses. The conclusions of the book can be generalized as follows:

I. Generally speaking, there are two lines dominating the restriction for MCP in the adverbial clauses and complement clauses in English and Chinese. Except for the movement and intervention proposal, the book shows that the parametric variations in splitting-CP between English and Chinese also plays a part.

II. In English adverbial and complement clauses, topicalization is a typical kind of MCP, while Chinese adverbial and complement clauses are compatible with topicalization. This compatibility is from the parametric variation in splitting CP. Because different constituents can project independently onto the CP layer in Chinese when CP is split, the full-fledged CP structure can provide enough positions for these fronted constituents like topics.

III. For the adverbial clauses derived by the operator movement, high modals are not compatible because of the intervention effect in English. This account can be applied to the related clauses in Chinese. And for those complement clauses that are not derived by the operator movement, the book indicates that the incompatibility of high modals with some complement clauses is from the semantic mismatch.

5.2 The innovations and highlights of the book

This book makes a contrastive study of MCP distribution in English and Chinese adverbial and complement clauses and tentatively provides a solution to the different MCP restrictions in these two languages. Because the previous linguists rarely notice the MCP restriction in Chinese, the proposal in this book fills the vacancies of the current linguistic research. As a supplement to the linguistic research, the book accounts for the different distributions of topicalization in English and Chinese and the similar distributions of high modal markers in English and Chinese, which have not been analyzed in the literature. The research in this book is the pioneering work of MCP research in Chinese and brings about a new domain of linguistic research in Chinese. The research outcomes are believed to be the foundation for future linguistic research in this domain.

When addressing the problem of the compatibility of topicalization in adverbial clauses and complement clauses. I put forward that the parametric variation in splitting CP is the reason for the absence of topics in the adverbial clauses and complement clauses in English and the contradictory behaviors in the corresponding clauses in Chinese. When CP is split, it can be further decomposed into different functional phrases. However, the compositions of these functional phrases can be varied among different languages, leading to the parametric variation. To be specific, there is only one syntactic position to host TopP and ForceP on the CP layer in English; while there are two separate and independent syntactic positions for TopP and ForceP on the CP layer in Chinese. This is the basic reason for the different distributions of topics in English and Chinese adverbial clauses and complement clauses. This discovery deepens the understanding of the left periphery of the clauses in different languages and is also a contribution to the cartographic research program.

Another significant discovery is the distinction between the *zai*-X structure and the *dang*-X structure. Noticing there are a series of differences in licensing high and low construals and resisting MCP in these two temporal preposition phrases, I systematically studied the syntactic structures and derivation patterns of these temporal preposition phrases by reference to the analyses of spatial preposition phrases. I argued that the Chinese prepositions *zai* and *dang* are on the different cartographic layers of the preposition phrase, and being on different cartographic layers is the source of their differences.

In the process of the discussion, firstly I explored the syntactic behaviors from the syntactic perspective and attempted to account for MCP restriction in terms of syntactic operations. However, with the depth of research, I realized that I should accommodate the semantic factors to explain MCP restriction since pure syntactic operations cannot be satisfactory solutions to the intricate problem of the compatibility of high modal markers in factive and noun complement clauses, while these problems are ignored by the previous linguists. High modal markers are compatible with some factive and noun complement clauses while incompatible with others. Aiming at this inconsistency, I introduced the property of referentiality and further distinguished factivity from referentiality. Based on these findings, I proposed that the semantic mismatch leads to the complicated situation of the compatibility of high modal markers. The research in this part solved two problems that hang over the previous linguists. The distinction between true factive predicates and referential (but not factive) predicates re-defined the term "factive" and "factivity". And the account of the semantic mismatch makes the bewilderment of the compatibility of high modals become self-evident.

The innovations and highlights of the research can be summarized as follows:

I. This book is the pioneering work in MCP research in Chinese adverbial clauses and structures and complement clauses and fills the vacancies of the linguistic research of MCP restriction in Chinese.

II. The book indicates that there is a parametric variation in splitting CP between English and Chinese and this is the reason for the different distributions of topics in English and Chinese embedded clauses. The discovery deepens the understanding of the left periphery of clauses in English and Chinese. And it can also be considered as a contribution to the cartographic program.

III. The cartographic analyses illustrate a fine-grained structure of temporal preposition phrases in Chinese. The different syntactic behaviors of the *zai*-X structure and the *dang*-X structure result from their being on different cartographic layers.

IV. The book distinguishes factivity from referentiality. Based on this, the book draws a clear demarcation line between the true factive predicates and the referential (but not factive) predicates and extends the analysis to head nouns in complement clauses. The terms "factive" and "factivity" that blur the eyes of the previous linguists are thus well defined. And this demarcation line is the key for MCP restriction in factive complement clauses and noun complement clauses.

V. The semantic mismatch is believed to be the source of the absence of high modal markers in some factive and noun complement clauses but not others.

5.3 The limitations of the present study

However, there are still many deficiencies in the research of this book. Due to the limited time and personal abilities, the present study does not cover all the adverbial clauses and complement clauses in English and Chinese. There are also many other related fields into which this book has not yet stepped. The distributions of MCP in other types of adverbials besides conditional and temporal clauses, for instance, are very complicated. While some of them can host MCP, others seem not that tolerant of the existence of these MCP. All of these different syntactic behaviors should be studied further in the future. And I truly hope that this book could be a starting point for the syntactic and cartographic research of MCP and even the complex sentences in Chinese.

References

[1] Abels, K. & P. Muriungi. (2008). The focus marker in Kîîtharaka: syntax and semantics. *Lingua 118*(5), 687-731.

[2] Abney, S. (1987). The English Noun Phrases in its Sentential Aspect. Ph.D. dissertation, MIT.

[3] Aboh, E. O. (2010). Event operator movement in factives: some facts from Gungbe. *Theoretical Linguistics 36*(2-3), 153-162.

[4] Aoun, J. & Y. H. A. Li. (2003). *Essays on the Representational and Derivational Nature of Grammar: The Diversity of Wh-constructions*. Cambridge, MA: The MIT Press.

[5] Arsenijević, B. (2009). Clausal complementation as relativization. *Lingua 119*(1), 39-50.

[6] Authier, J. M. & L. Haegeman. (2013). French adverbial clauses, rescue by ellipsis and the truncation versus intervention debate. *Probus: International Journal of Romance Linguistics 27*(1), 33-71.

[7] Basse, G. (2008). Factive complements as defective phase. In Abner, N. & J. Bishop (eds.), *Proceedings of the 27th West Coast Conference on Formal Linguistics* (pp. 54-62). Somerville, MA: Cascadilla Proceedings Project.

[8] Bentzen, K, G. Hrafnbjargarson., T. H. Hroarsdottir. & A. L. Wiklund. (2007). The tromsø guide to the force behind V2. *Working Papers in Scandinavian Syntax 79*, 99-118.

[9] Bhatt, R. & R. Pancheva. (2006). Conditionals. In Everaert, M. & H. V. Riemsdijk (eds.), *The Blackwell Companion to Syntax* vol.1 (pp. 638-687). Malden, MA: Blackwell Publishing.

[10] Bianchi, V. & M. Frascarelli. (2010). Is topic a root phenomenon? *An International Journal of Theoretical Linguistics 2*(1), 43-88.

[11] Bošković, Ž. (2011). Rescue by PF deletion, traces as (non)interveners, and the that-trace effect. *Linguistic Inquiry 42*(1), 1-44.

[12] Bošković, Ž. (2012). Phases Beyond Clauses. Ph.D. dissertation, University of Connecticut.

[13] Bošković, Ž. (2014). Now I'm a phase, now I'm not a phase: on the variability of phases with extraction and ellipsis. *Linguistic Inquiry 45*(1), 27-89.

[14] Büring, D. (2003). On D-trees, beans, and B-accents. *Linguistics and Philosophy 26*(5), 511-545.

[15] Caponigro, I. & M. Polinsky. (2011). Relative embeddings: a Circassian puzzle for the syntax/semantics interface. *Natural Language & Linguistic Theory 29*(1), 71-122.

[16] Cardinaletti, A. (2009). On a (wh-) moved topic in Italian, compared to Germanic. In Alexadou, A., J. Hankamer., T. Mcfadden., J. Nuger. & F. Schafer (eds.), *Advances in Comparative Germanic Syntax* (pp. 3-40). Amsterdam: John Benjamins.

[17] Carrilho, E. (2005). Expletive ele in European Portuguese Dialects. Ph.D. dissertation, Universidade de Lisboa.

[18] Carrilho, E. (2008). Beyond doubling: overt expletives in European Portuguese dialects. In Barbiers, S., O. Koeneman., M. Lekakou. & M. V. D. Ham (eds.), *Syntax and Semantics, vol. 36*: *Microvariation in Syntactic Doubling* (pp. 301-349). Bingley: Emerald Publishers.

[19] Chafe, W. (1995). The realis-irrealis distinction in Caddo, the northern Iroquoian languages, and English. In Bybee, J. L. & S. Fleischman (eds.), *Modality in Grammar and Discourse* (pp. 349-365). Amsterdam/Philadelphia: John Benjamins.

[20] Chao, Y. -R. (1968). *A Grammar of Spoken Chinese*. Los Angles: California University Press.

[21] Chen, Changlai. (2016). *Jieci yu Jieyin Gongneng* (Prepositions and the Introducing Functions). Hefei: Anhui Jiaoyu Chubanshe (Anhui Educational Press).

[22] Chen, Zongli. (2007). Hanyu guanxi jiegou de shengcheng jufa yanjiu (A generative analysis of Chinese relative constructions). *Xiandai Waiyu* (Modern Foreign Languages) *4*, 331-340.

[23] Chen, Zhenyu. & Zhen, Cheng. (2017). Xushixing de benzhi: cihui yuyi haishi xiuci yuyong (On the nature of factivity: a lexical-semantic phenomenon or a rhetoric-pragmatic one). *Dangdai Xiucixue* (Contemporary Rhetoric) *1*, 9-23.

[24] Chilton, P. (2014). *Language, Space and Mind: The Conceptual Geometry of Linguistic Meaning*. Cambridge: Cambridge University Press.

[25] Chomsky, N. (1964). *Current Issues in Linguistic Theory*. The Hague: Mouton.

[26] Chomsky, N. (1973). Conditions on transformations. In Anderson, S. & P. Kiparsky (eds.), *A Festschrift for Morris Halle* (pp. 232-286). New York: Holt, Reinhart and Winston.

[27] Chomsky, N. (1986). *Knowledge of Language*. New York: Praeger.

[28] Chomsky, N. (1995). *The Minimalist Program*. Cambridge, MA: The MIT Press.

[29] Chomsky, N. 2000. Minimalist inquires: the framework. In Martin, R., F. Michaels. & J. Uriagereka (eds.), S*tep by Step: Essays on Minimalist in Honor of Howard Lasnik* (pp. 89-155). Cambridge, MA: The MIT Press.

[30] Chomsky, N. (2001). Derivation by phase. In Kenstowicz, M. (ed.), *Ken Hale: A Life in Language* (pp. 1-52). Cambridge, MA: The MIT Press.

[31] Chomsky, N. (2004). Beyond explanatory adequacy. In Belletti, A. (ed.), *Structures and Beyond: The Cartography of Syntactic Structures* (pp. 104-131). Oxford: Oxford University Press.

[32] Cinque, G. (1999). *Adverbs and Functional Heads*. Oxford: Oxford University Press.

[33] Cinque, G. (2002). Mapping functional structure: a project. In Cinque, G. (ed.), *Functional Structure in DP and IP* (pp. 3-11). New York: Oxford University Press.

[34] Cinque, G. (2004). "Restructuring" and functional structure. In Belletti, A. (ed.), *Structures and Beyond: The Cartography of Syntactic Structure* (pp. 132-191). New York: Oxford University Press.

[35] Cinque, G. (2010a). Mapping spatial PPs: an introduction. In Beninca, P. & N. Munaro (eds.), *Mapping the Left Periphery* (pp. 1-27). New York: Oxford

University Press.

[36] Cinque, G. (2010b). *The Syntax of Adjectives: A comparison Study*. Cambridge, MA: The MIT Press.

[37] Cinque, G. & C. Rizzi. (2010). The cartography of syntactic structures. In Heine, B. & H. Narrog (eds.), *The Oxford Handbook of Grammatical Analysis* (pp. 51-65). Oxford: Oxford University Press.

[38] Citko, B. (2000). On the syntax and semantics of Polish and embedded clauses. *University of Venice Working Papers in Linguistics 17*, 1-32.

[39] Coates, J. (1983). *The Semantics of the Modal Auxiliaries*. London: Croom Helm.

[40] Comrie, B. (1985). *Tense*. Cambridge: Cambridge University Press.

[41] Coniglio, M. & I. Zegrean. (2012). Splitting up force: evidence from discourse particles. In Aelbrecht, L., L. Haegeman. & R. Nye (eds.), *Main Clause Phenomena: New Horizons* (pp. 229-256). Amsterdam: John Benjamins.

[42] Croft, W. (2001). *Radical Construction Grammar*. Oxford: Oxford University Press.

[43] Crystal, D. (2008). *A Dictionary of Linguistics and Phonetics 6th Edition*. Malden, MA: Blackwell Publishing.

[44] Culicover, P. (1991). Topicalization, inversion and complementizers in English. In Delfitto, D., M. Everaert., A. Evers. & F. Stuurman (eds.), *Going Romance and Beyond* (pp. 1-45). Utrecht: University of Utrecht.

[45] de Cat, C. (2007). French dislocation without movement. *Natural Language & Linguistic Theory 25*(3), 485-534.

[46] de Cat, C. (2012). Towards an interface definition of root phenomena. In Aelbrecht, L., L. Haegeman. & R. Nye (eds.), *Main Clause Phenomena: New Horizons* (pp. 135-158). Amsterdam: John Benjamins.

[47] de Cuba, C. (2006). The adjunction prohibition and extraction from non-factive CPs. In Baumer, D., D. Montero. & M. Scanlon (eds.), *Proceedings of the 25th West Coast Conference on Formal Linguistics* (pp. 123-131). Somerville, MA: Cascadilla Proceedings Project.

[48] de Cuba, C. (2007). On (Non)Factivity, Clausal Complementation and the CP-field. Ph.D. dissertation, Stony Brook University.

[49] de Cuba, C. (2010). On the intervention account of main clause phenomena

restrictions: NPI licensing and EV2. *Theoretical Linguistics 36*(2-3), 179-187.

[50] de Cuba, C. (2017). Noun complement clauses as referential modifiers. *Glossa: A Journal of General Linguistics 2*(1), 1-46.

[51] de Cuba, C. & B. Ürögdi. (2009). Eliminating factivity from syntax: sentential complements in Hungarian. In den Dikken, M. & R. Vago (eds.), *Approaches to Hungarian vol. 11* (pp. 29-64). Amsterdam and New York: Jonn Benjamins.

[52] de Cuba, C. & B. Ürögdi. (2010). Clearing up the "facts" on complementation. *University of Pennsylvania Working Papers in Linguistics 16*(1), 41-50.

[53] Declerck, R. (1997). *When-clauses and Temporal Structures*. London: Routledge.

[54] Declerck, R. & I. Depraetere. (1995). The double system of tense forms referring to future time in English. *Journal of Semantics 12*(3), 169-310.

[55] del Gobbo, F. (2003). Appositive at the Interface. Ph.D. dissertation, University of California, Irvine.

[56] Demirdache, H. & M. Uribe-Etxebarria. (2004). The syntax of time adverbs. In Guéron, J. & J. Lecarme (eds.), *The Syntax of Tense and Aspect* (pp. 143-179). Cambridge: The MIT Press.

[57] den Besten, H. (1983). On the interaction of root transformations and lexical deletive rules. In Abraham, W. (ed.), *On the Formal Syntax of the Westgermania* (pp. 47-131). Amsterdam: John Benjamins.

[58] den Dikken, M. (2006). *Relators and Linkers: The Syntax of Predication, Predicate Inversion, and Copulas*. Cambridge, Mass: The MIT Press.

[59] den Dikken, M. (2010). On the functional structure of locative and directional PPs. In Cinque, G. & L. Rizzi (eds.), *Mapping Spatial PPs: The Cartography of Syntactic Structures* (pp. 74-126). New York, Oxford University Press.

[60] Deng, Siying. (2016). Yingyu he hanyu yiwen weiju de jufa fenxi (A syntactic analysis of tag questions in English and Chinese). *Waiyu Jiaoxue yu Yanjiu* (Foreign Language Teaching and Research) *1*, 29-35.

[61] Dubinsky, S & K. Williams. (1995). Recategorization of prepositions as complementizers: the case of temporal prepositions in English. *Linguistic Inquiry 26*(1), 125-137.

[62] Emonds, J. (1970). Root and Structure-preserving Transformation. Ph.D. dissertation, MIT.

[63] Emonds, J. (1976). *A Transformational Approach to English Syntax*. New York: Academic Press.

[64] Emonds, J. (2004). Unspecified categories as the key to root construction. In Adger, D., C. de Cat. & G. Tsoulas (eds.), *Peripheries: Studies in Natural Language & Linguistic Theory* (pp. 75-120). Dordrecht: Springer.

[65] Emonds, J. (2012). Augmented Structure Preservation and the Tensed S Constraint. In Aelbrecht, L., L. Haegeman. & R. Nye (eds.), *Main Clause Phenomena: New Horizons* (pp. 23-46). Amsterdam: John Benjamins.

[66] Enç, M. (1987). Anchoring conditions for tense. *Linguistic Inquiry 18*(4), 633-657.

[67] Endo, Y. (2012). The syntax-discourse interface in adverbial clauses. In Aelbrecht, L., L. Haegeman. & R. Nye (eds.), *Main Clause Phenomena: New Horizons* (pp. 365-384). Amsterdam: John Benjamins.

[68] Endo, Y. & L. Haegeman. (2019). Adverbial clauses and adverbial concord. *Glossa: A Journal of General Linguistics 4*(1), 1-32.

[69] Engels, E. (2005). Adverb Placement: An Optimality Theoretic Approach. Ph.D. dissertation, University of Potsdam.

[70] Ernst, T. (2007). On the role of semantics in a theory of adverb syntax. *Lingua 117*(6), 1008-1033.

[71] Etxepare, R. (2010). From hearsay evidentiality to samesaying relations. *Lingua 120*(3), 604-627.

[72] Fang, Qingming. (2018). Xushi chouxiang mingci "shishi" de jufa, yuyi tanxi (An analysis of syntax and semantics of factive nouns in modern Chinese). *Yuyan Yanjiu Jikan* (Bulletin of Linguistic Studies) *22*, 17-36.

[73] Fernández, A. L. & S. Miyagawa. (2014). A feature-inheritance approach to root phenomena and parametric variation. *Lingua 145*(4), 276-302.

[74] Foley, W. & R. van Valin. (1984). *Function Syntax and Universal Grammar*. Cambridge: Cambridge University Press.

[75] Frascarelli, M. & R. Hinterhölzl. (2007). Types of topics in German and Italian. In Winkler, S. & K. Schwabe (eds.), *On Information Structure, Meaning and Form* (pp. 87-116). Amsterdam: John Benjamins.

[76] Frey, W. (2012). On two types of adverbial clauses allowing root-phenomena.

In Aelbrecht, L., L. Haegeman. & R. Nye (eds.), *Main Clause Phenomena: New Horizons* (pp. 405-430). Amsterdam: John Benjamins.

[77] Friedmann, N., A. Belletti. & L. Rizzi. (2009). Relativized relatives: types of intervention in the acquisition of A-bar dependencies. *Lingua 119*(1), 67-88.

[78] Gartner, H. M. & M. Steinbach. (2006). A skeptical note on the syntax of speech acts and point of view. In Brandt, P. & E. Fuss (eds.), *Form, Structure, Grammar* (pp. 213-222). Berlin: Academic Verlag.

[79] Geis, M. (1970). Adverbial Subordinate Clauses in English. Ph.D. dissertation, MIT.

[80] Geis, M. (1975). English time and place adverbials. *Ohio State University Working Papers in Linguistics 19*, 1-11.

[81] Giannakidou, A. (1999). Affective dependencies. *Linguistics and Philosophy 22*(4), 367-421.

[82] Green, G. (1976). Main clause phenomena in subordinate clauses. *Language 52*(2), 387-397.

[83] Green, G. (1980). Some wherefores of English inversion. *Language 56*(3), 582-601.

[84] Greenberg, J. 1995. The diachronic typological approach to language. In Shibatani, M. & T. Bynon (eds.), *Approaches to Language Typology* (pp. 145-166). Oxford, Clarendon Press.

[85] GuChuan, Yu. (1989). "De S" zi jiegou jiqi suoneng xiushi de mingci (The structure of de+self designation and the nouns it can modify) *Yuyan Jiaoxue yu Yanjiu* (Language Teaching and linguistic Studies) *1*, 10-25.

[86] Guo, Guang. & Chen, Zhenyu. (2019). "Zhidao" de feixushi yu fanxushi: jianlun zaozhidao de yufahua (A study on non-factivity and counter-factivity of *zhidao* and the grammaticalization of *zaozhidao*). *Yuyan Jiaoxue yu Yanjiu* (Language Teaching and linguistic Studies) *2*, 81-90.

[87] Haegeman, L. (2002). Anchoring to speaker, adverbial clauses and the structures of CP. *Georgetown University Working Papers in Theoretical Linguistics 2*, 117-180.

[88] Haegeman, L. (2003a). Conditional clauses: external and internal syntax. *Mind and Language 18*(4), 317-339.

[89] Haegeman, L. (2003b). Notes on long adverbial fronting in English and the left periphery. *Linguistic Inquiry 34*(4), 640-649.

[90] Haegeman, L. (2006a). Argument fronting in English, Romance CLLD and the left periphery. In Zanutt, H. C., E. Herburger. & P. Portner (eds.), *Cross-linguistic Research in Syntax and Semantics: Negation, Tense and Clausal Architecture* (pp. 27-52). Washington, DC: Georgetown University Press.

[91] Haegeman, L. (2006b). Conditionals, factives and the left periphery. *Lingua 116*(10), 1651-1669.

[92] Haegeman, L. (2007). Operator movement and topicalisation in adverbial clauses. *Folia Linguistica 41*(3-4), 279-325.

[93] Haegeman, L. (2009). The movement analysis of temporal adverbial clauses. *English Language and Linguistics 13*(3), 385-408.

[94] Haegeman, L. (2010a). The internal syntax of adverbial clauses. *Lingua 120*(3), 628-648.

[95] Haegeman, L. (2010b). The movement derivation of conditional clauses. *Linguistic Inquiry 41*(4), 595-621.

[96] Haegeman, L. (2012a). *Adverbial Clauses, Main Clause Phenomena, and the Composition of the Left Periphery*. New York: Oxford University Press.

[97] Haegeman, L. (2012b). The syntax of MCP: deriving the truncation account. In Aelbrecht, L., L. Haegeman. & R. Nye (eds.), *Main Clause Phenomena: New Horizons* (pp. 113-134). Amsterdam: John Benjamins.

[98] Haegeman, L. (2014a). Locality and the distribution of main clause phenomena. In Aboh, E. O., M. T. Guasti. & I. Roberts (eds.), *Locality* (pp. 186-222). New York: Oxford University Press.

[99] Haegeman, L. (2014b). West Flemish verb-based discourse markers and the articulation of the speech act layers. *Studia Linguistica 68*(1), 116-139.

[100] Haegeman, L. & B. Ürögdi. (2010a). Referential CPs and DPs: an operator movement account. *Theoretical Linguistics 36*(2-3), 111-152.

[101] Haegeman, L. & B. Ürögdi. (2010b). Operator movement, referentiality and intervention. *Theoretical Linguistics 36*(2), 233-246.

[102] Haiman, J. & S. Thompson. (1988). *Clause Combining in Grammar and Discourse*. Amsterdam: John Benjamins.

[103] Han, C. H. (2000). *The Structure and Interpretation of Imperatives: Mood and Force in Universal Grammar*. New York: Garland.

[104] Hegarty, M. (1992). Familiar Complements and Their Complementizers: On Some Determinants of A'-locality. Ms. dissertation, University of Pennsylvania.

[105] Heine, B. (2016). Extra-clausal constituents and language contact: The case of discourse markers. In Kaltenboeck, G., E. Keizer. & A. Lohmann (eds.), *Outside the Clause: Form and Function of Extra-clausal Constituents* (pp. 243-272). Amstrdam: Benjamins.

[106] Hernanz, M. L. (2007a). Emphatic polarity and C in Spanish. In Bruge, L. (ed.), *Studies in Spanish Syntax* (pp. 104-150). Venezia: Libreria Editrice Cafoscarina.

[107] Hernanz, M. L. (2007b). From polarity to modality: some (a)symmetries between bien and si in Spanish. In Eguren, L. & O. F. Sorinano (eds.), *Coreference, Modality and Focus* (pp. 133-169). Amstrdam: Benjamins.

[108] Heycock, C. (2006). Embedded root phenomena. In Everaert, M. & H. V. Riemsdijk (eds.), *The Blackwell Companion to Syntax vol. 2* (pp. 174-209). Oxford: Blackwell Publishing.

[109] Higgins, F. R. (1973). On. J. Emonds's analysis of extraposition. *Syntax and Semantics 2*(6), 149-195.

[110] Hill, V. (2007a). Romanian adverbs and the pragmatic field. *The Linguistic Riview 24*(3), 61-86.

[111] Hill, V. (2007b). Vocatives and the pragmatics-syntax interface. *Lingua 117*(12), 2077-2105.

[112] Hill, V. (2012). A main clause complementizer. In Aelbrecht, L., L. Haegeman. & R. Nye (eds.), *Main Clause Phenomena: New Horizons* (pp. 279-296). Amsterdam: John Benjamins.

[113] Hill, V. (2014). *Vocatives: How Syntax Meets with Pragmatics*. Leiden, Boston: Brill.

[114] Hiraiwa, K. (2010). Complement types and the CP/DP parallelism-a case of Japanese. *Theoretical linguistics 36*(2-3), 189-198.

[115] Hooper, J. (1975). On assertive predicates. In Kimball, J. (ed.), *Syntax & Semantics IV* (pp. 91-124). New York: Academic Press.

[116] Hooper, J. & S. Thompson. (1973). On the applicability of root transformation.

Linguistic Inquiry 4(4), 465-497.

[117] Hsu, C. -C. N. (2008). Revisit relative clause islands in Chinese. *Language and Linguistics 9*(1), 23-48.

[118] Huang, C.-T. J. (1982). Logical Relations in Chinese and the Theory of Grammar. Ph.D. dissertation, MIT.

[119] Huang, C. -T. J., Y. -H. A. Li. & & Y. -F, Li. (2009). *The Syntax of Chinese*. New York: Cambridge University Press.

[120] Huang, S. Z. (2005). *Universal Quantification with Skolemization as Evidence in Chinese and English*. New York: The Edwin Mellen Press.

[121] Jackendoff, R. (1972). *Semantic Interpretation in Generative Grammar*. Cambridge, MA: The MIT Press.

[122] Jackendoff, R. (1977). *X-bar Syntax*. Cambridge, MA: The MIT Press.

[123] Johnston, M. (1994). The Syntax and Semantics of Adverbial Adjuncts. Ph.D. dissertation, University of Massachusetts.

[124] Kayne, R. (1994). *The Antisymmetry of Syntax*. Cambridge, MA: The MIT Press.

[125] Kayne, R. (2004). Here and there. In Leclére, C., M. Piot. & M. Silberztein (eds.), *Lexique Syntaxe, et Lexique-Grammaire/Syntax, Lexis, & Lexicon-Grammar: Papers in Honor of Maurice Gross* (pp. 253-275). Amsterdam: John Benjamins.

[126] Kayne, R. (2007a). A short note on where vs. plac. In Maschi, R., N. Penello. & P. Rizzolatti (eds.), *Miscellanea di Studi Linguistici offerti a Laura Vanelli da amici e allievi padovani* (pp. 245-257). Udine, Forum Editrice.

[127] Kanye, R. (2007b). Several, few and many. *Lingua 117*(5), 832-858.

[128] Kayne, R. (2008). Antisymmetry and the lexicon. *Linguistic Variation Yearbook 8*(1), 1-31.

[129] Kayne, R. (2010a). More on relative pronouns. The Workshop on Adjectives and Relative Clauses: Syntax and Semantics, University of Venice.

[130] Kayne, R. (2010b). Why isn't this a complementizer. In Kayne, R. (ed.), *Comparisons and Contrasts* (pp. 190-227). Oxford: Oxford University Press.

[131] Kiparsky, P. & C. Kiparsky. (1970). Fact. In Bierwisch, M. & K. Heidolph (eds.), *Progress in Linguistics* (pp. 143-173). The Hague: Mouton.

[132] König, E. (1991). *The Meaning of Focus Particles: A Comparative Perspective*.

London: Routledge.

[133] Koopman, H. (2000). Prepositions, postpostions, circumpositions, and particles. In Koopman, H. (ed.), *The Syntax of Specifiers and Heads* (pp. 204-260). London, Routledge.

[134] Koster, J. (1975). Dutch as an SOV language. *Linguistic Analysis 1*(2), 111-136

[135] Kou, Xin. & Yuan Yulin. (2018). Hanyu xushi fanxushi mingci de jufa chayi jiqi renzhi jieshi (The syntactic difference between factive and counter-factive nouns: a cognitive explanation). *Yuyan Yanjiu Jikan* (Bulletin of Linguistic Studies) *22*, 1-14.

[136] Krifka, M. (2001). Quantifying into question acts. *Natural Language Semantics 9*(1), 1-40.

[137] Krifka, M. (2008). Basic notions of information structure. *Acta Linguistica Hungarica 55*(3), 243-276.

[138] Lahousse, K., C. Laenzlinger. & G. Soare. (2014). Contrast and intervention at the periphery. *Lingua 143*(3), 56-85.

[139] Lai, Weichen. & Zhang, Heyou. (2018). Xushi, zhicheng yu shidian (On factivity, reference and viewpoint). *Yuyan Yanjiu Jikan* (Bulletin of Linguistic Studies) *22*, 37-52.

[140] Lakoff, G. (1993). The contemporary theory of metaphor. In Ortony, A. (ed.), *Metaphor and Thought* (pp. 202-251). Cambridge: Cambridge University Press.

[141] Lang, Dadi. (1997). "Shihou" shiwei duochenshu pianzhengju (*Shihou*, the location of time and the multiple declarative subordinate sentences). *Yuyan Yanjiu* (Studies in Language and Linguistics) *1*, 50-58.

[142] Larson, R. K. (1987). "Missing prepositions" and the analysis of English free relative clauses. *Linguistic Inquiry 18*(2), 239-266.

[143] Larson, R. K. (1990). Extraction and multiple selection in PP. *The linguistic Review 7*(2), 169-182.

[144] Larson, R. K. (2004). Sentence-final adverbs and "scope". In Moulton, K. & M. Wolf (eds.), *Proceedings of NELS 34* (pp. 23-43). Amherst, MA: GLSA.

[145] Larson, R. K. & M. Sawada. (2012). Root transformations & quantificational structure. In Aelbrecht, L., L. Haegeman. & R. Nye (eds.), *Main Clause Phenomena: New Horizons* (pp. 47-78). Amsterdam: John Benjamins.

[146] Laskova, V. (2012). Subjunctive mood, epistemic modality and main clause phenomena in the analysis of adverbial clauses. In Aelbrecht, L., L. Haegeman. & R. Nye (eds.), *Main Clause Phenomena: New Horizons* (pp. 385-404). Amsterdam: John Benjamins.

[147] Lee, H. T. T. (1986). Studies on Quantification in Chinese. Ph.D. dissertation, University of California, Los Angeles.

[148] Li, C. -N. & S. A. Thompson. (1976). Subject and topic: a new typology of language. In Li. C. -N. (ed.), *Subject and Topic* (pp. 457-489). New York: Academic Press.

[149] Li, C. -N. & S. A. Thompson. (1981). *Mandarin Chinese: A Functional Reference Grammar*. Berkley/Los Angeles: University of California Press.

[150] Li, Jinxi. (1924/2007). *Xinzhu Guoyu Wenfa* (The New Chinese Grammar). Changsha: Hunan Jiaoyu Chubanshe (Hunan Education Publishing House).

[151] Li, X. -G. (1997). Deriving Distributivity in Mandarin Chinese. Ph.D. dissertation, University of California, Ivrine.

[152] Li, Xiangnong. (1997). *Xiandai Hanyu Shidian Shiduan Yanjiu* (The Study on Time Point and Time Range in Modern Chinese). Shanghai: Huazhong Shifan Daxue Chubanshe (Central China Normal University Press).

[153] Li, Xinliang. (2014). Xiandai Hanyu Dongci de Xushixing Yanjiu (Research on Factivity of Verbs in Modern Chinese). Ph.D. dissertation, Peking University.

[154] Li, Xinliang. (2015) Lizuyu hanyu shishi de dongci xushixing yanjiu (A modern Chinese based research on verb factivity). *Shijie Hanyu Jiaoxue* (Chinese Teaching in the World) *3*, 350-361.

[155] Li, Xinliang. (2016). Yiwenju yu hanyu dongci de xushixing (Factive verbs and interrogatives in modern Chinese). *Yuyan Jiaoxue yu Yanjiu* (Language Teaching and linguistic Studies) *2*, 92-102.

[156] Li, Xinliang. (2018). "Ganjue" lei dongci de xushixing jiqi piaoyi wenti yanjiu (On factivity shift of verbs of ganjue). *Yuyan Jiaoxue yu Yanjiu* (Language Teaching and linguistic Studies) *5*, 65-75.

[157] Li, Xinliang. & Yuan, Yulin. (2016). Fanxushi dongci binyu zhenjia de yufa tiaojian jiqi gainian dongyin (Conditions on the interpretation of the complement clauses of the counter-factive verbs). *Dangdai Yuyanxue* (Contemporary

Linguistics) *2*, 194-215.

[158] Li, Xinliang. & Yuan, Yulin. (2017). "Zhidao" de xushixing jiqi zhixindu bianyi de yufa huangjing (On the factivity of *zhidao* and its confidence variation under different grammatical environments). *Zhongguo Yuwen* (Studies of the Chinese Language) *1*, 42-52.

[159] Li, Yanhui. (2008). Duanyu jiegou yu yulei biaoji: "de" shi zhongxinci? (Phrase structures and categorial labeling: *de* as a head?). *Dangdai Yuyanxue* (Contemporary Linguistic) *2*, 97-108.

[160] Lipták, A. (2010). On event operator movement in English factives. *Theoretical Linguistics 36*(2-3), 225-231.

[161] Liu, Danqing. (2002). Hanyu zhong de kuangshi jieci (Circumpositions in Chinese). *Dangdai Yuyanxue* (Contemporary Linguistics) *4*, 241-253.

[162] Liu, Danqing. (2005). Yufa diaocha yu yanjiu zhong de congshu xiaoju wenti (Subordinate clauses as an issue in language investigation and description). *Dangdai Yuyanxue* (Contemporary Linguistics) *3*, 193-212.

[163] Liu, Danqing. (2008). *Yufa Diaocha Yanjiu Shouce* (A Handbook for Grammatical Investigation and Research). Shanghai: Shanghai Jiaoyu Chubanshe (Shanghai Educational Publishing House).

[164] Liu, Wei. & Zhang, Qingwen. (2019) Fenlie CP jiashuo yu ying, han tiaojianju de zhuju xianxiang chayi (Split CP hypothesis and distinctive behaviors of English and Chinese conditionals in main clause phenomenon). *Waiyu Jiaoxue yu Yanjiu* (Foreign Language Teaching and Research) *3*, 383-395.

[165] Lu, Jianming. (1991). Xiandai Hanyu shijianci shuolüe (An analysis of temporal words in modern Chinese). *Yuyan Jiaoxue yu Yanjiu* (Language Teaching and linguistic Studies) *1*, 24-37.

[166] Lu, Jianming. (2003). Dui "NP+de+VP" jiegou de chognxin renshi (A new approach to analysis on the Chinese "NP *de* VP" construction). *Zhongguo Yuwen* (Studies of the Chinese Language) *5*, 387-391.

[167] Lu, P. (2003). La Subordination Adverbial en Chinois Contemporain. Ph.D. dissertation. University Paris 7.

[168] Lu, P. (2008). *Les Phrases Complexes en Chinois*. Beijing: Waiwen Chubanshe (Foreign Languages Press).

[169] Lü, Shuxiang. (1980/2016). *Xiandai Hanyu Babai Ci* (800 Modern Chinese Words). Beijing: Shangwu Yinshuguan (The Commercial Press).

[170] Lü, Shuxiang. & Zhu, Dexi. (1952/2013). *Yufa Xiuci Jianghua* (The Speech on Grammar and Rhetoric). Beijing: Shangwu Yinshuguan (The Commercial Press).

[171] Lyons, J. (1995). *Linguistic Semantics: An Introduction.* Cambridge: Cambridge University Press.

[172] Maki, H., L. Kaiser. & M. Ochi. (1999). Embedded topicalization in English and Japanese. *Lingua 109*(1), 1-14.

[173] McCloskey, J. (2006). Questions and questioning in a local English. In Zanuttini, R., H. Campos., E. Herburger. & P. Portner (eds.), *Crosslinguistic Research in Syntax and Semantics: Negation, Tense and Clausal Architecture* (pp. 87-126). Washington, D.C., Georgetown University Press.

[174] Melvold, J. (1991). Factivity and definiteness. In Cheng, L. & H. Demirdache (eds.), *More Papers on Wh-movement: MIT Working Papers in Linguistics Vol 15* (pp. 97-117). Cambridge, MA: The MIT Press.

[175] Minami, F. (1974). *Gendai Nihongo no Koozoo* (The Structure of Modern Japanese). Tokyo: Taishuukan.

[176] Mithun, M. (1999). *The languages of native north America.* Cambridge: Cambridge University Press.

[177] Miyagawa, S. (2012). Agreements that occur mainly in the main clause. In Aelbrecht, L., L. Haegeman. & R. Nye (eds.), *Main Clause Phenomena: New Horizons* (pp. 79-112). Amsterdam: John Benjamins.

[178] Munaro, N. (2005). Computational puzzles of conditional clause preposing. In di Sciullo, A. M. (ed.), *UG and External Systems: Language, Brain and Computation* (pp. 73-94). Amsterdam: Benjamins.

[179] Nakajima, H. (1991). Transportability, scope ambiguity of adverbials, and the generalized binding theory. *Journal of Linguistics 27*(2), 337-374.

[180] Nasu, N. (2012). Topic particle stranding and the structure of CP. In Aelbrecht, L., L. Haegeman. & R. Nye (eds.), *Main Clause Phenomena: New Horizons* (pp. 205-228). Amsterdam: John Benjamins.

[181] Nichols, L. (2003). Attitude evaluation in complex NPs. In Carnie, A., H.

Harley. & M. Willie (eds.), *Formal Approaches to Function in Grammar* (pp. 155-164). Amsterdam: John Benjamins.

[182] Nilsen, O. (2004). Domains for adverbs. *Lingua 114* (6), 809-847.

[183] Ning, C. -Y. (1993). The Overt Syntax of Relativization and Topicalization in Chinese. Ph.D. dissertation. University of California, Irvine.

[184] Noda, H. (1989). Nun Koosee (Clause structures). In Miyazi, Y. (ed.), *Nihongo to nihongo kyooiku* (Japanese and Japanese education) (pp. 67-95). Tokyo: Meizi-syoin.

[185] Noda, H. (2002). Tanbun Hukubun to Tekisuto (Simple sentences, complex sentences and the text). In Noda, H., M. Takasi., S. Mayumi. & Y. Takubo (eds.), *Hukubbun to Danwa* (Complex sentences and the discourse) (pp. 3-62). Tokyo: Iwanimi.

[186] Norrick, N. (1976). Two kinds of factive presuppositions. *Linguistiche Berichte 46*(1), 84-89.

[187] Palmer, F. R. (1986). *Mood and Modality*. Cambridge: Cambridge University Press.

[188] Palmer, F. R. (2001). *Mood and Modality* (2nd edn.). Cambridge: Cambridge University Press.

[189] Pan, Haihua & Lu, Shuo. (2013). Dep fenxi suo dailai de wenti jiqi keneng de jiejue fangan (The problems of the DeP analysis and its possible solution). *Yuyan Yanjiu* (Studies in Language and Linguistics) *4*, 53-61.

[190] Pan, V. J. (2015). Mandarin peripheral construals at the syntax-discourse interface. *Linguistic Review 32*(4), 819-868.

[191] Pan, V. J. & W. Paul. (2018). The syntax of complex sentences in Mandarin Chinese: a comprehensive overview with analyses. *Linguistic Analysis 42*(1-2), 63-161

[192] Payne, T. (1997). *Describing Morphosyntax: A Guide for Field Linguistics*. Cambridge: Cambridge University Press.

[193] Peng, Lizhen. (2005). Xiandai Hanyu Qingtai Yanjiu (On Modality of Modern Chinese). Ph.D. dissertation, Fudan University.

[194] Penner, Z. & T. Bader. (1995). Issues in the syntax of subordination: a comparative study of the complementizer system in Germanic, Romance, and

Semitic Languages with special reference to Bernese Swiss German. In Perner, Z. (ed.), *Topics in Swiss German Syntax* (pp. 73-290). Bern: Peter Lang.

[195] Pesetsky, D. & E. Torrego. (2007). The syntax of valuation and the interpretability of features. In Karimi, S., V. Samiian. & W. Wilkins (eds.), *Phrasal and Clausal Architecture: Syntactic Derivation and Interpretation* (pp. 262-294). Amsterdam: John Benjamins.

[196] Platzack, C. & I. Rosengren. (1998). On the subject of imperatives: a minimalist account of the imperative clause. *Journal of Comparative Germanic Linguistics* *1*(3), 177-224.

[197] Pollock, J. -Y. (1989). Verb movement, universal grammar and the structure of IP. *Linguistic Inquiry 20*(3), 365-424.

[198] Portner, P. (2009). *Modality*. New York: Oxford University Press.

[199] Quirk, R., S. Greenbaum., G. Leech. & J. Svartvik. (1985). *A Comprehensive Grammar of the English Language*. London: Longman.

[200] Radford, A. (2009). *Minimalist Syntax: Exploring the Structure of English*. Cambridge: Cambridge University Press.

[201] Reinhart, T. (1981). Pragmatics and linguistics: an analysis of sentence topics. *Philosophica 27*(1), 53-94.

[202] Rivero, M. L. & A. Terzi. (1995). Imperatives, V-movement, and logical mood. *Journal of Linguistics 31*(2), 301-332.

[203] Rizzi, L. (1990). *Relativized Minimality*. Cambridge, MA: The MIT Press.

[204] Rizzi, L. (1997). The fine structure of the left periphery. In Haegeman, L. (ed.), *Elements of Grammar* (pp. 281-337). Dordrecht: Kluwer.

[205] Rizzi, L. (2004). Locality and left periphery. In Belletti, A. (ed.), *Structures and Beyond* (pp. 223-251). Oxford: Oxford University Press.

[206] Rizzi, L. (2013). Locality. *Lingua 130*(2), 169-186.

[207] Rizzi, L. & G. Cinque. (2016). Functional categories and syntactic theory. *The Annual Review of Linguistics 2*(1), 417-429.

[208] Roberts, J. (1990). Modality in Amele and other Papuan languages. *Journal of Linguistics 26*(2), 363-401.

[209] Rooth, M. (1992). A theory of focus interpretation. *Natural Language Semantics* *1*(1), 75-116.

[210] Roussou, A. (2000). On the left periphery: Modal particles and complementizers. Jounral of Greek Linguistics *1*(1), 65-94.

[211] Sadock, J. & A. M. Zwicky. (1985). Speech act distinction in discourse. In Shopen, T. (ed.), *Language Typology and Syntactic Description* (pp. 155-196). Cambridge: Cambridge University Press.

[212] Schachter, P. (1973). Focus and relativization. *Language 49*(1), 19-46.

[213] Schachter, P. (1992). Comments on Bresnan and Kanerva's "locative inversion in Chichewa: a case study of factorization in Grammar". In Stowell, T. & E. Wehrli (eds.), *Syntax and semantics vol. 26* (pp. 103-110). New York: Academic Press.

[214] Searle, J. (1975). A taxonomy of illocutionary acts. In Gunderson, K. (ed.), *Language, Mind, and Knowledge, vol. 7* (pp. 344-369). Minneapolis: University of Minnesota Press.

[215] Shen, Jiaxuan. (1995). "Youjie" yu "wujie" ("Bounded" and "unbounded"). *Zhongguo Yuwen* (Studies of the Chinese Language) *5*, 367-380.

[216] Shi, Dingxu. (2008). "De" he "de" zi jiegou (*De* and *de* Construction). *Dangdai Yuyanxue* (Contemporary Linguistics) *4*, 298-307.

[217] Shi, Yuzhi. (2000). *Yufa de Renzhi Yuyi Jichu* (Cognitive and Semantic Foundations of Grammar). Nanchang: Jiangxi Jiaoyu Chubanshe (Jiangxi Educational Publishing House).

[218] Si, Fuzhen. (2002). Hanyu de biaojuci "de" ji xianguan de jufa wenti (The Chinese complementizer "De" and the related syntactic problems). *Yuyan Jiaoxue yu Yanjiu* (Language Teaching and linguistic Studies) *2*, 35-40.

[219] Si, Fuzhen. (2004). Zhongxinyu lilun he hanyu de DeP (Head theory and DeP in Chinese). *Dangdai Yuyanxue* (Contemporary Linguistics) *1*, 26-34.

[220] Si, Fuzhen. (2006). Zhongxinyu lilun he "Bulongfeierde nanti"—jianda Zhou Guoguang (The head theory and the Bloomfieldian puzzle—a response to Zhou Guoguang). *Dangdai Yuyanxue* (Contemporary Linguistics) *1*, 60-70.

[221] Simpson, A. (2002). On the status of modifying DE and the syntax of Chinese DP. In Tang, S. W. & C. S. Liu (eds.), *On the Formal Way to Chinese Languages* (pp. 74-101). Stanford, CSLI.

[222] Sinclair, J. (2011). *Collins Cobuild English Grammar Third Edition*. London:

Collins Publishers.

[223] Speas, P. & C. Tenny. (2003). Configurational properties of point of view roles. In Maria, D. A. (ed.), *Asymmetry in Grammar* (pp. 315-344). Amsterdam: John Benjamins.

[224] Stowell, T. (1981). Origins of Structure. Ph.D. dissertation, Cambridge University.

[225] Strake, M. (2001). Move Dissolves into Merge. Ph.D. dissertation, University of Geneva.

[226] Svenonius, P. (2006). The emergence of axial parts. In Svenonius, P. & M. Pantcheva (eds.), *Adpositions. Special Issues of Nordlyd: Tromsø Working Papers in Linguistics 33*(1-2) (pp. 49-77). Tromsø: University of Tromsø Press.

[227] Svenonius, P. (2007). Adpositions, particles, and the arguments they introduce. In Reuland, E., T. Bhattacharya. & G. Spathas (eds.), *Argument Structure* (pp. 71-110). Amsterdam: John Benjamins.

[228] Svenonius, P. (2008a). Projections of P. In Asbury, A., J. Dotlačil., B. Gehrke. & R. Nouwen (eds.), *Syntax and Semantics of Spatial P* (pp. 63-84). Amsterdam: John Benjamins.

[229] Svenonius, P. (2008b). The position of adjectives and other phrasal modifiers in the decomposition of DP. In McNally, L. & C. Kennedy (eds.), *Adjectives and Adverbs: Syntax, Semantics and Discourse* (pp. 16-42). New York: Oxford University Press.

[230] Svenonius, P. (2010). Spatial P in English. In Cinque, G. & L. Rizzi (eds.), *Mapping Spatial PPs: The Cartography of Syntactic Structures* (pp. 127-160). New York: Oxford University Press.

[231] Tang, S.W. (2015). A generalized syntactic schema for utterance particles in Chinese. *Lingua Sinica 1*(3), 1-23.

[232] Tang, Zhengda. (2008). Hanyu zhuju xianxiang jinru guanxi congju chutan (A discussion on the embedded main clause phenomena in Chinese relative constructions). In Zhongguo Yuwen Zazhishe (Periodical Office of Studies of the Chinese Language) (ed.), *Yufa Yanjiu he Tansuo, vol. 14* (The Study and Exploration of Grammar, vol. 14) (pp. 194-216). Beijing: Shangwu Yinshuguan (The Commercial Press).

[233] Tsai, W.-T. D. (2019). Zhitu lilun he hanyu yufa (Cartographic approach and the syntax of Chinese). *Yuyanxue Yanjiu* (Linguistic Research) *19*(1), 28-44.

[234] Van Gelderen, E. (2004). *Grammaticalization as Economy*. New York, John Benjamins.

[235] Vergnaud, J. R. (1974). French Relative Clauses. Ph.D. dissertation, MIT.

[236] Wang, Li. (1943/1985). *Zhongguo Xiandai Yufa* (Chinese Modern Grammar). Beijing: Shangwu Yinshuguan (The Commercial Press).

[237] Wang, Wenbin. (2013). Lun yingyu de shijianxing tezhi he hanyu de kongjianxing tezhi (On the trait of temporality in English and that of spatiality in Chinese). *Waiyu Jiaoxue yu Yanjiu* (Foreign Language Teaching and Research) *2*, 163-173.

[238] Watanabe, A. (1993). Larsonian CP recursion, factive complements, and selection. In Schafer, A. J. (ed.), *Proceedings of the North East Linguitic Society 23* (pp. 523-537). Amherst, MA: GLSA.

[239] Watanabe, A. (1996). Nominative-genitive conversion and agreement in Japanese: a cross-linguistic perspective. *Journal of East Asian Linguistics 5*(4), 373-410.

[240] Wei, H. W. & Y. A. Li. (2018a). Adverbial clauses in Mandarin Chinese part 1: preverbal adverbial PPs and clauses. *Linguistic Analysis 42*(1-2), 163-233.

[241] Wei, H. W. & Y. A. Li. (2018b). Adverbial clauses in Mandarin Chinese part 2: ordering and syntax-discourse-prosody interface. *Linguistic Analysis 42*(1-2), 235-297.

[242] Wei, H. W. & Y. A. Li. (2018c). Adverbial clauses in Mandarin Chinese part 3: postverbal purpose clauses: complementation vs. adjunction. *Linguistic Analysis 42*(1-2), 299-330.

[243] Wiklund, A. L., K. Bentzen., H. Hrafnbjargarson. & T. Hroarsdottir. (2009). On the distribution and illocution of V2 in Scandinavian *that*-clause. *Lingua 119*(12), 1914-1938.

[244] Williams, E. (1974). Rule Ordering in Syntax. Ph.D. dissertation, MIT.

[245] Xing, Fuyi. (2001). *Hanyu Fuju Yanjiu* (Research on Chinese Complex Sentences). Beijing: Shangwu Yinshuguan (The Commercial Press).

[246] Xiong, Zhongru. (2005). Yi "de" wei hexin de DP jiegou (A DP structure headed

by *de*). *Dangdai Yuyanxue* (Contemporary Linguistics) 2, 148-165.

[247] Yuan, Yulin. (2014). Yinxing fouding dongci de xushixing he jixiang yunzhun gongneng (On the factivity and NPI-licensing function of the implicit negative verbs in Mandarin Chinese). *Yuyan Kexue* (Linguistic Sciences) *6*, 575-586.

[248] Yuan, Yulin. & Kou, Xin. (2018). Xiandai hanyu mingci de xushixing yanjiu (Research on factivity of nouns in Mandarin Chinese). *Yuyan Yanjiu* (Studies in Language and Linguistics) *2*, 1-13.

[249] Zanuttini, R. & P. Portner. (2003). Exclamative clause: at the syntax-semantics interface. *Language 79*(1), 39-81.

[250] Zhang, N. -N. (2008). Gapless relative clauses as clausal licensors of relational nouns. *Language and Linguistics 9*(4), 1003-1026.

[251] Zhang, N. -N. (2010). *Coordination in Syntax. Cambridge Studies in Linguistics, Series 123.* Cambridge: Cambridge University Press.

[252] Zhang, Qingwen & Lin, Huayong (2021). Dang fangwei yushang chongdie: Lianjiang Yueyu chongdie fangwei duanyu yanjiu (When location meets reduplication: A study of reduplicated locative phrases in Lianjiang Yue dialect). *Journal of Chinese Linguistics 49*(1), 194-225.

[253] Zhang, Xinhua. (2015). Ganzhi lei xushi dongci yanjiu (On the perception factive verb). *Yuyan Jiaoxue yu Yanjiu* (Language Teaching and Linguistic Studies) *1*, 69-77.

[254] Zhang, Xinhua. (2018). "Ganxie" lei xushi dongci ju de huati, jiaodian he mingcihua xianxiang (On the topic, focus, and nominalization of sentences with *ganxie* "thank"-type factive verbs). *Yuyan Yanjiu Jikan* (Bulletin of Linguistic Studies) *20*, 55-76.

[255] Zhu, Dexi. (1982). *Yufa Jiangyi* (Lecture Notes of Grammar). Beijing: Shangwu Yinshuguan (The Commercial Press).

[256] Zribi-Hertz, A. & L. Diagne. (2003). Deficience flexionnelle et temps topical en wolof. In Sauzet, P. & A. Zribi-Hertz (eds.), *Typologie des Langues d'Afrique et Universaux de la Grammarire vol. 2: Berue-Kwa et wolof* (pp. 205-231). Paris: L'Harmattan.